Windows 2000®
Active Directory™

Other Books by New Riders Publishing

Windows NT Power Toolkit
Stu Sjouwerman and Ed Tittel,
0-7357-0922-x

Planning for Windows 2000
Eric Cone, Jon Boggs, and Sergio Perez,
0-7357-0048-6

Windows NT DNS
Michael Masterson, Herman Kneif, Scott
Vinick, and Eric Roul, 1-56205-943-2

Windows NT Network Management:
Reducing Total Cost of Ownership
Anil Desai, 1-56205-946-7

Windows NT Performance
Monitoring, Benchmarking and Tuning
Mark Edmead and Paul Hinsburg,
1-56205-942-4

Windows NT Registry: A Settings
Reference
Sandra Osborne, 1-56205-941-6

Windows NT TCP/IP
Karanjit Siyan, 1-56205-887-8

Windows NT Terminal Server and
Citrix MetaFrame
Ted Harwood, 1-56205-944-0

Cisco Router Configuration and
Troubleshooting
Mark Tripod, 0-7357-0024-9

Exchange System Administration
Janice Rice Howd, 0-7357-0081-8

Implementing Exchange Server
Doug Hauger, Marywynne Leon, and
William C. Wade III, 1-56205-931-9

Network Intrusion Detection: An
Analyst's Handbook
Stephen Northcutt, 0-7357-0868-1

Understanding Data Communications,
Sixth Ed.
Gilbert Held, 0-7357-0036-2

Windows 2000® Active Directory™

201 West 103rd Street,
Indianapolis, Indiana 46290

Edgar Brovick,
Doug Hauger, and
William C. Wade III

Windows 2000® Active Directory™

Edgar Brovick, Doug Hauger, and William C. Wade III

International Standard Book Number: 0-7357-0870-3

Library of Congress Catalog Card Number: 99-068970

Printed in the United States of America

First Printing: *February, 2000*

03   02   01   00   7   6   5   4   3   2   1

Interpretation of the printing code: The rightmost double-digit number is the year of the book's printing; the rightmost single-digit number is the number of the book's printing. For example, the printing code 00-1 shows that the first printing of the book occurred in 2000.

Trademarks

All terms mentioned in this book that are known to be trademarks or service marks have been appropriately capitalized. New Riders Publishing cannot attest to the accuracy of this information. Use of a term in this book should not be regarded as affecting the validity of any trademark or service mark.

Windows 2000, Active Directory, BackOffice, and Exchange Server are trademarks of Microsoft Corporation.

Warning and Disclaimer

Every effort has been made to make this book as complete and accurate as possible but no warranty or fitness is implied. The information provided is on an "as is" basis. The authors and the publisher shall have neither liability nor responsibility to any person or entity with respect to any loss or damages arising from the information contained in this book.

Publisher
David Dwyer

Associate Publisher
Brad Koch

Executive Editor
Al Valvano

Managing Editor
Gina Brown

Product Marketing Manager
Stephanie Layton

Development Editor
Katherine Pendergast

Project Editor
Laura Loveall

Copy Editor
Christy Parrish

Indexer
Larry Sweazy

Technical Reviewers
Desmond Banks
Mary McLaughlin
Ross Yeatman

Proofreader
Debbie Williams

Compositor
Amy Parker

Contents

About the Authors

Edgar Brovick is the national director for Cambridge's Network Solutions Practice. Ed's experience started in development on a team creating an SNA PUT2 for NCR Systems. Most recently, Ed was a founding member of Excel Data's network services organization before its acquisition by Cambridge Technology Partners. Ed has a B.A. and M.S. in computer science, and he received his M.B.A. from the University of California, Irvine.

Doug Hauger is the director of the Knowledge Management Group for Microsoft's Worldwide Enterprise Group. The Knowledge Management Group focuses on business uses of Microsoft's knowledge management solution in such areas as intranets, extranets, and the Internet by evangelizing both the technology and the methodology necessary to develop and deploy knowledge management solutions. Before joining Microsoft, Doug was Director of Technology at Cambridge Technology Partners, focusing on implementing Microsoft technology in large enterprise environments. Doug has worked extensively in the Middle East, and he will someday be drawn back there by his wife's career—at which point, he will work harder than ever taking care of the home and children. Doug holds a B.A. from St. Olaf College and a M.A. from Boston University.

William C. Wade III has been a networking and systems consultant for several years. From a big-six consulting firm, Bill's interests and talents lead him into the MCSE and MCT channels. Along the way, he worked for several solution providers, big and small, where he gained a great deal of experience implementing Microsoft solutions. Today, as an independent contractor *available for hire*, Bill works closely with Microsoft and other companies on Windows 2000 and Exchange 2000 projects. In his spare time, he writes articles, white papers, and books on new Microsoft technologies. Bill can be reached at `bill@wadeware.net`.

About the Technical Reviewers

Desmond Banks is a Microsoft Certified Systems Engineer (MCSE) and Novell Master CNE who has been working in the computer industry for over 13 years. He has an extensive background in designing Windows NT and Novell Networks for large enterprises.

Mary McLaughlin, MCSE+I, MCT, ASE, ACT, lives in the Boston area with her beloved daughter, Margaret. She started as a systems administrator 10 years ago, and she has worked consistently on small to medium-sized LANs and WANs for profit and non-profit organizations. In the past 5 years, her focus has been training individuals in Windows 2000, Windows NT, and Compaq technologies. Currently, she has been involved in security solutions, such as firewall, Virtual Private Network (VPN), and public key infrastructure (PKI) technologies. Mary has a B.A. in economics, summa cum laude.

Ross Yeatman has worked in the computer industry for over 5 years. He is currently assistant director of computing services at the University of Arkansas, Fayetteville. One of his primary responsibilities is planning, implementing, and managing Microsoft Networking resources on the campus network. Ross is a MCSE with a degree in business administration with an emphasis on information systems.

To my colleagues in this endeavor:

Bill—I knew you were strong technically, but when the direction of the book was wavering and there were doubts about completion, you held fast. You are more than a bronze medallist in the William C. Wade legacy.

Doug—Thanks. Whether it is hauling my sorry city-boy body up the side of a mountain or dragging my fatigued brain through this book, it is always an adventure.

And to:

Avery, Sydney (Nini), and Austin Paul—you are always an inspiration. A big commitment made for a short summer. Your voices were always on my mind—"But why?"

Ed Brovick

Thanks to Dean for keeping me moving on the narrow path toward what really matters, and to Indigo, Aiden, and Christine for the love that turns the journey itself into the true reward.

Doug Hauger

As I sit in a random hotel room, two weeks into a three-week business trip, I try to come up with the words to properly thank my wife for her support on this project and on my career— none are adequate. Thanks Julie, I couldn't have done it without you.

William C. Wade

Acknowledgments

Writing a design and implementation book on a new and dynamic product, such as Active Directory, requires the efforts of many people. Foremost in this effort are the reviewers. Mary McLaughlin, Desmond Banks, and Ross Yeatman kept us honest, offered us the benefit of their experience, and challenged our opinions when appropriate. They added tremendous value to this book.

Next, the Team Coordinator, Jen Garrett, and Development Editor, Katie Pendergast, showed great patience with our struggling deadlines and held our feet to the fire when we would begin to stray. This book would not have been ready until December of 2001 without them.

Charles Bartley provided valuable insight into group policies and workstation interaction with Active Directory. We also want to thank Brett "Infrastructure" Dean, whose knowledge of networking and networking infrastructure filled a void in the pages of this book. Brett has always been the go-to guy for the authors on issues relating to infrastructure and enterprise computing. He provided significant value investigating how Active Directory affects network infrastructures and how those infrastructures benefit from Active Directory. Brett can be reached at `brettwdean@aol.com`.

Finally, we would like to thank Microsoft. Despite being constantly attacked by friend and foe alike, Microsoft continues to produce best-of-breed products that have offered us careers doing something we love and writing books as well.

Your Feedback Is Valuable

As the reader of this book, you are our most important critic and commentator. We value your opinion and want to know what we're doing right, what we could do better, what areas you'd like to see us publish in, and any other words of wisdom you're willing to pass our way.

As the Executive Editor for the Networking team at New Riders Publishing, I welcome your comments. You can fax, email, or write me directly to let me know what you did or didn't like about this book—as well as what we can do to make our books stronger.

Please note that I cannot help you with technical problems related to the topic of this book, and that because of the high volume of mail I receive, I might not be able to reply to every message.

When you write, please be sure to include this book's title and author, as well as your name and phone or fax number. I will carefully review your comments and share them with the authors and editors who worked on the book.

Fax: 317-581-4663
Email: nrfeedback@newriders.com
Mail: Al Valvano
        Executive Editor
        New Riders Publishing
        201 West 103rd Street
        Indianapolis, IN 46290 USA

Introduction

Welcome to *Windows 2000 Active Directory: Design and Implementation*, a book designed to provide you with the information you need to begin preparing for Windows 2000 Active Directory. Your Active Directory project will encompass multiple facets of your organization, bringing together various technologies into a unified directory solution. To what extent Active Directory will play a role in your organization will depend on your business and technical requirements. This book is intended to help you discover those requirements and couple them with functionality provided by Active Directory. After your requirements are identified, the chapters of this book will assist you in designing your Active Directory to meet your defined requirements.

This book is divided in to three parts: Part I, "Introduction and Overview;" Part II, "Planning;" and Part III, "Implementation." Although the book is designed to be read from start to finish, the configuration of the three main sections, as well as each individual chapter, is such that you can pick and chose the material most relevant to your needs.

Who This Book Is Written For

This book is designed specifically for technical architects and implementers already familiar with Windows NT. It is expected that concepts, such as domains, trusts, namespace, and Internet technologies are familiar to the reader. This book is not targeted at the individual who will be tasked with administering and maintaining an Active Directory environment.

Finally, this book is primarily focused on individuals working for medium- to large-size organizations of one thousand desktops or more. Many of the design issues discussed in this book might not apply to organizations smaller than this.

What's in This Book

This book discusses the information needed to begin to prepare for Active Directory, to design an adequate architecture for the directory, and finally how to go about implementing that design in your organization. This book is not a "how-to" manual on Active Directory, nor is it a book that explains the property pages of Active Directory objects or the various User Interfaces. It is not designed to be an entry-level reference book for people who are not familiar with Window NT or Windows 2000.

To make the book easier to read and provide a structure to the material, the chapters are arranged in three sections:

Part I: Introduction and Overview

This part of the book contains five chapters, which provide an overview of steps that should be taken and the issues to consider before beginning the planning process for implementing Active Directory. Chapter 1, "How Active Directory Will Affect Your Organization," provides an overview of this topic. Chapter 2, "Introducing Active Directory," provides a basic primer of terms and concepts used in the book. Those readers already familiar with Active Directory and Windows 2000 can skip this chapter. Chapter 3, "Active Directory as a Meta-Directory," discusses the different approaches to utilizing Active Directory as a meta-directory and examines what a meta-directory actually is. Chapter 4, "Defining and Meeting Your Directory Requirements," lays out all the business requirements that will need to be identified before the Active Directory planning process can take place. Chapter 5, "Scoping the Project," helps the reader scope what effort will be needed to design Active Directory architecture.

Part II: Planning

This part of the book contains six chapters that walk you through the steps for designing your environment. These chapters are not intended to be a cookbook, but instead to give you an outline of the major components and considerations for your design. Chapter 6, "Planning for Coexistence," starts where most installations of Active Directory start—with considering coexistence between existing directory structures and Active Directory. Chapter 7, "Designing the Windows 2000 Domain Structure," addresses the design of the namespace. This chapter is probably the most rich in discussing the core considerations of Active Directory because the namespace is one of the primary elements of a successful deployment of Active Directory. Chapter 8, "Designing the DNS Namespace," considers domain name system's (DNS's) integration and impact on Active Directory. Chapter 9, "Group Policies," reviews the use of group policies, a key feature of Active Directory and one of the primary reasons for considering a migration from Windows NT. Chapter 10, "The Physical Topology: Sites and Replication," addresses how physical topology affects the design of sites and Active Directory replication. Chapter 11, "Active Directory and Scalability," considers the scalability of your Active Directory design.

Part III: Implementation

The final part of the book provides you with the considerations for moving your design into a practical reality. In some ways, this phase can be the most challenging. It requires developing the implementation plan for translating your Active Directory design in to a tangible aspect of your organization's computing environment. Chapter 12, "Managing the Desktop," addresses the many issues that need to be considered when developing a plan for controlling the desktop with Active Directory. Chapter 13, "Developing an Administration Strategy;" Chapter 14, "Windows 2000 Networking Services;" Chapter 15, "Developing and Network Security Strategy;" and Chapter 16, "Developing a Remote Access Solution," review the substantive capabilities of Active Directory, including flexibility of administration, core network services, security, and remote access.

Developing that plan is addressed in Chapter 17, "Developing an Implementation Plan." Microsoft Exchange 2000 will be one of the primary application drivers for implementing Windows 2000 and Active Directory. In Chapter 18, "Windows 2000 and Exchange Server," we address how to coexist with Active Directory and Exchange 5.5 before a rollout of Exchange 2000. Chapter 19, "Scripting with Active Directory," discusses how to leverage scripting to simplify the administration of Active Directory and your Windows 2000 environment. Chapter 20, "Designing Active Directory Hierarchies," identifies the key issues to be addressed when implementing an Active Directory organizational hierarchy, which then should be tested in a lab environment before it is deployed in production. Building that lab is discussed in Chapter 21, "Creating a Lab." Finally, Chapter 22, "Upgrading from Windows NT 4.0," takes you to one of the tactical issues regarding implementing Active Directory.

How to Use This Book

You can use this book in any of a variety of ways. If you have limited experience with Windows 2000 or Active Directory, you'll benefit from reading the book in sequence, chapter by chapter.

If you have been experimenting with early releases of Windows 2000 and Active Directory, look for chapters on topics of interest and tackle them as you please. If you are already a Windows 2000 expert, I recommend that you use the book's index and table of contents to point your reading to more precise topics.

We, the authors, welcome any comments, criticism, and free advice you have regarding the book. We can be reached at authors@wadeware.net. Thanks for buying our book. We hope you enjoy it and that it provides you with the technical expertise necessary to implement a fruitful Active Directory in your organization.

I

Introduction and Overview

1

How Active Directory Will
Affect Your Organization

MANY ORGANIZATIONS TODAY HAVE MULTIPLE DIRECTORIES IN PLACE. There are phone directories, email directories, and human resource directories. Each of these directories is typically maintained and managed by different groups. This guarantees that at any one time the information contained in any one directory is different than the information in each of the other directories.

With the prevalence of multiple directories, many organizations have established the goal of implementing a single, consolidated directory. This consolidation promises to ensure greater accuracy, increase productivity, and facilitate more efficient and effective directory administration. Microsoft's Active Directory is a compelling technology for achieving the goal of a single organization-wide directory.

Active Directory can be viewed from two different perspectives. One perspective is that of the Information Technology (IT) department, including administrations, operations, and development. The second perspective is that of the end user. This chapter will examine how the implementation of Active Directory impacts individuals and groups in your organization—your customers. It also provides recommendations for how the IT department should adjust to take the best advantage of Active Directory.

The Customer—How Active Directory Affects the Users

Active Directory is a new paradigm for most organizations. Today, organizations have lists for everything from phone numbers to books to the physical inventory. Developers and systems analysts, with the advent of object-oriented design and its supporting technology, are trying to develop applications that more closely mimic the real world. The hope is that it is easier to translate real-world requirements into productive applications. The other hope is that application maintenance and changes are made easier by making adjustments that reflect the way the real world changed. Active Directory is based on object-oriented technology, which enables Active Directory to reflect the way information is intuitively interpreted—the way you perceive it in the real world.

Rather than fumbling through lists and multiple resources, an end user might want to move through the tree looking for someone who exists in Miami and who is part of the finance group. This is easy with Active Directory. As an end user, you are able to move through the tree from the US to Florida to Miami and then to the finance group and search through a relatively short list for the person you are seeking. Alternatively, you look through the corporate administration group to the finance group and then select those that are located in Miami. Each of these navigations represents a different view of the "world." The design of your Active Directory tree and the end user's view of the real world have an impact on how easy your users traverse and use the Active Directory tree. In the best case, your design and a good understanding of your end user community lead to an Active Directory design that is intuitive to the end user.

One Stop Shopping

Active Directory provides the ability to find information by going to a single location. So, how does this help a user in modern day computing? Rather than searching with multiple tools, the user can use a single tool. If we look at today's implementation, we find

- We use Explorer to traverse file system repositories.
- We use Microsoft Exchange for recipient data.
- We use Explorer for enterprise resources, such as printers.
- We use Windows Internet Naming Service (WINS) for NetBios name resolution.
- We use Domain Name Service (DNS) to find information about local and remote resources.

Information Technology Impacts

Currently, several directory service tasks are managed across the organization and kept in a variety of forms. The reality is that each of these directories is based on a different technology. To staff the administration of all the directories requires the skills from a variety of technologies. This predicament almost ensures a variety of directory systems. There is no single repository to support all the needs—that is, until Active Directory.

If you look at a typical scenario, there are the network operating system (NOS) administrators. These people perform additions, deletions, and modifications to the administration of the NOS resources. The NOS administrators use a tool specifically designed for the NOS or a customized script. For email administration, a person performs additions, deletions, and modifications to users in the email directory. The administrators use the tool specifically designed for each directory system, as shown in Table 1.1

Table 1.1   **Directory Tools and Skills**

Directory	Skill SET
NOS User administration	■ NOS trained and NOS administration tool.
	■ Familiar with the networking infrastructure and the attributes of the network user.
	■ Some scripting skills for network login scripts.
Email directory	■ Email administration tool familiarity. Ability to understand message flow.
On-line Web directory	■ Skills with HTML, FrontPage 98, or Word 2000.
	■ The ability to create Web pages with links.

With a quick view of the preceding table, you can see that there is no common skill across these relatively simple directory systems. Unfortunately, to consolidate these environments today would require expertise in a variety of tools. If you had a single tool that could support the needs of all these directories, you would have greater consensus on moving to a single directory. Active Directory provides an environment for integrating the directory requirements. With a single directory system, you are able to use a single tool for administering your environment.

Administration

Unfortunately, for directory administrators the workload is undetermined and ongoing. There could be no changes for a week, or there could be a hundred in a single day. The challenge never ends, and with all this effort the directory is viewed as a resource but not an accurate source for directory data. Thus, individuals start creating their own private directories. Excel spreadsheets with subsets of the information are on desktops everywhere. In the ideal case, all the information you need to know could be obtained by a simple query of the larger directory.

The impact to your organization is three-fold. *There is duplication of effort.* Staff in your organization are creating and inputting the same information in multiple instances. *The available information is not used consistently as a resource.* The directories are viewed as suspect. Because there are different sources with different update frequencies, information appears out-of-date on a regular basis. *The directory is not being used as an enterprise service, and thus, not leveraged across the applications, users, customers, and partners.* Other factors that are indirectly compromised are security and the underlying network. Multiple directories contribute to multiple data sources. With multiple copies of similar information and without centralized control, these sources can be compromised, which lead to other compromises. Searching and retrieving the directory information from multiple sources can lead to network impacts.

Before horizontal enterprise application use, most applications existed for a specific departmental need. The finance department had accounting applications, and people who needed accounting information requested reports that were churned out by the applications and typically delivered in paper reports. The administration and users of these systems resided largely in the department that they existed. Specific systems including hardware, software and eventually small local area networks (LANs) were created for departmental use.

The first horizontal uses of technology included the telephone, followed by mainframe application services (including email), some time later by LANs that were interconnected, and most recently by email systems with post offices in multiple locations. These systems started having impacts on networks because of passing messaging and directory information back and forth. Each of these systems developed centralized staff for the design, administration, deployment, and support of these systems. One can make the argument that this was not true with early email integration as distributed Network Administrators worked with each other to implement email enterprise wide. This system had limited effectiveness because the directory was always out of synchronization. This drove the requirement for a single email system. This is similar to what we have seen with network directories. There are many disparate systems today. Active Directory is the opportunity for migration to a single system.

With the implementation of Active Directory, Microsoft introduces another horizontal enterprise-wide service. The impact on the organization is similar to that of phone systems, network infrastructure, and email systems and may be even larger. As mentioned earlier, to realize the full promise of the enterprise directory there should be application integration. This requires development and integration expertise. To maintain the directory, the organization requires administration expertise, and policies and processes for an effective system surrounding the administration.

Roles

Active Directory has a large impact on the organization. Similar to early LAN/WAN designs for connecting the organization, Active Directory is a pervasive horizontal service in the organization used by some users unknowingly.

To support this new service, a new administration group should be formed. Although you can make the argument that directory services are an extension of existing network administration responsibilities, the reality is that Active Directory is pervasive, and Microsoft's implementation has integration requirements with a variety of services. Some of the requirements might be outside the typical Network Administrator's responsibilities.

The other key reason for implementation of a separate group responsible for the directory is that you will then have a driving force for the advocacy of the use of the directory, guidance in application implementation of the directory, and development of the policies and processes necessary to leverage this technology. It would be all too easy for Active Directory to mimic early directory services as a simple repository for network file- and print-service directory requirements. The objective with an Active Directory implementation is to create a value for the directory that is used in many aspects of the computing environment, which leverages the organizational and business objectives.

With the advent of a new group, there needs to be clear role definition. The roles are defined so that they can be integrated. We define roles that, in larger organizations, might require three staffs, and in small organization might need to be combined with other directory service roles to create a single position. This section outlines the need for specific roles in the management of the directory and relationships with existing functions in most corporate and computing organizations.

First, the roles and responsibilities are described, followed with an example in a fictional company.

Directory Services Manager/Lead

Depending on the size of the organization, either a directory services manager or a lead position should exist. The directory services manager provides the single point of contact for all aspects of Active Directory implementation, as well as some influence, if not participation, in the design, implementation, and operational procedures for other directory services that exist in the organization. The directory services manager should manage the following services:

- Design of Active Directory
- Identification of the business requirements for the implementation of Active Directory and related services
- Implementation of Active Directory
- Customization of Active Directory

- Project plan for
  Design enhancement
  Business requirements gathering
  Enhancements

- Development of the interaction with use of Active Directory
  Develops standards for the organization and use by applications
  Quality Assurance program for application use of Active Directory

- Operations and maintenance
- Backup and disaster recovery
- Staffing of the directory services team
- Organizational alliances
- Program for Active Directory service use within the organization and externally in support of e-business connectivity

Although the directory service manager surely cannot perform all the functions describe in the preceding list, the directory services manager is responsible for driving these tasks and programs to completion and general use by the organization.

Directory Services Management Emphasis

The top five priorities of Active Directory tasks previously described are the initial design, proper implementation, operations, disaster recovery, and application use of the directory. Although it might be easy for the directory services manager to be distracted with all the responsibilities and requirements, this section is designed to help identify and explain the top priorities of the directory services manager.

Design of Your Active Directory Environment

The design of Active Directory is critical to its use and function. By designing Active Directory properly, the user is able to use the directory intuitively. Although future chapters discuss the design in more depth, it is safe to say that creating a metaphor for the directory is important. The directory design should reflect some design that makes sense for the end users. An example of a common metaphor for an Active Directory design is the physical locations of the organization. Another example is the organizational structure of the company.

Administration of the directory is also affected by the design. The performance of centralized or decentralized administration is impacted by the Active Directory design. The administrators should consider the topology, bandwidth, and delegation of administration as part of the design.

Proper Implementation

After the design of your Active Directory is complete, the implementation is important as with any complex technology. The implementation must adhere to the designs or the design must be changed to reflect the implementation. An implementation of this nature requires some adjustments.

You can do several things to ensure a proper implementation. Again, these topics will be covered in more detail in later chapters, but the high-level of intent of "proper implementation" is to develop a process in the implementation. Hardware should be consistent and within specification. Validation testing should be performed to demonstrate key features of the design as the implementation moves forward. As an example: Is the directory replicating properly? Can remote users access their accounts from a distant location? Does the training add value to the understanding of the technology?

Operations

The focus on operations by the directory services manager is to emphasize the need for process and validation. This relates to the need for a design that can be administered. In addition, there is the need for reviewing capacity, performance, and "what if" scenarios.

The Operations group needs to ensure availability for the enterprise-critical service, predict future needs, and plan appropriately. Regular reporting and trend analysis on the system goes a long way toward keeping the focus on the operational environment.

Disaster Recovery

Disaster recovery of Active Directory is important for the survival of the directory services manager. Regardless of the reason for the disaster, you must be prepared to get the system up and running again. As part of your design, you should consider how you would recover from a disaster. This includes everything from a downed server to some loss of data or functionality in the system.

Because Active Directory is a horizontal service that traverses the entire organization, it is important to remember that a simple outage of service can affect a large community. The capability to recover quickly, or at a minimum to be able to communicate a process and timeline for recovery, has prevented the need for many resume updates.

Application User of Active Directory

Leveraging Active Directory naturally follows an implementation. First, users rely on it for everyday use. Active Directory provides applications with an enterprise-wide repository of information. Applications have the capability to use standard interfaces for access to information that remains consistent throughout the organization.

Some examples of the use of the directory by applications would include a Human Resources (HR) benefits application, or any type of business application that would include or integrate workflow.

Active Directory Engineer

The Active Directory engineer is the primary design engineer for Active Directory. He works to create and re-create the design as appropriate, based on the changing business requirements of the organization.

Active Directory Operations Specialist (ADOS)

The ADOS is responsible for the on-going support of Active Directory. The ADOS should have a firm understanding of the underlying architecture for the project. With the architectural understanding, the ADOS provides information on the stability, performance, and capacity of the environment.

The ADOS's daily tasks include the following items:

- Adding/deleting users and other objects
- Implementing directory design changes, as decided by the directory services engineer
- Performing backups
- Performing backup fire drills
- Reporting on performance and utilization
- Implementing changes to the directory based on design changes made by the directory services engineer

The ratio of ADOS is about 1 per 1000 end users. This ratio might change based on the wide range of locations an organization might have and the mature use of the Active Directory implementation. Simplification of directory tools and use can reduce the ratio of ADOS to end users.

Directory Services Application Specialist (DSAS)

The DSAS is the technical specialist for application development using Active Directory. This responsibility requires the ability to understand and influence the design of Active Directory in collaboration with the directory services engineer. Although the directory services engineer focuses on the function of Active Directory, based on both the underlying architecture and the information that end users need and want, the ADAS also focuses on how to use this information in conjunction with application goals.

The ADAS should understand the requirements for Active Directory. These requirements map to the features and ultimately the design. The ADAS's responsibilities include understanding the Active Directory design of the organization, developing, documenting, and reviewing applications development standards for the use of Active Directory in the organization. This should be clearly stated in the Active Directory architecture document. (The Active Directory architecture documents the business requirements for the implementation and the implementation details of the installation.)

The primary goals of the ADAS is to improve the ongoing use of the directory and to ensure that the directory provides for a consistent service. Working collaboratively with his or her peer, the directory services engineer, the Directory Services Application Specialist (DSAS) is responsible for the consistent use of Active Directory. As Active Directory becomes a horizontal service of the organization, the DSAS provides guidance for the development teams in how to use Active Directory and leverage it as an enterprise repository.

There might be the need for compromises between the DSAS and the directory services engineer to create a robust environment that provides desired performance levels for applications and end users, and ease of use for application developers, end users, and administration.

The DSAS should be responsible for identifying initiatives around the following areas.

Working with the Directory Services Engineer

The DSAS should work with directory services engineers to clearly understand the Active Directory implementation and provide insight into application use. This is a collaborative effort.

Establish Application Development Standards

The DSAS should develop standards for application development. Application use of the directory is a key leveraging point for Active Directory. The hope is to have clearly defined use of the Active Directory to ensure consistent use and support easier modifications should interfaces change later. This effort includes documenting the standards, providing sample code for typical uses, and even internal training on lessons learned from projects implemented in the organization.

Define High-Level Application Functionality Requirements

This effort is to provide the directory services engineer and developers with a clear understanding of the high-level functionality required by applications. This is particularly beneficial if setting expectations as to what can be accomplished with directory interfaces. In addition, should there be a need to migrate to another interface/technology; the migration should be identified in the context of the current high-level functionality requirements, and eventually, to the specific interface translations.

Examples of high-level functionality requirements are: 1) the capability to search the directory based on any field; 2) the capability to update the directory; and 3) the capability to limit access of directory fields based on application security context. Again, the capability to establish high-level requirements helps to support any future migrations or application programming interface changes. The high-level definitions also provide a clear way to communicate the functionality available in the interface without diving into the detailed specifications. The DSAS provides guidance for the development teams in how to use Active Directory. Figure 1.1 depicts the organization of the directory services team.

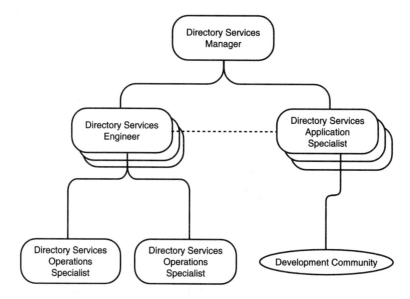

Figure 1.1   The directory services organization.

Organizing and Evolving the Active Directory Team

As you embark on building the Active Directory team to design, implement, deploy, and eventually leverage your investment in Active Directory, it is important to recognize the evolution that takes place within the team and the team's relationship with the organization.

In the beginning, Active Directory design started with some fact finding about the requirements for the directory and about the types of directories currently existing in the organization. This activity starts the first phase of developing the directory. Phase 1 is called "Understanding, Labbing, and Prototyping." Phase 1 is the learning phase in which the team works together to understand Active Directory and to determine how to implement it in the organization.

Phase 1: Understanding, Labbing, and Prototyping

During Phase 1, the Active Directory team consists of the directory services manager/lead, Active Directory engineer, Active Directory Operations Specialist (ADOS), and a DSAS. The team is striving to create an architecture document that identifies the requirements for Active Directory. These might include reduced administrative costs and greater consistency of information across the enterprise. As the team might be new to the technology, there should be some time planned for taking the ideas and technology into the lab and validating functionality based on the requirements. The lab portion should result in a reasonable architecture document.

This type of discovery process, close to the beginning, requires an action-oriented staff. It also requires analysis of how to balance the requirements. This first phase requires senior staff in the organization for identifying the needs of the organization, most likely through some type of interview process. The results should be documented and integrated into the architecture document. The team should document all the findings and develop standards for implementation.

Now that you have an understanding about the requirements, the next step is to create a lab environment to validate the functionality and demonstrate to those in various roles how the product actually works against the requirements. This is a time for the Directory Services Operations Specialist (DSOS) to validate some of the administrative tasks.

In the third part of this phase, the organization should work to establish a preproduction prototype for a small representative group of users. The objective of this phase is to provide the users with an understanding of the function of the design in a real-world environment. Performance and operational procedures surrounding the implementation should also be noted for any unusual variances to what might be expected.

During this phase, a directory services manager/lead needs to be identified to deal with all the logistics for rolling out the product and through the preproduction pilots. Training requirements need to be identified for staff, end users, and developers.

Phase 2: Implementation of Active Directory and Applications

During this phase of the development, the team changes the focus from investigation, discovery, and documentation to the actual building of the systems and processes for the directory. Initially, the directory services team focused on design and design validation. With design complete, the team focuses on rolling out Active Directory and providing a structured operation for supporting the new environment.

The jump from planning to implementing creates a dramatic change for the complexion of the team. Depending on the size of the organization, there might be a need for temporary staff during the role out. In any case, there is the challenge of moving from a largely analytical phase to a largely "can-do" phase, during which the focus is on getting the product rolled out.

In conjunction with the roll out of the directory, there should be special consideration for rolling out an application that takes advantage of the enterprise directory. This application should have been in development and tested during the preproduction pilot, and it should go through the typical application quality-assurance process. As the directory scales to the enterprise's size, you can deploy the application. We would recommend that at least 50 percent of the deployment is completed, and that the 50 percent that is completed is representative of the organization as a whole. In addition, the first application that uses the directory should be a simple application, and one that is used by only a small population within the organization.

You can deploy applications that use Active Directory after the initial installation and stabilization of Active Directory. The use of Active Directory by applications is a great leveraging point for the new directory service, but it is understandable that some organizations are reluctant to deploy a new operating system, directory infrastructure, and a custom application at the same time.

The objective of the implementation phase is to deploy a clean, relatively simple implementation of the directory across the organizations. It is realistic to expect less than the entire organization moving to Active Directory during the initial implementation. Primary for this phase is deploying an implementation that is reliable as a platform for the organization. The organization should not see some new intrinsic benefit of the directory at this phase. Although this might occur, this phase focuses on laying a strong foundation for more expanded uses of Active Directory.

In Phase 2, the directory services team has moved from analytic and discovery driven to task–oriented and process driven. This is a challenging transition. Most architects are interested in seeing their designs come to fruition, but dealing with the rigors of a day-to-day installation is not an ideal situation. As Table 1.2 demonstrates, the directory services engineer and the DSAS are supporting the roll out and doing some planning for future enhancements. Enhancements include exposing features that you did not initially implement, adding third-party software, and customizing the directory.

Table 1.2 **Directory Services Team Responsibilities by Phase**

Role	Phase 1	Phase 2	Phase 3
DSE	Design . initial functionality	Support design modifications, as required for implementation.	Support design changes as needed.
		Start on future design enhancements.	Continue with future design enhancements.

Role	Phase 1	Phase 2	Phase 3
		Provide Tier 3 support.	Work with directory services manager to develop a directory services vision for future phases.
DSAS	Participate in designing initial functionality.	Support . application implementations using directory services	Develop roadmap for directory-enabled applications.
DSOS	Understand the design.	Support implementation /roll out.	Operate directory services.
		Provide Tier 2 support.	
Project Manager	None	Drive effective implementation.	Conduct post mortem and evaluate lessons learned.

Phase 3: Maturity, Leverage, and Evolution

In Phase 3, the team defines a new mission. After the implementation is complete, the foundation for leveraging directory services is in place. This does not constitute the end but only the beginning of the challenge. After directory services are in place, the team has learned many things about the product and its use. This phase of the project is to truly create an operating environment. The design phase provided a vision for the implementation. The implementation phase built Active Directory to that vision, and in turn, most likely leads to many lessons about the product, end users, application use, and directory services team. In Phase 3, the directory is fine-tuned, based on what we learned.

Maturity

The directory services environment and the directory services team matures during this phase. The implementation phase probably encouraged many individuals to work together to get things done, regardless of the responsibility. The Project Manager is now gone, and he or she has turned over the outstanding issues of the implementation. During Phase 3, the team should mature the system based on the outstanding issues. Regular performance, system utilization, and problem summaries should be captured for trend analysis and proactive resolution of problems.

Just as the system matures, the directory services team matures. The team now has a firm understanding of how the system works. The Active Directory design team should expand to include some if not all the DSOSs. The DSOSs are a vital link to the day-to-day operational functions and challenges.

Working directly with the DSOS, the DSAS can identify opportunities for developing tools to enhance the support of the enterprise system.

Leverage

At this point, you have several pieces in place. Active Directory is running and stable. The organization is using the directory. At least one custom application is up and running on the directory. Now, you are prepared to leverage the directory. This effort should be lead by the directory services manager and the DSAS for application development. The opportunity is to identify applications, both those currently in place and new ones, which can take advantage of the directory for more effective and dynamic use in the organization.

Several application uses come to mind. Applications that are used in HR and need to kept track of, or communicated with employees. A common example would be the new employee interface. After the new employee has finished orientation, a HR person would be able to programmatically enable the new employee's email and network account. On exit, the HR person could disable the account. With regular employee-benefits information sent out, communications could be sent to users based on a location that is identified in the company's directory. This is a short list, but the directory probably has hundreds of uses that are valuable—now that we know the directory is run and maintained by an organization chartered with that responsibility.

Evolution

Now that the directory has matured and is starting to be used to an advantage in the organization, the process of evolving the directory (just as the organization and industry are also evolving) is important. The evolution of the directory starts from the beginning. The directory services manager, the directory services engineer, and the DSAS should work together to define the evolution. Questions about the direction of this mission critical service need to be answered.

- Will this service scale with the organization's direction?
- What are the emerging service standards that are going to be required as the service becomes integral to all the activities of the organization?
- Are we ready for the next release of the product?
- Are there features in the current product that we are ready to expose?
- Does the current application functionality need to be increased?

The answers to these questions help to define the evolution that will undoubtedly take place as directory services takes an increasingly important role in your organization.

Now we have covered the organization, the directory services team, and the various roles they play in your organization. There is also an important design requirement that can have an impact on your organization and how your IT staff organizes around these requirements.

Central Versus Distributed Administration

Centralized administration and distributed administration have long been the debate amongst LAN and email administrators. Centralized administration provides for greater control and consistency. This is important from an operational standpoint. Historically, systems that were tightly held provided a reliable and stable environment. Unfortunately, the tightly held systems also reduced the responsiveness that the more distributed systems provided. Whether it was a password change or a logon script modification, having the capability to get this done locally, or at least in the same time zone, provided greater responsiveness.

In addition to responsiveness, distributed administration provided a forum for communicating the requirements of the system from many of the remote environments and users. A distributed system had the benefit of enabling users to have access to an environment that would best meet the needs of the local operating environment. Today, many of the systems have been brought under some sort of centralized control either through a strict policy of adherence to standards or through direct central administration—all changes are made from a single location.

With Active Directory, both centralized and distributed administration can occur simultaneously. Centralized architecture and design can take place for the benefit of consistent operations, reliability, and performance. Distributed administration of data can take place by enabling the end users and/or directory services lead the capability to modify specific fields in the directory. A simple example of this is to enable end users to modify the address field or phone number field in Active Directory for their entry.

In the initiation of the directory, the recommendation is to have representatives from several of the remote or distributed locations. Failing to gather feedback or to understand concerns about the design or operations of the environment can lead to mis-expectations and simple lack of use. Remote site involvement can also help in developing effective training. Training your users about the possible uses of the directory proves important in getting the most out of directory services.

Small Organizations

Based on the size of your organization, you might need to consolidate some of the roles of the directory services team. A small organization might have the directory services manager and engineer responsibilities integrated with the Network Manager's and Network Administrator's responsibilities, respectively. The Network Operations Specialist could also be integrated with the Network Administrator's responsibility.

If the small organization is performing custom development, an effective strategy is to use an external consultant specializing in directory services for the DSAS. This approach would avoid the need for additional staff.

Security

Active Directory provides features that improve security. Active Directory provides support for single sign-on. Integration is possible with Active Directory and Windows 2000's support for Kerberos, an industry standard for authentication.

Active Directory has an impact on public key infrastructure (PKI). With Active Directory as part of Windows 2000, the PKI capability is integrated into Active Directory. Active Directory provides the capability to mirror and replicate certificate information. Smart cards are able to hold certificates and are able to take advantage of Active Directory's PKI support.

Infrastructure

Active Directory's replication and redundancy help reduce network traffic. With replicated Domain Controllers (DCs), a user is able to authenticate to a device that is close to the user. This minimizes network traffic.

DNS plays a role in resolving hostnames. The Windows 2000 implementation of DNS takes advantage of Active Directory's capability to replicate and mirror DNS information. In addition, if using dynamic DNS (DDNS), DNS updates need only to travel to the closest DC. This is a big improvement over typical DNS implementations. The primary domain master functions as the central location for updating the environment. If your environment is across a WAN, the DNS updates need to travel to a single location, causing a networking bottleneck.

Summary

Active Directory has an impact on your IT organization. Active Directory affects the infrastructure group, the operations group, and the application development group. The initial impact of this horizontal service can appear overwhelming, and without an organization to support the variety of effects, Active Directory might be used ineffectively. This chapter suggests how to organize for the creation and support of Active Directory.

Whether you create a formal organization to deal directly with the implementation and support of directory services in your organization, someone should be given the responsibilities described in this chapter. The size and complexity of your organization and your interest in leveraging the benefits of Active Directory play a large role in your decision.

2

Introducing Active Directory

ALL MAJOR NETWORK OPERATING SYSTEM (NOS) manufacturers include some form of a directory that stores information about network resources, such as users, groups, computers, printers, and so forth. One of the distinguishing factors for choosing a NOS in large enterprises is the directory. An enterprise directory must scale itself to support hundreds of thousands and even millions of objects, and it must be available for rapid and secure access across a distributed network environment, using a variety of different network transmission mediums and speeds.

There are a number of solid directory products on the market today. Netscape provides a directory called the Netscape Directory Server; Novell's is called Novell Directory Services (NDS); Banyan's is called StreetTalk; and *Meta* vendors, such as Entevio and Isocore, offer meta-directories that are designed to manage multiple directories using common directory protocols, such as Lightweight Directory Access Protocol (LDAP).

When Microsoft set out to build arguably one of the most comprehensive and complete operating systems available—Windows 2000—developing a solid directory was central to their design specifications. Active Directory is fundamental to Windows 2000. Like all directories, Active Directory provides a directory of objects (users, groups, computers, printers, and so on) and object attributes (email addresses, telephone numbers, locations, and so on) that enable users on a network to access information and resources easily. Because Active Directory stores all this information in a data store that is fast, efficient, and replicated throughout a distributed enterprise, the management and support of the enterprise can be tailored to suit any organization's specific business needs; users can easily access information assets from anywhere, at anytime.

The benefits of a directory are now clear. Just a few years ago, directory manufacturers, such as Novell, had to work hard to articulate the value, importance, and benefits of a directory. Today, directories are core components of large enterprises and are now beginning to be exploited for their benefits and potential. Like Windows 2000, Active Directory is built on standards, and it delivers a number of distinct benefits. Active Directory uses LDAP as the core directory protocol, RPC and SMTP for directory replication, domain name system (DNS) for name resolution, and Kerberos and a X.509 public key infrastructure (PKI) for authentication and encryption.

Active Directory is like the nervous system for Windows 2000. It functions as the *security enabler* for the network, the *resource locator* for users, and the *policy implementer* for businesses. Active Directory benefits an organization by

- Storing critical information about computer networks, users, and groups in a single *data store*

- Providing consistent and accurate information about the network and its resources

- Extending interoperability to application vendors so that they can leverage and utilize the directory

- Eliminating the duplication of data and data entry

- Reducing the time required to develop applications and to administer and support the network

- Improving an organization's ability to secure access to network resources and information assets

- Enabling organizations to automate business processes for e-business

- Providing for enhanced customer service to both users and customers

- Providing redundancy through a multi-master directory, which replicates changes throughout the enterprise

- Enabling flexibility for directory-enabled applications by allowing the directory schema to be modified for specific packaged or custom applications

- Providing a scalable directory solution through decentralized directory services, which supports replication

Active Directory simplifies management, strengthens security, improves productivity, leverages existing investments, enhances availability, and can lower overall support costs. In addition, Active Directory has been built using lessons learned form other, older directories.

Finally, an important aspect of Active Directory has to do with directory consolidation. All of Microsoft's BackOffice and core application services, such as Exchange, SQL Server, System Management Servers (SMS), Dynamic Host Configuration Protocol (DHCP), and DNS, use, or rely on Active Directory for interoperability and administration. When you plan and design Active Directory for your organization, you define much of your enterprise-computing environment's structure. The structures that you define determine the level of availability and fault-tolerance, usage characteristics for clients and servers, methods that users use to view and access information in the directory, and capability of your directory to scale and evolve as your organization changes; they determine how to effectively manage the directory's contents.

Throughout this book, we introduce and discuss the major components of Active Directory. We explore several design considerations and present information that can help you make correct decisions when designing Active Directory to meet your specific needs. However, before we continue with this book, it is important to discuss some fundamentals of Active Directory.

In this chapter, we introduce the core components of Active Directory, explain how each component relates to each other, and explain how each component can affect your Active Directory design.

Active Directory Components

There are four principle components to an Active Directory design:

1. Forest
2. domain
3. organizational unit (OU)
4. site

Each design component builds on the others to produce the overall Active Directory design. For example, although the OU design and the domain design can account for the geographic needs and the administration needs of the organization, respectively, without a site design, a user, who needs to authenticate and access information from a remote office over a slow link, could suffer poor performance. In addition, if Active Directory domain, OU, and site designs are solid but the organization needs to replicate directory data to another subsidiary that needs to use a different namespace, Active Directory Forest design needs to be included for your Active Directory design to be considered accurate and complete.

Terminology and Context

Before we discuss each of the four principle components of Active Directory, let us first introduce some Active Directory terminology and define the context for proper Active Directory design.

Active Directory Forest

The Active Directory Forest is a group of one or more Active Directory domain trees that trust each other. In a Forest, domains are organized into trees. All domains share a common schema, configuration, and Global Catalog (GC). Unlike directory domain trees, a Forest does not share a contiguous namespace. Therefore, Forests do not need a distinct namespace, like microsoft.com or msn.com. This means that multiple name-spaces can be supported in a single Forest. If you plan to deploy an enterprise network comprised of numerous businesses, you might want to consider designing an Active Directory Forest as a way to logically represent and organize your business, business operations, and geographic structures.

Active Directory Tree

The Active Directory tree is a collection of one or more Windows 2000 domains that share a common schema, configuration, and GC. There can be multiple trees within a single Forest. Active Directory trees share a contiguous namespace resulting in a parent-child namespace relationship, like microsoft.com and sales.microsoft.com. The Active Directory tree design is the basis for Windows 2000; it helps define the namespace and the logical structure of your network.

Active Directory Domain

The Active Directory domain is an administrative boundary for a Windows 2000 envi-ronment. An Active Directory domain can span one or more locations, and it has its own security policies. A collection of domains that trust each other and that have a common namespace form a Directory Tree. All trees in the Forest share a common schema, configuration, and GC. It is important to model your Active Directory domain design in such a way that aligns with your administrative and security models so that the Windows 2000 enterprise is both easy to administer and to manage and secure from unauthorized access.

Global Catalog (GC)

Each domain replicates objects amongst its Domain Controllers (DCs). Domain objects are not replicated between domains. To provide object visibility between domains, the GC is a partial replica of every Windows 2000 domain in Active Directory. The GC stores a replica of the entire directory. In addition, it also contains a partial list of attributes so that information (users, computers, and printers) can be quickly found and "sourced" in Active Directory and across domains. If you do not consider which Windows 2000 servers will function as Active Directory GC servers, you could severely affect a user's ability to locate important network resources.

Active Directory Partition

Active Directory servers always store at least three partitions: the schema partition, the configuration partition, and the directory partition, which contains the subtree information. The domain partition only replicates between DCs within the same domain. The schema and configuration partitions replicate between all DCs in Active Directory. Active Directory partitions replicate, therefore, you need to consider your physical network topology and your users' computing needs and characteristics when designing Active Directory partition schemes.

Organizational Unit (OU)

The OU is a container in the Active Directory domain that can contain other OUs, user objects, group objects, computer objects, and more. OUs are a way to organize your objects into logical containers based on organizational structure, geographic structure, or any combination of the two. Defining a solid OU design enables you to assign a flexible administrative model that eases the support and management of a large, distributed enterprise. The OU design is also used for applying group policy.

Active Directory Site

The Active Directory site defines a set of Windows 2000 Servers holding Active Directory partitions, which are considered well-connected LAN speeds, such as 10Mbps Ethernet. Designing a solid Active Directory site, which is based on your physical network topology, ensures that Active Directory and all dependent applications and service operate with high-performance and high reliability. How DCs replicate and which DCs Windows 2000 clients prefer is based on your Active Directory site topology.

Active Directory Forest Design

Active Directory domains are identified by DNS names, for example `wadeware.net`. A domain always contains one or more DCs. A collection of Active Directory domains refers to a *Forest*. The primary purpose of an Active Directory Forest is to improve the management of multiple domains—typically a daunting task in prior versions of Windows NT—and simplify user access to network resources in the directory. In a Forest, all domains share a common schema, configuration, and GC. When the domains in a Forest have a contiguous namespace, they are referred to as a domain tree; when they do not share a contiguous namespace, they form separate domain trees within a Forest.

Figure 2.1 illustrates a typical Active Directory Forest design—one with a contiguous namespace and one with a discontiguous namespace.

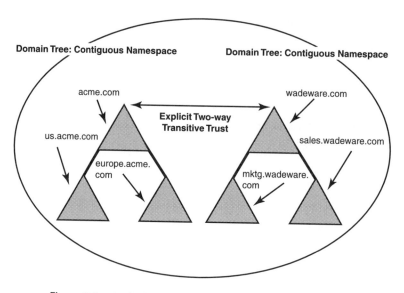

Figure 2.1 An Active Directory Forest with two domain trees.

The first domain in an Active Directory Forest is referred to as the *forest root.* You create the forest root when you install the first Active Directory DC and establish a new Active Directory Forest. Once established, you can create additional DCs in the same domain, additional domain trees, or a child domain of an existing domain tree. In certain circumstances, you might want to establish new Active Directory Forests.

When designing your Active Directory design, the first step is to define your Forest design. A key decision factor is whether to define a single Forest, which is most typical and easiest to manage and support, or multiple Forests, which although more difficult to manage, offers distinct advantages based on the specific characteristics of an organization. Considerations of an Active Directory Forest design include

- **Organizational Structure**—The structure of each business entity, such as partnership, joint ventures, and conglomerates, must be considered. Depending on the organizational structure of each business entity, you might need to create either multiple Forests or a single Forest.

- **Administrative and Security Model**—Each business entity's administration and security model can affect the design. For example, in a partnership, each business can have its own identity, business processes, Information Systems (IS) support organization, and security policies. In this case, it probably makes sense to create a separate Forest for each business in the partnership, especially if their security policies prohibit a trust relationship or if changes in one business, in other words new user objects, should not manifest themselves in the other business. When considering a multi-Forest design, it is important to know the trade-offs with regard to the user experience and the administrative complexities that come with having multiple Forests.

- **Organizational Changes**—Creating multiple Active Directory Forests could have a significant impact if you foresee organizational changes. Merging Active Directory Forests is not a one-step process. Creating trusts is more difficult to manage if you need to provide access to network resources located within another Active Directory Forest. Try to anticipate these changes when designing your Active Directory Forest.

- **Namespace Design**—Namespace design is based on your defined organizational structure. This process involves defining the Global Namespace, which is the combination of the DNS namespace and the Active Directory namespace. Defining your namespace correctly, both internal and external, is a key component that drives the decisions around your Active Directory Forest design. Some common models for namespace design include

  Geographic—when the namespace is based solely on the geographic attributes of the organization

  Political—when the namespace reflects the organizational structure of an organization

  Geo-Political—when the namespace reflects a mixture of the geographic and political structures of an organization

  Political-Geo—when the namespace reflects the political structure of the organization first and then the geographic structure of an organization

  Functional—when the only consideration for the namespace is operational necessity

- **Trust Relationships**—In prior versions of Windows NT, establishing and managing trusts between domains was difficult, especially if you had a master domain model with a number of resource domains. When you create domains or domain trees within an Active Directory Forest, two-way transitive trusts are automatically created between each domain in the Forest, making administration much easier. Understanding the trust relationships required for your organization helps to define the Active Directory Forest design. Multiple Active Directory Forests require explicit trusts to perform inter-Forest lookups, and even then, objects need to be imported from one Forest to another.

- **Global Catalog (GC)**—Because directory searches reference the GC and because the GC is replicated throughout the domains and domain trees in an Active Directory Forest, the GC server placement and the quantity of GC servers are critical for fast directory-wide lookups. Knowing what type of access to resources located on the network that your users would need helps to determine your Active Directory Forest design.

By understanding the specific components of Active Directory and the terminology associated with each component and by factoring in the considerations previously described, you will be able to successfully define your Active Directory Forest design. After you have completed this task, you are ready to go a step deeper in the Active Directory design process and focus on defining the Active Directory domain design.

Active Directory Domain Design

Like the Forest design, the Active Directory domain design is an essential part of Active Directory. As a second step, you need to carefully consider your domain structure. Many factors can affect your Active Directory domain design:

- **Active Directory is a distributed database**—with parts of the directory (represented by domains) stored on DCs within a domain tree or a Forest. Given this fact, it is important to correctly partition the directory in such a way that stores relevant data close to the users of that data, while ensuring fault-tolerance and reliability.

- **A domain is an administrative boundary**—meaning that domain administrators have full access to objects in their domain but not to other domains within the Forest.

- **A domain is a unit of authentication**—which requires a DC to service authentication requests.

- **A domain has a common database partition**—which replicates between all DCs in the domain. Therefore, if a domain spans multiple physical locations, the domain database partition replicates itself to those physical locations. This replication can be managed using Active Directory sites, but the replication is inevitable.

To define your Active Directory domain design, you should use the following process:

1. Verify that the Active Directory Forest design is complete and bought-off by the organization.
2. Define the number of domains in each Forest.
3. Select the Forest's root domain.
4. Determine the DNS name for each domain.
5. Determine the DNS server deployment.
6. Identify trust relationships—explicit or automatic two-way transitive trusts.
7. Understand the impact of future changes to the organization after the Active Directory domain design is defined and in place.

In previous versions of Windows NT Server, the Security Account Management (SAM) database had a limitation of storing no more than 40,000 objects. This limitation required large organizations to build and maintain elaborate domain structures, using a variety of domain models, including single, master, and multi-master domain models. Furthermore, a read-write replica of the SAM was stored on a single machine called the Primary Domain Controller (PDC). This meant that all domain changes, such as creating user accounts, needed to be accomplished on the PDC, and these changes would then replicate to backup DCs, called BDCs. With Active Directory, Windows 2000 can now scale up to millions of objects, and changes to the directory can now be made on any number of DCs because the directory is now a distributed database that replicates throughout the domain, domain trees, and Forest. This model is called a multi-master domain because all DCs are equal, and they can have their objects modified. These modifications are then replicated to all other appropriate DCs.

Active Directory also offers a flexible administrative model because the domains are not the only method of granting or delegating administrative responsibilities. With Active Directory, you can create OUs that represent containers within Active Directory hierarchy. OUs provide the capability to administer portions of the directory and to organize objects (users, groups, printers, computers, and so on) into sub-units. This is especially helpful in large, distributed enterprises.

Figure 2.2 illustrates a couple of typical Active Directory domain designs. One is a single domain model made up of OUs, and the other is a multi-domain model made up of multiple domains forming a domain tree.

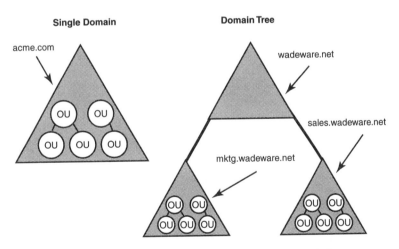

Figure 2.2 Two examples of Active Directory domain designs.

There are a number of ways to define your specific domain design. There is no single, right design; however, there are some common reasons for creating multiple domains. We always recommend starting with an assumption of a single domain (for simplicity), and then identify reasons why this domain model would need to change. For example, if you needed to preserve legacy Windows NT domains to create multiple domains because of physical limitations in your network or geographic structure, or if you need to portion administration to separate *units* within a large organization, you might need a multiple domain structure.

Like a Forest design, the key to a successful Active Directory domain design is to make sure you factor as many considerations—network, administration, security, organizational—and possibilities for change as possible. Many of these considerations are discussed in Chapter 7, "Designing the Windows 2000 Domain Structure." Typically, you need to come up with a number of different design alternatives and apply each design to your specific considerations before you can validate the best design for your organization.

Unlike the Forest design, Active Directory domain designs offer a bit more flexibility for change. With Windows 2000 and Active Directory, you can promote and demote DCs, and you can add and remove DCs with little effort or risk. You can partition and re-partition the directory and configure replication in a way that aligns with your organizational structure and network topology.

After you have completed the Active Directory domain design, you are ready to move on to define the OU structure of the directory.

Active Directory Organizational Unit Design

The OU design is another critical component to your overall Active Directory design. A number of factors need to be determined before you decide on a final design, for example the domain design. There is no single, *right* way to define your OU structure; there are only some common techniques and best practices.

Before we discuss these, let's define some of the basic properties of OUs:

- **OUs are not security principles**—They cannot be added to security groups. Furthermore, you cannot assign permissions or rights to OUs and, therefore, apply those rights (through inheritance) down the hierarchy to objects within the OU.

- **OUs are used to delegate administration and control directory objects within the OU**—This means that you can assign security to objects within the OU and then assign access control lists (ACLs) to these objects for further administrative granularity and control.

- **OUs can contain other OUs**—These are often referred to as nested OUs.

- **OUs can be assigned a group policy**—This allows for greater control and administration.

- **OUs do not need to represent an *intuitive* structure**—Users do not navigate the OU structure; they *virtually* view the resources that they have access to based on the cumulative security, policy, and permissions applied to them from the Active Directory design. Although a common OU structure across domains is simpler to administer, it is not required.

Active Directory OU design can take on several forms. Because OUs are used to delegate administration and because users won't necessarily see the OU structure, the OU design is typically based on the Administrative Mode. Who is responsible for administering and managing certain portions (containers) of the directory?

Typically, administration can be delegated in three ways:

1. By physical location
2. By business unit or department
3. By role/task

Because Active Directory can contain nested OUs and because OUs can contain multiple objects with assigned security and object attributes, it is easy to create a granular administrative model that meets the most specific needs of an organization, such as resetting passwords on user objects without being able to change or modify anything else about that object. However, just because OUs can be nested, it does not mean that they should be. The more OUs in a domain the more complex the administration of the domain will be. OUs should exist to satisfy a business requirement.

The Active Directory OU design needs to be carefully planned. If you do not have a complex organization or a highly distributed work force or administrative model, it is probably not wise to create a complex OU structure. Often Network Administrators, who know NDS, create Active Directory OU structure based on their organizational structure because they think that Active Directory's OU structure is used for "walking the tree;" this is not the case.

Typically, the OU structure is driven by the need to delegate administration or to apply group policy. Both of these design considerations are explained in two different chapters, Chapter 9, "Group Policies," and Chapter 13, "Developing an Administrative Strategy."

With the Forest design, the domain design, and now the OU design complete, you are ready to move on to the final component of your Active Directory design: the site design.

Active Directory Site Design

As mentioned at the beginning of this chapter, Active Directory site design is based on the physical topology of your network. One of the distinct advantages of Active Directory over other major directory service products is the notion of a site. Microsoft first implemented a site structure with Exchange and SMS. Although the definition and use of a site was slightly different with each product, the intention for defining a site was always based around an area of high-speed connectivity.

In Windows 2000, Active Directory uses a site structure to partition Active Directory based on high- and low-speed communications. For example, if you have a remote office that has a LAN comprising 100 users, which operates autonomously but requires access to corporate applications and email over a 56Kbps frame relay circuit, you'll probably want to consider defining this portion of the network, or the subnet for that location, as a separate site.

In this example, the site would enable Network Administrators to define explicit directory replication intervals and to apply configuration to the replication processes using more resilient transport protocols for slow-speed networks, such as SMTP.

Active Directory site design has several components. Each component has special configuration properties and requirements. A *site link* is a connection between two sites that uses a slow network connection, less than LAN speeds of 10Mbps. Site links can be configured based on a replication schedule, a costing model, a replication interval, and the type of transport protocol used for site-to-site Active Directory replication.

To define your Active Directory site design, you should start by defining or documenting your physical network topology. With this in hand, you can then identify the number of sites and the connections between sites, and then define the site links and the associated configuration properties of each site link.

By designing a solid Active Directory site structure, you are able to control how and where users authenticate to the Windows 2000 Active Directory domain. This means that users first try to locate a DC within their site, which is (by definition) connected at LAN speeds, before they attempt to locate another DC across a slow-link to another site. In prior versions of Windows NT Server, authentication to the NT domain over a slow link was slow and painful for end users. With the capability to define sites, Network Administrators can now define areas of high-speed connectivity and direct users transparently to authenticate with a *preferred* DC. The process for designing an Active Directory site topology is outlined in Chapter 10, "The Physical Topology: Sites and Replication."

Summary

This chapter presented and discussed a brief overview of Active Directory and some of the core components that comprise a successful Active Directory design. The remaining chapters of this book delve into the details of Active Directory and identify how the components of Windows 2000 interact, rely on, and use Active Directory for improved functionality, scalability, and reliability.

3

Active Directory as a Meta-Directory

Eᴀʀʟɪᴇʀ ɪɴ ᴛʜɪs ʙᴏᴏᴋ, ᴛʜᴇ ɪᴍᴘᴏʀᴛᴀɴᴄᴇ ᴏғ ᴅɪʀᴇᴄᴛᴏʀɪᴇs in our everyday lives was discussed. We need to look up phone numbers and email addresses. Applications that we use store profiled information in a directory. Our ability to log in to our workstation is governed by information in a directory. Not only are directories central to our ability to function in an electronic society, *multiple* directories are important. Consequently, the integration of directories, and the information in them, is a critical success factor for the knowledge worker in today's business environment.

This chapter focuses on Active Directory as the central technology in a meta-directory strategy. This includes using Active Directory as a central repository for application and organization data, as well as examining integration with Novell Directory Services (NDS) and X.500.

What is a meta-directory? The first section of this chapter addresses the fundamentals of what a meta-directory is and how Active Directory can begin to meet the criteria of a meta-directory. These criteria include

- Integration with other directories via an industry-recognized standard interface
- Extensibility
- Reliability
- Scalability

How will Active Directory integrate as a meta-directory with a directory based on NetWare directory services? The second section of this chapter addresses some of the technical requirements to integrate Active Directory with an NDS solution in a long-term coexistence environment.

How will Active Directory integrate with and leverage X.500 directory standards? In the words of Microsoft, Active Directory is "X.500-like." What this means is that Active Directory uses X.500 elements, such as organizational units (OUs) and given names (GNs), but it does not fully comply with the X.500 standards. The third section of this chapter addresses some of the challenges of integrating Active Directory with a directory based on the X.500 standard.

How can Active Directory be integrated in a heterogeneous environment? The final section describes how someone might put Active Directory into a corporate environment that might have other defacto standards. In addition, it addresses how to use Active Directory as the central directory resource within a heterogeneous environment.

Defining a Meta-Directory

When discussing a meta-directory strategy, it is important not to confuse the concept of a meta-directory with that of directory coexistence. In the case of a true meta-directory, there is a single directory (the meta-directory) that is integrated with other directories and that is the single point of contact for all directory clients—whether they be users, applications, or hardware. Figure 3.1 illustrates a meta-directory integrated into an infrastructure that includes other directories. The meta-directory is the single point of contact for all these directory users. The meta-directory then references the other directories to gain the necessary data.

This chapter primarily focuses on examples in which Active Directory is the meta-directory in a directory coexistence (or synchronization) configuration.

Directory integration is not restricted to classic directories. It is also possible to configure a meta-directory system that includes both directories and other data sources. For example, Active Directory might be used to integrate application data between a Human Resources (HR) application and Microsoft Exchange. In Figure 3.2, Active Directory is the intersection between the two disparate data sources. A Web application that integrates information from both the HR application and Microsoft Exchange can query the Active Directory for the information, rather than having to query both Microsoft Exchange and the HR application.

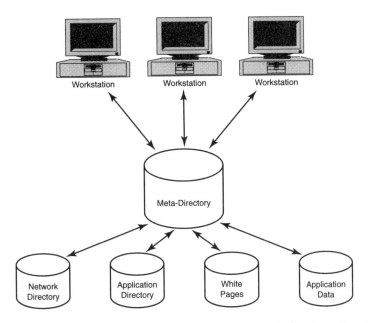

Figure 3.1   In the case of a true meta-directory strategy, multiple directories might contain information required by network users, applications, or network hosts.

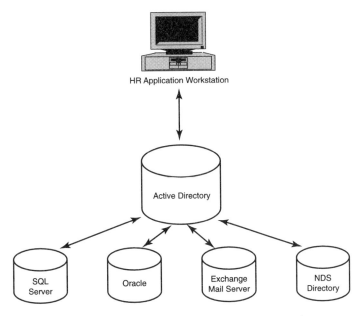

Figure 3.2   Active Directory can serve as a central point of contact for applications seeking data from distributed data sources.

This type of directory integration should not be confused with the concept of directory coexistence. Directory coexistence exists if two or more directories synchronize data or share data elements while, at the same time, servicing their own directory clients. For example, Active Directory might be an intersection point for Windows NT 4.0, NetWare with NDS, and UNIX Network Information Service (NIS) directories, as in Figure 3.3. However, each of the respective network clients and users do not access Active Directory for their network authentication information. Instead, they access their own native directory. Directory-coexistence strategies are discussed in Chapter 6, "Planning for Coexistence."

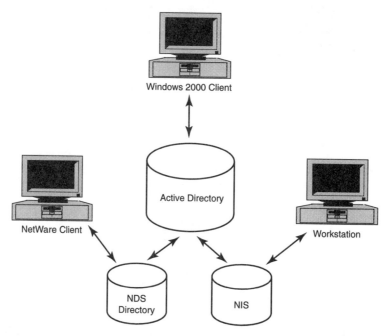

Figure 3.3   Active Directory can also be used as a central element in a directory-coexistence scheme. This should not be confused with a meta-directory strategy as previously outlined.

A meta-directory is a central repository for many types of data, such as telephone numbers, user network logon names and passwords, manager's names, office locations, and so on. Because there are so many different types of data that can be stored in a meta-directory, it is critical that the structure of the directory schema be planned carefully. In some cases, the data might not actually be stored in the directory. Instead, there might be pointers in the directory to data that is stored in other databases or directories. For example, Active Directory could include a Globally Unique Identifier (GUID) and a Lightweight Directory Access Protocol (LDAP) query string that identifies a specific set of data in a HR database that is accessible by using the LDAP

Application Programming Interface (API). In this way, the HR department would not have to modify the data in Active Directory, but it could simply modify the data in the local application. If a directory client queries Active Directory for the data string, the meta-directory issues a LDAP query to the HR application, which then returns the data to Active Directory and finally to the client.

Figure 3.4 illustrates a meta-directory that is accessing information stored in both SQL Server and Oracle. Active Directory, as a meta-directory, can be used to access and integrate data from a wide range of back-end data sources.

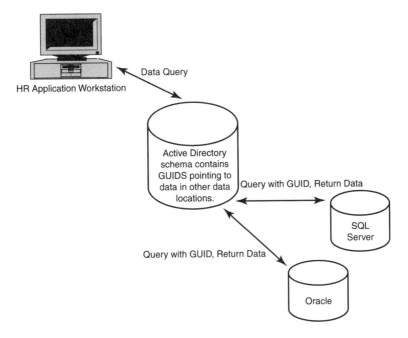

Figure 3.4   A meta-directory accessing information from both SQL Server and Oracle.

A meta-directory can contain pointers to data in other directories, thus distributing the required space for data storage, as well as the administration requirements. It is important to note that other types of data do not belong in a directory. Stock quotes, for example, represent data that is so dynamic that storing them in a directory is not practical. Stock quote information changes so often that the replication traffic caused by the system trying to replicate changes between directory servers would, in most cases, bring the system down. Stock ticker symbols, however, represent data that is static in nature and that users can use as a reference to query other data sources.

Integration

As you begin to plan the structure of your directory, you must take into account all the different types of data you want to include, as well as all the different sources of that data. Active Directory is simply another database in your Information Technology (IT) infrastructure. You need to employ the same planning methods that you would to deploy a new SQL database. In the case of our sample company, Wadeware, many different types of data will eventually be included in Active Directory, after it is established as the central directory in a meta-directory architecture. The sales force uses a sales-force automation tool that requires a separate user name and password. This information is stored in Active Directory. One of the subsidiaries of Wadeware currently uses NetWare as a primary network operating system (NOS). There is a requirement to synchronize network authentication information between Active Directory and NDS on NetWare.

Determining all the data that needs to go in to Active Directory can be overwhelming. The best way to start is to develop a table that contains all the data elements that you plan to include in Active Directory. You want to capture several properties for each data element. These include

- **Data Type**—The type of data that is in the field. This is defined as ASCII, binary large object (BLOB), numeric, alphabetic, currency, and so on. This determines the formatting of the field and the configuration of how the data should be presented.

- **Field Length**—The size of the data field is important to determine at the outset. When determining the length of the data filed, it is extremely important to take in to account all the possible configurations of the data. For example, a phone number might be represented as *425-555-1212, (425) 555-1212, +1 (425) 555-1212*, or even *1.425.555.1212*. Each one of these configurations represents a different requirement for the length of the data field. Another way to control the length of the data entered in any specific field is to provide a field mask for the data. In the case of the phone number previously listed, you could provide a mask that exposed only the character places required for the area code and the seven digit phone number. You could then present the data in any format you wanted.

- **Current Source of Data**—When establishing a new meta-directory, you should always identify the current source of the data that you put in the directory. This helps you to determine data synchronization requirements.

- **Data Owner**—It is important to determine at the outset who is the owner of the data. In large organizations, it is typical for multiple people to claim ownership of data. When considering your design for a meta-directory solution using Active Directory, it is critical that you determine who owns what data so that you assign the correct administrative rights to the individuals or departments for changing the data in the directory.

- **Synchronization Method**—There are several ways to design synchronization in a meta-directory environment. The easiest way to jumpstart data synchronization between two directory systems is a one-time data extraction from a legacy data source. This is adequate for dealing with a legacy data source that will be retired as soon as the meta-directory is in production. It is obviously not adequate for synchronizing data between a legacy data source and the meta-directory in a situation in which the legacy data source coexist with Active Directory for an extended period of time. Although it is possible to conduct on-going data extractions from a legacy data source by using a batch process, those processes are often cumbersome and time-consuming. In addition, when large blocks of data are added wholesale to a directory, it can significantly affect the amount of replication traffic between directory servers on the network.

Table 3.1 is representative of one used for developing a meta-directory architecture.

Table 3.1   **Examples of Data Used When Developing a Meta-Directory**

Data Type	Field Length (chars)	Current Source	Data Owner	Synchronization Method
User Name	50	NDS	NetWare Admin	MS Directory Synchronization (DirSync)
Access Authentication Level	2	Siebel Sales Force Automation	Sales IT Admin	ADSI Script

Extensibility

For a directory to meet the requirements of a meta-directory, it must be extensible. In the case of Active Directory, it is possible to extend the schema by using the directory snap-in for the Microsoft Management Console (MMC) or programmatically by using a script. The extensibility of a meta-directory is important for external applications to take advantage of the directory as a repository for application data or as a pointer to external sources for the data. In the case of the next version of Microsoft Exchange, for example, the Active Directory schema is modified significantly to provide directory services for Exchange.

The schema in Active Directory is fully extensible and can be used as an object store for data, or as a store for pointers to other data locations. However, although the schema can be extended (if needed), it is important that Active Directory administrators fully understand the implications of extending the schema and develop a schema modification policy. Because schema extensions can have a dramatic impact on performance of Active Directory, it is well worth your time expanding on schema management at this point. When discussing schema extensibility, it is important to understand

- How to modify the schema
- When to modify the schema
- How to develop a policy for modifying the schema

How to Modify the Schema

The Active Directory schema is comprised of components. These components are classes, attributes, and syntax. It is important to note that when a new user is added to the directory, the schema is not modified; in other words, a new component is not added. Instead, an object of the User class is created. New objects in Active Directory should be a relatively routine task for administrators. Modifying the schema should be a task that happens rarely—and one that is done only with a significant amount of consideration.

Classes in the schema are groupings of objects that share a set of attributes, such as Users or Computers. Attributes are the data elements that collectively define an object. In the case of a user, the attributes would include `displayName` and `name`. These attributes are also referred to as properties (see Figure 3.5).

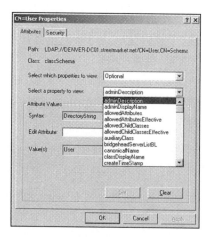

Figure 3.5   Attribute objects within the directory schema can be
modified by using Active Directory schema in MMC.

Each one of these attributes also contains a definition for syntax. The syntax of an attribute determines the type and format of the data that is required. For example, the syntax rules for the attribute `displayName` might require that the value be alpha, rather than numeric. The syntax rules for the attribute `Telephone-Number` might require a numeric value.

The schema can be modified by using the Active Directory schema snap-in found in MMC. Members of the Schema Admins group can use the snap-in to manage the schema by creating, deactivating, and modifying classes and attributes. It is extremely important to note that after a schema extension has been enacted, it is not possible to delete it. It is possible to deactivate classes and attributes, but not to delete them.

Scripting is also a possible method for modifying the schema. By using ADSI, a script can perform all the same schema modification tasks as the schema snap-in.

There is also a third way to modify the schema. When new applications are installed, the installation process can modify the schema based upon the needs of the application. If an application is installed that requires a modification to the schema, it is necessary for a member of the Schema Admins group to perform the installation.

Not all schema objects can be modified. Any classes and attributes defined as systems cannot be modified or deactivated. In addition, certain restrictions are enforced if the classes or attributes are part of the default schema configuration. Objects that are in deactivated classes still appear in directory searches. Consequently, to eliminate deactivated objects from search results, you must search for all objects in deactivated classes and then delete the objects themselves.

When to Modify the Schema

Deciding when to modify the schema is an important decision because of the dramatic impact on performance that a schema modification can have. Because of the large number and the range of classes and attributes in the default schema, modifications should be a rare occurrence. However, there might be times at which the default schema does not meet your needs. The following are some situations in which the schema might need to be modified:

- **No existing class meets your needs**—There might be times when there is no existing class that meets your needs in the default schema. This might be the case if you are creating a new, homegrown application or installing an application that does not include schema modification as part of the installation process. In these cases, you should add an entire new class to the schema.

- **An existing class lacks attributes**—An existing class might nearly fit your needs, but it might lack specific attributes that you need. In this case, you can add new attributes to the existing call or derive a child class from the existing class and add attributes as needed.

- **A set of unique attributes is needed**—There might be times that a unique set of attributes is needed, but an entire new class or child class is not required. In these cases, you can create an auxiliary class that is connected to the original class.

- **Classes or attributes are no longer needed**—In the case where a class or attribute is no longer needed, use the snap-in or a script to deactivate the class or attribute.

Regardless of how the schema is modified, it is important to always consider the concept of inheritance between classes. Classes inherit the properties of the classes from which they are derived. The parent class from which a child class is derived affects all future objects created in that class type. Consequently, it is important to plan correctly when deriving new child classes.

Policy for Schema Modification

Developing a policy for schema modification is less about technology than it is about good project management and planning. Schema modifications can have widespread effects that might impair or disable Active Directory across entire organizations. Consequently, it is important to follow a rigid set of steps if reviewing and approving modifications. These steps might include

- **Initiating modification request**—Requests for any schema modification should be reviewed by a committee that represents all the stakeholders in the organization. Any group that is affected by the schema modification should have a say in the review process. After the request is reviewed and validated, the committee is the body to approve the request.

- **Planning implementation**—After the modification is approved, a plan must be developed for implementing the modification. The plan should include testing to ensure that the modification meets the requirements of the requestor. The plan should also ensure that an effective roll-back process is in place.

- **Modification**—Modification of the schema should also be tested in a lab environment first. The lab should be completely separated from the production environment. The lab schema should accurately represent the production schema.

Reliability

Reliability is a critical feature for any directory—and even more so for a meta-directory. A meta-directory by definition is used by multiple applications, systems, network services, and other directories. Consequently, any directory outage can have a significant impact on business performance and, ultimately, on the bottom-line revenue of the company.

Several levels of fault-tolerance can be implemented so that Active Directory is highly available. Because it is a multi-master directory, it can withstand Domain Controller (DC) outages by having multiple DCs located in strategic locations around the organization. As a best practice, DCs should be located on every major segment of the network. In addition, the physical layer configuration of the network should provide for multiple path connectivity between DCs whenever possible. This type of configuration, enables continued directory replication if a single network segment fails. In Figure 3.6, if one WAN segment fails, connectivity between DCs is still possible by using a secondary link. In this example, any one of the three sites has two network paths to the other two sites.

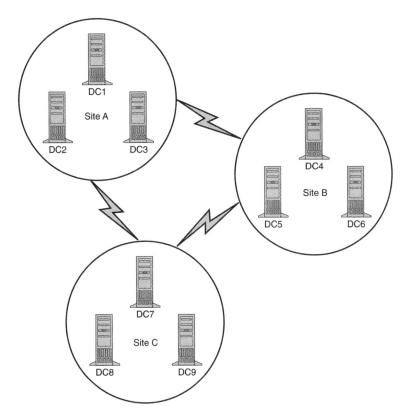

Figure 3.6   A redundant network helps to augment the reliability of Active Directory.

In addition to providing multi-master replication between DCs within Active Directory, each Active Directory DC can function as a zone-master domain name system (DNS) server to external clients and other DNS servers. This is radically different from the standard configuration of DNS, which has only one zone master and multiple secondary, or caching, servers. Configuration of DNS as part of Active Directory is covered in more depth in Chapter 8, "Designing the DNS Namespace."

In addition to directory reliability and redundancy, Active Directory leverages Windows 2000 Advanced Server clustering, which provides an additional level of reliability. Advanced Server and Data Center Server provide hardware clustering services for two-node and multi-node systems, respectively. Active Directory is used to publish information about the cluster configuration.

Scalability

Scalability is another critical aspect of a meta-directory. Active Directory provides for scalability through multi-master domains, multi-domain trees, and multi-tree Forests. This is a marked contrast to Windows NT 4.0, which had a practical limitations on the number of domains that could be linked together by using explicit trust relationships. With Active Directory, it is possible to configure the domain environment in a way that matches business needs, rather than having to force business requirements into an inferior domain design, as was often the case with Windows NT 3.51 or 4.0.

As discussed at length earlier in this chapter, Active Directory also meets scalability requirements through an extensible schema and a fault-tolerant schema. Unlike earlier versions of Windows NT, Active Directory does not have a specific limitation on the size of the directory database. However, although there is no specific limitation on the size of the database, there are practical limits. The speed of connectivity between DCs both within the same site and in different sites, limits the actual size of the directory database.

Integration with NetWare Directory Services

Windows NT Server included several tools for integrating with a Novell NetWare environment, including Gateway Services for NetWare (GSNW), File and Print for NetWare (FPNW), and NetWare Convert. Of these three utilities, NetWare Convert was the only tool designed to actually integrate and migrate directory information between a NetWare directory and a Windows NT 4.0 directory. Windows 2000 Server includes a new version of NetWare Convert. The tool is now called the Directory Services Migration Tool (DSMT). In addition to DSMT, there is an important tool for integrating NDS, as well as other directories, and Active Directory for long-term coexistence. This tool is called the DirSync Server. This is an add-on tool to Windows 2000.

The Active Directory DirSync Server is a Windows 2000 service that runs on a Windows 2000 DC. DirSync Server is actually a collection of components that integrate to provide directory synchronization (see Figure 3.7). These components are

- **DirSync session manager**—The session manager manages the sessions between disparate directories. Each session includes a pair of directories and a set of parameters for synchronizing the two directories.

- **Directory providers**—Each directory has a directory provider that reads changes incrementally or writes changes incrementally to the directory that the provider supports. There is a directory provider for NetWare directory services.

- **Object mappers**—Object mappers provide a mapping of objects in the directory schema, access rights and permissions, and namespace for each directory.

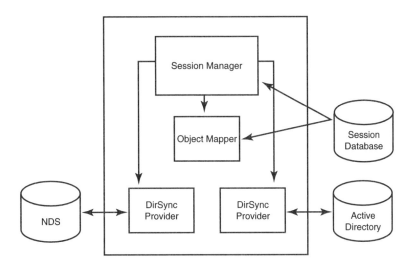

Figure 3.7   The DirSync server architecture provides an integrated environment for synchronizing NDS and Active Directory.

Session Manager and Sessions

The session manager coordinates the synchronization process between directories. The session manager provides logging, error handling, recovery, and performance counters.

Sessions are defined by a set of session parameters. A sample of the most common session parameters follows:

- **Session owner**—The session owner is the identification of the DC on which DirSync is running. Only one DirSync process can run on a DC computer.

- **Session ID**—The session ID is a unique identifier for the session on the DC that owns it.

- **Session name**—The session name is a friendly name provided by the administrator for the session.

- **Session flags**—The session flags specify if two-way synchronization is enabled and if the session is enabled or disabled. Disabled sessions are not started automatically.

- **Source directory**—The source directory identifies the source directory type, server location, and logon credentials.

- **Target directory**—The target directory identifies the target directory type, server location, and logon credentials.

- **Schedule**—The schedule specifies when sessions are to be executed.

- **Log level**—The log level specifies the level of logging needed for each session.

Challenges

Implementing synchronization architecture between NDS and Active Directory has several challenges. Both NDS and Active Directory are biased on the X.500 directory standard. Consequently, there can be some confusion between the semantics used to describe a directory structure in NDS versus a directory structure in Active Directory. For example, containers in NDS are equivalent to OUs in Active Directory.

The first step in developing a plan for integrating NDS and Active Directory is to map the NDS directory hierarchy that exists and to map the Active Directory hierarchy that either already exists or is in development. This includes mapping all objects and attributes, as well as security and access rights on each container in the directory. After the directories have been mapped, the next step is to identify the master/slave relationships between objects in each directory.

There are limitations to the services that the DirSync Server can provide. These limitations include

- There is support for only one-to-one mapping of object IDs. It is not possible to map a one-to-many relationship between an object in an NDS directory and Active Directory.

- Synchronization takes place on a container level, not on an object level. This means that all objects in a container and all child containers are synchronized between the two directory environments. It is not possible to synchronize a single object in a container.

Integration with X.500

True integration with an X.500 directory can be extremely hard to achieve. There are multiple reasons for this. First, there are not many X.500 directories in production today. This is because the X.500 standard is cumbersome to deploy and manage. Second, the Directory Access Protocol requires a lot of overhead and is difficult to configure.

Consequently, one of the best ways to integrate with an X.500 directory is to find an X.500 directory that supports LDAP and that uses LDAP as the protocol for reading and writing data between Active Directory and the X.500 directory. This type of directory architecture has been used for the past several years as LDAP has gained more popularity. Without exception, all the major X.500 directory services on the market today support LDAP (see Figure 3.8).

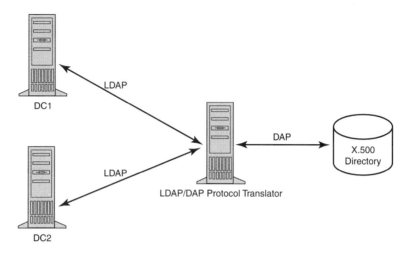

Figure 3.8 LDAP can be used as a protocol for communication between
Active Directory and existing X.500-based directories. All major
X.500 directories on the market today support LDAP.

If you are planning for integration and coexistence between Active Directory and an
existing X.500 directory, it is likely that the directory interchange architecture and
Active Directory structure are derived from the existing X.500 directory structure.
This is because X.500 directories are typically designed and developed from the top
down. Because of this, the directory structure can be rigid and difficult to modify. This
is not to say, however, that the Active Directory structure will be the same as the existing X.500 directory structure. If implementing Active Directory in an environment
that already has a directory in place, it is important to consider implementing the best
design for a directory—not to simply mirror what is already in place.

  Active Directory hierarchies and the best design properties for that hierarchy are
discussed later in the book. That discussion focuses primarily on establishing a simple
hierarchy. In many cases, X.500 hierarchies are multi-layered and can be complicated
in nature.

Summary

A meta-directory is a single directory in an organization that provides users
one stop for their directory needs. Directory data may reside in several directories
across the organization, but the meta-directory brings this disparate data together,
while leaving the data in its native directory. This is accomplished by representing
directory objects in the meta-directory but referring queries to the directory where
the data is stored. Careful planning of how your Active Directory will integrate with
Windows NT 4.0, NetWare with NDS, and UNIX NIS will make this meta-directory
the enterprise directory.

4

Defining and Meeting Your Directory Requirements

"WHY?"IT IS A SIMPLE QUESTION REALLY, but one that is not asked often enough. Many organizations are in the habit of upgrading to the latest version of an application or operating system without really defining why. Some organizations that do articulate their reasons for upgrading restrict those reasons to specific Information Systems (IS) requirements without much consideration to user requirements. Usually there are several good reasons, both technical and business related, to upgrade software. However, those reasons should be balanced against the benefit to the organization and the cost of upgrading.

From this analysis comes a list of requirements that justifies the upgrade or migration to the new software—in this case Windows 2000 and Active Directory. This list of requirements is an integral part of the Active Directory architecture. If the items on this list are not met, then Active Directory does not provide the cost benefit promised.

This chapter describes how to create a list of requirements and how to map those requirements to Active Directory functionality.

Defining Requirements

In any business decision-making process, there are costs and benefits. As with yin and yang, they must compliment one another. If one outweighs the other, and costs outweigh benefits, then everything becomes unbalanced; the decision to buy, or not to buy, becomes self-evident.

Requirements can come from several different levels of an organization. When considering an operating system such as Windows 2000, most requirements typically come from the IS department. Business requirements are most often the driving factor behind the implementation of applications. However, Windows 2000 and Active Directory have functionality that reaches out past the IS department and into the front office. Therefore, defining requirements for Active Directory should extend beyond the back office and into the business that Active Directory supports.

Business Requirements

Identifying business requirements helps solidify executive sponsorship for the expenditure necessary to implement a system like Active Directory. Articulating business requirements, such as single seat administration, BackOffice application integration, or organizing resources, and how these applications increase productivity and reduce costs, makes the decision to implement Active Directory more palatable. After executive sponsorship is secure, the executives not only understand the reasons for proceeding with the Active Directory project, but they also have some skin in the game.

Single Seat Administration

High up on the wish list of Windows NT 4.0 administrators is the ability for an administrator, anywhere in the organization, to manage the directory. This gives organizations the ability to adopt a variety of administrative models. If you are implementing a directory, it is important to devise an administrative model that makes sense for your organization. It is likely that some administrative tasks are centralized in a few locations, whereas other administrative tasks are decentralized across the enterprise. For example, take the organization that has several remote offices, each with someone responsible for maintaining the local servers. The administrators in those locations should have the permissions and rights necessary to perform their jobs, but they don't need all available permissions. The local administrator, although responsible for the local servers, might not be responsible for user account maintenance. User account maintenance might be centralized at a corporate Helpdesk. Hence, the local administrators do not need to have permissions to change user accounts. If a centralized user account administration and distributed server administration model is ideal for an organization, the directory must be flexible enough to support that model.

Therefore, as a business requirement, the directory should be flexible enough to adopt the IS administrative model that makes sense for an organization. An organization's administrative model should not have to be defined based on the inflexibility of the directory service.

Infrastructure for Business Applications

A directory within an organization should be the central point of user and resource information. It makes sense to leverage this data beyond just providing information to users. The directory should also be a source of information for applications.

Applications that rely on user information for functionality or controlled access should be able to access the directory for this user data. This means that the directory should be available throughout the organization along with the applications that require this user data.

How applications use the directory must be analyzed. Enabling applications to write to the directory, for example, can be dangerous, depending on the application and the information it stores in the directory. There need to be guidelines for the types of information stored in the directory and for when data should be stored on a file server or database.

As a business requirement, the directory should provide an infrastructure that allows business specific applications access to rich directory services. The directory service should also provide guidelines for application development.

Integration with BackOffice Applications

Extending the previous requirement that the directory integrate with applications in an organization, the directory should easily integrate with some core enterprise-wide applications. Many organizations, which currently use Windows NT and/or Novell NetWare also use Microsoft BackOffice applications. If your organization is one of these, your directory should integrate with these Microsoft BackOffice applications.

As a business requirement, Active Directory is the future directory for BackOffice. If an organization wants to benefit from the evolution of Microsoft BackOffice, Active Directory is a critical aspect to that evolution.

Directory Integration

Most organizations have more than one directory and, perhaps, more than one directory service. To provide users with a single source of directory information, the directory service that users rely upon should allow for integration with other directories in the organization. This provides users with a single source of directory information.

Centralized Resources

A directory should also be able to host several types of objects, not just users. Computers, printers, and conference rooms are but some of the types of objects that a directory should be able to host. By including resources other than users in the directory, it becomes a service that can meet a broader range of requirements across an organization. After these resources are in the directory, they are objects that can be administered in the directory, taking advantage of the centralized or distributed administrative model that has been deployed.

As a business requirement, centralized resources allow for the administration of corporate resources based on a defined and deployed administrative model.

Security and Controlled Access

As with most applications across the enterprise today, the directory must be secure. However, if the directory is to grant or deny access to resources, the directory must provide the security components necessary to assure that resources are only accessed by those who are allowed access. To foil unauthorized access to a resource, that resource must be managed by a secured system—one that cannot be manipulated at any level by someone or something that has not been granted permissions or rights to manipulate the directory. This means that access between the client and the directory must be secured, access into the directory must be secured, and policies must be configured that make it difficult for an imposter to gain access to a resource as someone they are not.

Flexible to Business Changes

Today more than ever companies are reorganizing, downsizing, and merging with other companies. There are several causes for these changes, many of which are based on the bottom-line. It's not that an organization is losing money and must layoff employees; it's that technology or some other factor has changed the way they do business. To meet that change, the organization needs to be reorganized in some fashion. It has also recently become common for organizations to grow through mergers and acquisitions. Capital of some kind is used to buy resources or talent, a portion of a market, or a name to supplement an organization's menu of products and services.

Whatever the case, an organization's directory needs to be able to expand and contract along with an organization. It needs to be flexible enough to meet the need of an ever-evolving company. X.500, as a standard, is good at allowing for changes. It is important, however, to make sure that the X.500 directory being analyzed for your organization is also flexible to changes.

Executive Requirements

Coupling executive requirements with business requirements and their benefits to the organization helps weigh the decision scale in favor of implementing Active Directory. What executives themselves want out of a service like Active Directory is for the directory to be available and easy to use. A good example of this is the telephone. The executive picks up the receiver and hears a dial tone every time. They don't care about the infrastructure required to provide that service; they just want it available 24 hours a day, seven days a week. They want it to sound the same, no matter which phone receiver they pick up, and they want it to be able to take the service with them when they leave the office.

Executive business requirements are usually less specific than most other business requirements. Executive requirements are usually basic and fundamental: increase productivity, reduce total cost of ownership (TCO), increase competitive advantage, and give me a dial tone whenever I need it.

Increased User Productivity

Increasing user productivity decreases the amount of time it takes a user to perform his or her job, thus increasing the amount of work a user can accomplish in a week. If a technology can be used to make users more productive by streamlining their work processes, then that technology is a good investment.

Pointing to units of productivity and stating that they will increase by 25 percent as a result of a new technology is difficult. Some organizations go to great lengths to record what their users do on their workstations. They install software that measures how much time is spent in an application, how much keyboard activity occurs while in the application, what Web sites are visited, and so on. They use this data to determine the amount of time a user spends performing certain tasks. Whatever the method for measuring productivity, if a technology decreases the time it takes to perform tasks, decreases the time a user spends in training, and increases the time a service is available, then that technology is a good investment.

Reduced TCO

Pinpointing TCO is like obtaining enlightenment. If you question whether you've obtained it, you haven't. What TCO actually means depends on whom you ask, and its definition depends on the philosophy of your environment. Microsoft is good at identifying how their products can reduce TCO in a Microsoft environment, but it is rare for an organization to have only Microsoft products on the desktop or in the back office. TCO is a function of many things, including the cost of hardware and software, maintenance costs, and administrative costs. The most fruitful method for reducing TCO is to implement systems in a way that logically reduces the maintenance and administrative overhead associated with the workstation.

Opportunity for Competitive Advantage

By decreasing the TCO, theoretic competitive advantage can be had over an organization's competitors. Assuming all things are equal and two organizations supply the same quality products and services, by reducing TCO, users produce those products and services in less time than their competitor (and for less cost). This reduces overhead and increases margin, allowing for several areas of competitive advantage. For example, overhead could be shifted to other areas in the organization, such as research and development. Alternatively, if no additional overhead is needed, an increase in margin can be had, making the organization more profitable. Finally, the organization could keep the same overhead and margin but reduce the sales price of the products or service. Any of these options can provide a competitive advantage. By reducing TCO, making users more efficient, and reducing administrative overhead, the financial metrics of an organization can shift enough to provide a competitive advantage.

IS Requirements

IS requirements, for the most part, support business and executive requirements. *IS, make us more efficient, deliver us from this maintenance nightmare, and give us the tools and functionality necessary to implement an IS model that is ideal for our organization.*

Windows 2000 and Active Directory go a long way toward this utopia. Identifying the ideal IS model and mapping Active Directory functionality to that model is the point at which the design becomes critical. Some common IS requirements that compose the ideal IS model, such as controlling the environment and providing efficient, fault tolerant services to the client, are identified in this section.

Controlling the Environment

When client/server environments sprouted throughout organizations, the server portion of that relationship was reigned in to the computer room and controlled by IS. Security was soon applied and services were made accessible only to predefined users or clients. For the most part, however, the client side of client/server remains under the control of the end user. Users think the computer at their desk is *their* portal onto the network, to be configured and changed to meet their personal tastes. Nevertheless, the end user does expect a timely response from the Helpdesk when something fails, even if it is a result of their "customization." Moreover, in some organizations, the culture is such that this philosophy is accepted. However, this philosophy has its price. Non-standard client configurations increase cost of maintenance, software deployment, inventory control, software licensing, and in many cases, reduce user productivity.

By taking control of the desktop, the client/server environment becomes a single distributed system with standardized policies and security applied. The client is not an outsider looking in; the client becomes the controlled interface to services provided to the end users that make the user more efficient. How does allowing a user to browse the Internet (for example, make that user more productive)? Well, it can be argued that the Internet is a source of services itself, and it allows users to perform tasks, both personal and professional, more efficiently. Imagine that a user is planning a vacation. What takes less time: Purchasing airline tickets and reserving a hotel room and car online over the Internet, or having that user leave the office, drive to a travel agent, make travel arrangements, and then drive back to the office to resume work?

Therefore, the business requirement is to control the desktop in such a way that maintenance of that desktop is reduced, and the user becomes more productive and secure.

Providing Services to the Client

With a managed client, it becomes easier to automate the distribution of applications because you know what to expect on each desktop. Constructing software distribution packages for clients whose hardware and software configurations are known to IS has a much better chance for success than for those clients where available disk space, operating system, and client configurations are variable. As problems do arise, the capability for applications to fix themselves or for the Helpdesk to view what is happening on the desktop increases availability and reduces maintenance costs. The business requirement is to provide an efficient way to distribute software, and for software to recognize when something is wrong and to take appropriate steps to resolve the problem. This functionality is reliant on a reliable security-based directory service.

Fault Tolerance

When a server fails, it affects several users. When a client workstation fails, it only affects the user at the client workstation. Therefore, it is common practice for server-based systems to have some level of redundancy in either hardware or software that provides a fail-safe against loss of service on a single server. This is a huge and complex topic, with costs increasing exponentially as systems become closer to 100 percent availability. Active Directory, as a mission critical system that many applications and services rely upon for their operation and functionality, needs certain levels of fault tolerance. As a business requirement, when a directory service or one of its supporting services, such as domain name system (DNS), fails, users and applications must still be able to access directory services.

Administrative Requirements

Windows NT is a successful server operating system. As such, it evolved to meet customer requirements as best it could despite some design limitations. Multiple domain models appeared allowing some amount of scalability, but still there were design limitations that kept Windows NT from being implemented across the enterprise in a way that fits each organization's ideal client/server model. Windows NT dictated the administrative model to the organization. There wasn't a lot of choice concerning how an organization could administer Windows NT out of the box, so many organizations had to compromise when it came to the administrative model that best fit their organization. They typically had to adopt the Windows NT domain topology administrative model that best suited them.

Starting fresh, with a new server operating system and directory, allows organizations to re-evaluate their administrative model and adopt one that makes sense for their organization.

The business requirement here is driven from an organization's re-evaluation of its administrative model. The adopted directory must fit that model to the greatest extent possible. Be it a centralized administration model, distributed administration model, or something in between (which most are), the directory service should be able to mirror your administrative model.

Automated Administration

Automated administration is one of the ways to make directory administration more efficient. There are a couple of different approaches that can be taken when trying to offload administrative tasks from IS. One approach is to delegate administration of directory data down to the department that owns the data. For example, Human Resources (HR) would own user data, whereas Helpdesk and security would own and manage security data. To mitigate the risk of having non-IS people changing directory information, scripts can be used by the administrators in these groups to ensure that the data written to Active Directory meets naming and other organization-defined standards.

Scripts can also be used to process directory changes in batches during off-hours. For example, user additions and deletions to the directory made throughout the day can be batched to actually post changes to Active Directory in the evening, when network utilization is low, allowing replication between Domain Controllers (DCs) in the domain to occur primarily at night.

The capability to do automated administration should be an option for any directory service installed in an organization. The administrative model might not call for it immediately, especially if it was not part of the previous administrative model; but as scripting becomes more commonplace in organizations, administrative tasks also are candidates for automated scripts. It is also beneficial to be able to have the script run with administrative authority without making the user an administrator.

Delegated Administration

To decentralize administration without having to create multiple security contexts with multiple domains, administrative delegation becomes necessary. Administrative delegation is the ability to grant groups of appointed users specific permissions on groups of objects; specific permissions down to the rights and object attributes levels. Therefore, delegated administration is a prerequisite for decentralized administration.

Security Requirements

Security is always a requirement. Directory security can be broken down into these categories:

- The directory's capability to secure the resources it represents
- The directory's capability to secure the directory database
- The directory's capability to secure communications between the directory client and the directory service
- The directory's capability to secure resources
- The directory's capability to secure its own database
- The directory's capability to secure communications between itself and the client

For each of these categories there should be a minimum level of security required. Ideally, security would also be based on industry standards, which would make interoperability between directories and access by various standards-based clients possible.

Another aspect of security is the ability to tighten or relax it based on an organization's security policy. Some organizations thrive on the information they keep, and security is a very important aspect of these organizations' computing environment. Other organizations, such as colleges, have never had much security and probably never will. Whatever the requirements of your organization, be it Smart Card authentication or anonymous authentication, it is important that the directory provide the level of security you require.

Desktop Management

Desktop management was identified earlier as an integral part of reducing the cost of desktop management. To fully realize the financial benefit of desktop management, the desktop should be locked-down to some degree. By locking down the desktop, users can't add or break software on their computer. This keeps the corporate computer a resource for the user, not a source of entertainment, and it reduces maintenance costs. Locking down the desktop also makes it easier to deploy software. Most software deployment systems, such as Microsoft's System Management Servers (SMS), are more successful at deploying software if they know the environment to which the software is deploying. By locking down the desktop, many of the variables and unknowns that can cause a software deployment to fail are eliminated.

As a business requirement, Desktop Management should be an option that uses the directory as a source of security information. Based on the user or administrator using the client computer or the computer itself, different polices should be applied that determine what type of changes can be made.

End User Requirements

Most directory services, especially the Windows NT directory, had little interaction with the end user. Therefore, most of the functionality and requirements that came from the Windows NT directory were administrative and security based. The user and how they used the directory were not often considered because their only insight into the directory was at the point of logging on. More advanced directory services, such as those based on X.500, have a charter that goes beyond just authenticating users; the directory is a source of end user information. How the directory is designed determines how useful the directory is to end users.

As an end user requirement, the directory should be an easily accessible source of information. There should be a single, familiar, interface to the directory that is available to users whether they are online or offline.

Mapping Requirements to Functionality

After the business requirements are defined, it is necessary to map those business requirements to functionality. It is also necessary to assign a priority to each business requirement. This priority is used when multiple business requirements are considered in the design as a particular aspect of Active Directory. The best example of this is the organizational unit (OU) structure within a domain. Administrative requirements, end user requirements, and group policy requirements must all be considered when designing the OU structure. The priority helps determine which design consideration, or requirement, takes precedence over the others.

Table 4.1 summarizes the business requirements accumulated thus far in this chapter.

Table 4.1 **Business Requirements**

Category	Requirement(s)
Business Operations	Single seat administration infrastructure for business applications
	Integration with BackOffice centralized resources
	Security and controlled access
	Flexible to business changes
Executive Requirements	Increased user productivity
	Reduced cost of ownership
	Competitive advantage
IS Requirements	Controlling the environment
	Providing services to the client
	Fault tolerance
	Directory Integration

Category	Requirement(s)
Administrative Requirements	Automated administration
	Delegated administration
	Attribute level security
Security Requirements	Single per-user logon
	Strong passwords
	Secure database
	Secure client/server communications
Desktop Management	Application control
	Desktop lock-down
	Inventory management
End User Requirements	Easy access
	Familiar interface

Business Requirements

Business requirements, the lengthiest list, are supported by various features and functionality within Active Directory. Business requirements are also IS requirements in a solid IS environment, but they are still business requirements. Things like simplified administration, application integration, security, flexibility, and availability all top the list of business requirements that must exist before an investment should be made in an application or operating system—especially one that has the far-reaching affects of an application like Active Directory.

Single Seat Administration

Windows 2000 and Active Directory enable a single seat administration model. With Active Directory being a multi-master database, all the DCs in a domain replicate changes between each other. Any changes made by an administrator or user to any DC in the domain are replicated to all other DCs in that domain. The multi-master relationship is not limited to domain data, such as users and passwords, but the Active Directory configuration, Global Catalog (GC), and schema database partitions are replicated between DCs. Although the domain database partition is replicated between all DCs in the domain, the GC between all GC servers in the forest; the configuration and schema database partitions are replicated between all DCs in the forest. This allows for a centralized administrative model in which administrative tasks can be delegated to predefined administrative groups; each is granted specific administrative rights. In earlier version of Windows NT, administration was not flexible. The domain model had to reflect the administrative structure of an organization. With Windows 2000, the domain model is not overly influenced by the desired administrative model because administrative responsibilities can be delegated within a domain through groups and OUs.

Infrastructure for Business Applications

Active Directory is a distributed database that serves as a directory. As such, it provides a directory infrastructure for business applications. Several applications, such as Microsoft Exchange, use Active Directory as their sole directory. Other business applications can also take advantage of this unified directory, not only as a source of directory information, but also as a repository for application specific directory information. Microsoft is publishing an Active Directory development guide that outlines the types of information that can and should be stored in Active Directory. Businesses can use this as a guideline in developing applications that take advantage of this investment.

Another example of an application that should be integrated with Active Directory is the average HR application. An interface between a company's HR database and Active Directory can move the administrative burden of updating the user portion of the directory from IS and to HR (where it belongs), allowing HR personnel or the HR application to administer the objects that they have permission to administer. As users come and go, Active Directory automatically reflects these changes and accesses to resources are granted or denied based on the type of employee hired or fired.

Integration with BackOffice

It is only logical that Microsoft BackOffice applications evolve into a model that uses Active Directory. Microsoft Exchange, System Management Servers (SMS), Site Server, Proxy Server, and SNA Server are examples of applications that adopt the Active Directory security subsystem as their primary security interface. The resources and services these applications provide are subject to Active Directory security and security principals (users and computers). The rights that a security principal has either allow or deny access to BackOffice services. Active Directory also provides directory services to BackOffice applications as appropriate.

Again, Microsoft Exchange uses Active Directory as its directory, no longer supporting its own directory as in earlier versions. Users access Active Directory to resolve mail recipients (such as other users), mail enabled contacts (Custom Recipients), and distribution groups (distribution lists). Exchange, therefore, becomes a message store providing various protocol accesses to message store services for Active Directory users.

Directory Integration

Directory integration is available through the tools included with Windows 2000 and third-party products. Tools support application coexistence with Active Directory. For example, the Active Directory Connector (ADC) synchronizes Active Directory with the Exchange 5.5 directory. Tools, such as the Microsoft Directory Synchronization tool (MS DirSync), allow for synchronization between Active Directory and Novell Directory Services (NDS) version 4.1x or greater. These tools facilitate Active Directory in becoming the single source of directory information for users and the single source of directory administration for administrators.

Centralized Resources

As Active Directory centralizes users in a single, distributed directory, it also centralizes resources. There are several object-classes that Active Directory can host, such as computers, printers, and DCs, which give users and administrators the ability to locate and access these resources through Active Directory. After Active Directory contains these resources, they can be managed through Active Directory. For example, policies can be set at the domain, OU, and site level that define what can be done on a computer or resource. Depending on the location of the computer in the domain, different policies can be enforced. Say you have a group of workstations that are in an unsecured area within your organization and are used for anonymous access to public resources. Policies can be set for those workstations that limit how they can be used, such as preventing the floppy drives form being accessed or software from being installed.

Security and Controlled Access

Active Directory is the Windows 2000 security subsystem. Not only does it define the users and resources in an organization, but what those users and resources can do within an organization. Through access control lists (ACL), users are granted or denied access to resources. Kerberos is used to provide authentication between client and server when accessing Active Directory. As a business requirement, user access to resources should be tightly controlled based on granted permissions that a user inherits through group membership or permissions a user has explicitly defined. The authentication process is also secured, through Kerberos, which guarantees the user accessing a resource is actually that user, and the computer being accessed is actually the intended computer. Chapter 15,"Developing a Network Security Strategy," gives a full explanation of Kerberos, and how it is used.

Flexible to Business Changes

Active Directory, if designed correctly, is flexible to business changes. It can support multiple organizations with unique identities (DNS namespaces) in the same directory.

Objects within a domain can also be moved with a click of the mouse. Between domains, objects can be moved (when in Native Mode) using tools included with Windows 2000. As users move between departments, groups, or locations, their location in Active Directory can also move. This is important in today's business environment. As a business requirement, a directory needs to be able to change with an organization. How Active Directory is designed depends on the amount of changes an organization goes through. If an organization, for example, is growing through mergers and acquisitions, Active Directory should be designed to be extensible and allow for distributed administration.

Executive Requirements

Executive requirements are general in nature, as are the aspects of Active Directory that satisfy them. Identifying these requirements legitimizes Windows 2000 with Active Directory as a next generation operating system that can add value to the way an organization does business.

Increased User Productivity

Many aspects of Windows 2000, other than Active Directory, help to increase user efficiency and productivity: Microsoft Installer, IntelliMirror, Plug-and-Play, Distributed File System (DFS), and high availability through clustering, just to name a few. Active Directory, specifically, helps increase user efficiency by virtue of being a single source for directory information, distributed across the enterprise, and available through multiple user applications. By having a single source of directory information available to users, regardless of their location, Active Directory provides a familiar, information-rich, directory to all parts of the enterprise.

Reduced TCO

Reducing cost of ownership entails reducing the cost of the workstation and software, along with reducing the maintenance and administrative overhead spent on each workstation. Simply upgrading an existing Windows NT domain structure to an Active Directory domain structure is not likely to reduce the cost of ownership. However, implementing Active Directory in such a way that increases service availability, reduces administrative overhead, and streamlines user and computer maintenance does have an overall effect of reducing the amount of resources necessary to support a computing environment.

Implementing Active Directory provides services to end users that are common across multiple applications. This makes users more productive by giving them more time to do their job because they are spending less time negotiating each application's directory. As a business requirement, a case can be made that Active Directory reduces administrative overhead and increases user efficiency, thus reducing TCO.

Competitive Advantage

A reduction in cost of ownership and an increase in user productivity can reduce the overhead in an organization, making it more competitive. Active Directory as a service is easy to use, has high availability, and provides the functionality that reduces maintenance costs; this has the effect of increasing user performance and reducing maintenance costs.

Maintenance costs are reduced by using Windows 2000, Active Directory Group Policy Objects (GPOs), and even SMS to deploy applications to specific groups within the enterprise. Rather than having a technician visit each workstation to upgrade Microsoft Office, the application is published or deployed automatically. Locking down the workstation with policies so that users cannot break their software reduces the amount of Helpdesk calls, which also reduces maintenance costs.

Administrative costs are reduced by developing and implementing an administrative model that fits an organization's requirements. Delegating administrative tasks to those groups who require them can reduce administrative costs by decentralizing some administrative functions to specific groups in an organization.

IS Requirements

The requirement of the business, its customers, and employees are rolled up into IS requirements; because after all, IS is the organization that designs, deploys, and supports the technologies that provide functionality to the business. Active Directory satisfies some IS specific business requirements.

Controlling the Environment

Active Directory, through the domain and OU structure, enables group policies to be deployed and enforced throughout the directory. An OU structure is devised that meets an organization's administrative model *and* allows group policies to be applied in such a way that users in specific OUs adhere to the policies of that OU *and all the OUs that are above it*. Through inheritance, group policies flow down through the domain, site, and OU structure and are cumulative.

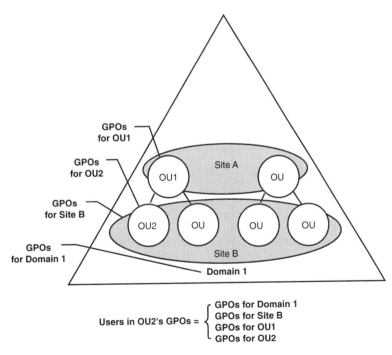

Figure 4.1   Group policies are cumulative.

In Figure 4.1, policies can be applied at the site, domain, and OU level. If a user exists in the OU2, they are subject to the group policies of the Domain 1, the Site B, and OU1 *and* OU2. This means that the applications that are applied to OU1 are also inherited down to OU2. Policies that are applied to Site B are applied to the users and computers in that site. It is this type of domain, site, and OU structure that can be designed and deployed to give IS control of the environment.

Providing Services to the Client

The software distribution functionality that comes with Windows 2000 is dependent on Active Directory. Active Directory provides the security context necessary to determine if a user or workstation is eligible to receive a software distribution. Software can be published to that user so that he or she can install it if necessary, or it can be mandatory so that it is installed upon startup. This decision point uses Active Directory to determine what applications a user has available.

Fault Tolerance

Active Directory is a fault tolerant service by virtue of its distributed databases. When a DC fails, clients attempt to contact other DCs for directory services. Therefore, as long as there is more than one DC, directory services are available to the client. Now there are additional considerations, such as the placement of the DCs and the other services that Active Directory clients are reliant on, like DNS and the GC. If the Active Directory architecture is designed correctly, each of these services has built-in redundancy. This enables the DC to service clients in the event of another failed DC or other failed Active Directory reliant service.

Administrative Requirements

Administrative requirements are defined on a per organization basis through an administrative model developed as part of the Active Directory architecture each organization deploys. The administrative model can be centralized or distributed, depending on the organization and its physical and internal structure. Active Directory has the capability to meet the requirements of either a centralized or a decentralized administrative model through its domain and OU structure by delegating authority based on that specific model.

Automated Administration

To help streamline administration, Windows 2000 has a script engine that allows Active Directory administrative tasks to be automated. As administrative responsibility is delegated throughout an organization, different support or administrative groups are responsible for specific administrative tasks. It is possible to develop scripts, using ADSI, that walk these groups through their administrative tasks. For example, a script could be written that would be fed by an HR system. The HR system would upload updates that a script would use later to change Active Directory. This would be a move toward automating account creation and deletion within Active Directory. Active Directory, out of the box, gives an organization everything necessary to administer their environment. However, the scripting capabilities of Active Directory greatly expand the administrative possibilities that Active Directory provides. A more detailed description of scripting Active Directory can be found in Chapter 19, "Scripting with Active Directory."

Delegated Administration

Delegating administrative authority allows for a distributed, or partially distributed, administrative model. Defining administrative groups and delegating administrative authority to those groups is how an administrative model is implemented.

As with group policies, permissions are also inherited down the OU hierarchy. When you apply permission to an object, that permission can be propagated to that object's sub-objects (or child objects).

Administrative function can be delegated by assigning permissions in a specific OU or by assigning permission to change the permissions on objects at the attribute level. By delegating permissions at the OU level and allowing the appropriate users or administrators to administer that OU, administrative responsibility is distributed.

Attribute Level Security

Within Active Directory, administration can be specified beyond the object level to the attribute level. Administrators can be granted the ability to only change passwords on user objects for example, without having the ability to change the other attributes contained in the user object.

Security Requirements

Security in Active Directory is paramount. Active Directory is the security subsystem for Windows 2000. As such, it is important that each aspect of Active Directory, from the database to client communications, be secure.

Single Sign-On

Because Active Directory is a single distributed directory, which can be utilized by applications for user information, it is possible to have a single user logon or single sign-on. After a user is authenticated by Active Directory, that user has access to the resources to which they have been granted permission (inherited or otherwise). The user is also able to access services provided by Active Directory integrated applications without having to logon again. This means only one security policy need be maintained, one password managed by the user, and one account managed by the user administrators.

Strong Passwords

Because Active Directory aspires to be the single source of directory information and to grant or deny access to resources, it is important that a strong password policy be an option. Active Directory supports a strong policy option.

Secure Database

The Active Directory database, when hosted on an NTFS partition, is encrypted and secured. An Active Directory database cannot be copied to another Windows 2000 server with a different administrator password because that would allow that administrator to take control of the directory.

Secure Client/Server Communications

Kerberos is a secure method for authenticating a request for a service. Through Kerberos, a user or process requests an encrypted ticket from an authentication process, which can then be used to request a particular service from a server. The user's password does not have to pass through the network. This keeps passwords and other traffic between the client and server secure.

Desktop Management

Desktop management, through application control and maintenance, and desktop lock-down, helps reduce desktop maintenance and make users more productive. This has the intended result of lowering TCO and improving user efficiency.

Application Control

Through the Active Directory structure, GPOs can be created that dictate to which applications a user has access. Again, designing an Active Directory structure, which meets the application requirements for certain groups, provides those users with the applications they require, but nothing more. Moreover, users can be denied the ability to install their own applications based on their location in Active Directory. This can have the effect of increasing user performance and reducing desktop maintenance costs.

Windows 2000 and Active Directory can also be used to ensure users have applications that work. If a user or application deletes or corrupts a file that is necessary for an application to run, the deleted or corrupt file can automatically be replaced on that desktop. This reduces the number of Helpdesk calls, thus reducing maintenance costs and increasing user efficiency.

Desktop Lock-down

Desktop lock-down is achieved through GPOs. The ability to lock-down the desktop can have a significant impact on the cost of ownership. Through GPOs, desktops can be locked-down so that users can only change things for which they have permission. Designing an Active Directory structure which allows resources to be grouped in Active Directory in such a way that group policies can be applied in a logical fashion, enables desktops to be locked-down when and where appropriate.

Inventory Management

Locking down the desktop so that users only have access to applications assigned to them, makes it easier to maintain an accurate application inventory. This can allow organizations to maintain application licenses for only a subset of users and allow users to roam from computer to computer with their assigned applications always available to them.

End User Requirements

It is true that Active Directory, and the design considerations around the domain and OU design, is mainly driven by administrative requirements. However, it is important to also consider the end user. Not only can end users query Active Directory, but they can also browse Active Directory. If they are looking for a printer in a certain location or a group of users in a department, browsing Active Directory can be the most efficient way to locate these resources. If Active Directory is not designed in a way that compliments how users browse it, Active Directory's usefulness to the end user is compromised.

Summary

It is important to understand the capabilities of Windows 2000 and Active Directory. This understanding makes it easier to map the business requirements of an organization to Windows 2000 and Active Directory functionality. With a list of business requirements and the Windows 2000 and Active Directory functionality that meets those business requirements, decision makers in an organization can justify the expense of migrating to Windows 2000 and see the value that is added to the organization.

5

Scoping the Project

AS WITH ANY MAJOR UNDERTAKING, WHETHER IT IS MOTORCYCLE repair under desert heat or cooking your first turkey, the first step is scoping the project. The process of scoping the effort usually helps in prioritizing the components, as well as defining alternative approaches. Getting a caterer to cook your turkey might be the right approach if the real effort is exposed. Scoping the project helps you to identify the breadth and depth of the goal and, subsequently, the choices available to obtain objectives and to reach the goal. Ultimately, you determine the best path to travel to obtain your goal and complete the project. As with any undertaking, creating an effective Active Directory design requires a scoping that bounds the project and further defines the challenges.

This chapter provides an overview for identifying the issues involved in scoping an Active Directory project. In developing the roadmap, this chapter travels through a series of components that can affect the design and implementation of Active Directory. As a foundation for many enterprise services and applications, Active Directory's scope affects this technology's capability to leverage its promise in the enterprise.

With a limited scope, Active Directory's effect on your organization might be transparent. As the implementers, you might decide that it is better to have a simple introduction to the technology than provide the user with a new technology that might cause problems that put the move to Active Directory in question. New technology usually has stability problems and limited integration with other technologies. In Active Directory's case, it might be prudent to limit the introduction of new capabilities because this might expose the latest generation of code in the product. In addition, there are a limited number of commercially available applications that can take advantage of the technology.

If you look to the early adopters of Novell Directory Services (NDS), there was some pain in the initial installation. This was further complicated by the limited support of commercial applications and tools. Most administrators who have lived through the implementation of a well-thought-out NetWare 4.X installation will remind you of the tools that were not available.

So, with all this said, the key decision in identifying the scope is, "How much do you want to leverage the promise of Active Directory?" If you answer "fully," the risk is greater, but the reward might also be greater, creating value that differentiates your organization from your competitors. You need to evaluate it.

I had a business strategy professor who mentioned a consulting gig for a small manure business. The owner wanted to develop a strategic plan for improving his business, something that would give him a strategic advantage. After careful analysis, the conclusion was that getting individuals who could shovel the manure into the bags faster would have the greatest impact on the business. The point is choosing your features carefully. Don't become caught up in implementing the "cool" features just for technology's sake. You can always do that in the lab where it won't have long-term effects on your career.

After your strategy has been identified, you need to look at a variety of factors to determine the impact of the scope of your project. These include the following:

- Current applications in your organization
- Analysis of the administrative structure
- Analysis of the computing environment

Analysis of Current Applications

In looking at how you want to implement Active Directory in your organization, one of the greatest impacts is how your applications use Active Directory. In reviewing this, you look at the applications in your organization based on the use of the application. The point of this section is to help devise a reasonable methodology for breaking down the application effort and coming up with not only a scope, but an insight into the reality of what can be done within the time and risk parameters that you have set for your project.

Enterprise-Wide Applications

One of the greatest benefits of Active Directory is the integration with applications that span the organization. A directory service is an enterprise resource; therefore, it comes as no surprise that enterprise applications can make good use of an enterprise source of information. I don't know how many times I have used the phone list for the group I worked in as the starting point for keeping track of everything from who has completed what training, to who is bringing what to the company picnic. Similarly, planning a trip on the open road requires a map, and on that map, one typically chooses from the key points of interest when deciding the path to take. With this Active Directory scoping, look at the horizon with a focus on those objectives (applications) that will have the greatest impact on the desired destination or goal.

The applications that have an immediate use of an Active Directory are those that view the organization as a whole. Human Resource (HR) applications typically have a view of all the users in the organization. One can imagine the need for sending information automatically to a group of users based on their time of service or their time with their current employer. By creating an attribute for all employees that has start date, a simple query would return all those employees that started before July 1, 1982, for example. Another possible use would be for users to authenticate to Active Directory. Based on who you are, you would be authorized access to personal HR information like benefit spending account information or 401K asset accruals. The result is better service and reduced impact to the HR organization.

These examples represent benefits and possible scenarios, but in moving forward with defining a scope for the project, a planner for Active Directory needs to identify those applications that will be affected during the "Phase 1" implementation. The Phase 1 implementation is the set of features that have been defined as being supported in the initial implementation. It is rare that a new product is implemented to include all the features of the product. The implementation is divided into phases that gradually increase the production functionality of the product.

The first step is to determine which of your applications are enterprise applications. In a small company this can take a few minutes, and in a large company this can take 12 months. Regardless of the size of the company, a few key applications come to mind. These are the applications that that run the business. They are typically the financial applications or HR applications. In a manufacturing organization, they are the production control system. In a retail environment, it would be the point-of-sale and inventory systems. With this list of applications in hand, do some research on the complexity of the applications. For example, is it a package from another third-party or is it a custom application?

With third-party applications, you can research what the plans are for the integration with and the use of Active Directory. After this is determined, you can evaluate whether the release of the new product, or feature upgrade, fits into the window of your release. As you work through this, you should be getting some feel for the magnitude of the effort. Some questions that help determine the effort include

- What is the complexity of the application? What is the complexity of the use of Active Directory?

- Is the application going to use Active Directory to validate whether resources are available, or is it going to modify the directory entries?

A more complex undertaking would be to modify the directory. Modifying the directory means modifying the schema by adding new classes or attributes.

To help organize the findings, a simple table has been created to start scoping the effort involved in implementing Active Directory. Throughout this chapter, additional estimating parameters are added to create a final estimate. Using Wadeware as a test, Table 5.1 is created to develop an initial scope for five applications.

The first application is a custom HR application that keeps track of communications with employees, which is based on region. The employee's regional information was maintained within the application, but with the use of Active Directory, this information can be retrieved and maintained as part of the directory.

The second application is a legacy application that has been through many maintenance and enhancement changes. The result is complex code, which is fragile when changed. There is risk in modifying it, and the effort required to make the changes is undetermined.

The third application is a financial application developed outside the company as a packaged solution. This is a relatively new application in the organization. The application currently has its own directory for all current and past employees to track benefits information. Because of the recent release and installation of the product, integration with Active Directory is not available in time for Phase 1 participation.

The fourth application is a complex financial and operational application that uses project-scheduling information provided by project managers and project members coupled with standardized costs to create project scheduling and Profit/Loss statements. This application requires moderate changes for integration with Active Directory. Timing is critical for participation in Phase 1.

The fifth application is an Excel spreadsheet coupled with a process. This application keeps track of different classes of users and administrators. This information, contained in the spreadsheet, is used to set rights to resources throughout the network. When individuals change roles, the spreadsheet is updated, and then the changes are made to the network resources. This process is error-prone and does not provide any logging capability. Based on the simplicity of the technology component in place, some parts of the application can be put in place using Active Directory.

Table 5.1 **Summary of Wadeware Enterprise Applications**

Application	Complexity of Application	Complexity of Using Active Directory	Effort	Phase 1	Future Features
HR Application 1	Simple: VB application with a single interface.	Moderate: Email status based on the location in directory.	Moderate.	Yes.	
HR Application 2	Complex: C, Legacy application.	Simple: Create. The call to AD is focused in one part of the application, and it only needs to create users in AD.	Undetermined.	No.	Possible.
Financial Application 1	Third Party.	Update directory with benefits information.	Just released. Future integration with AD is considered.	No.	Possible. Promote with vendor.
Financial Application 2/ Operations	Complex: VB application.	Moderate: Use directory information and calendar information to determine project costs.	Moderate.	Considered. Timing is critical.	Potential.
Operations	Excel spreadsheet coupled with undocumented complex processes. Company resource security is managed by a variety of administrators.	Moderate: Use of directory supplied roles. Apply to predetermined directory scheme.	Undetermined.	Partial implementation.	Further implementation.

After some analysis of the enterprise applications, Wadeware is prepared to have some participation of enterprise applications in Phase 1 of the Active Directory migration. This provides a solid foundation for additional leverage in the future in two ways: the current applications that migrate are likely candidates to take advantage of additional information in Active Directory; the applications that are migrated also serve as an example for new and existing applications to take advantage of Active Directory.

Workgroup Applications

Workgroup applications are those applications that only affect a specific workgroup, from both a user and span of influence position. This differs from some of the previous applications in that most have only a small user community, but the application has an impact on the entire enterprise's staff.

It is anticipated that Wadeware will have many workgroup level applications. They might be Access databases, Excel spreadsheets, or shrink-wrapped solutions. With the effort of modifying these applications to use Active Directory, you want to identify some groups that have flexibility and provide an enthusiastic interest in making the change. This might be difficult, but finding a group that is interested in a better way of computing goes a long way toward overcoming any challenges that the migration might create. Remember, it is not how bumpy the road but how soft the seat you're sitting on, and a cooperative and enthusiastic team can make the seat softer.

Wadeware has identified two applications for consideration. The first application is used in the marketing department to keep track of resources used for events. The current application is used by a small group of event coordinators to identify resource availability and to match that with a team of event presenters. The objective is to make sure that all the resources are available, and if not, external vendors can be used to lease equipment.

The second application is in the product distribution department. This application keeps track of supplier orders for a specific line of products only manufactured at the Miami location. Two shipping department personnel and three resource planners in the manufacturing department use this application. Currently, they shuffle paper around, which is entered in a simple Microsoft Access database with all the customers' names and addresses in it. This database replicates the information in the billing applications used by the finance department.

Both of these applications are candidates for integration with Active Directory. These applications have a small group using the product, and they affect a small number of contacts internally. Each of the groups using their new application has an interest in simplifying their workflow, and they are enthusiastic about the potential to simplify their already busy schedules with an easier interface and more accurate reporting. By leveraging Active Directory in both of these applications, the maintenance of the directory information is passed on to another organization, rather than being replicated with each user community. In addition, the information becomes more reliable because changes in addresses go directly from Human Resources (HR) to Active Directory. In this example, using Active Directory reduces your total cost of ownership.

A first attempt at the estimates for making some improvements that use Active Directory are that they can be made in time for Phase 1. Wadeware now has four applications: three from the Enterprise pool and one from the workgroup pool, that are part of Phase 1 of the Active Directory implementation. Expecting that at least one, and possibly two, applications will still not make the deadline leaves two applications for a success story. This is important. There is the opportunity for a success even with minor setbacks. A failure to get any applications using Active Directory as part of the implementation plan is not leveraging the full value of Active Directory. Yet, having too many applications involved during the onset is too ambitious.

Stand-Alone Applications

Stand-alone applications are applications that are used by a single user. The output from the application is typically input for another application or for use by a single user. The application developer might even be the user. In the initial phase, it might be best to see if you can find an application that is totally controlled by a single user; both the input and the output are in the total control of the user of the application.

Wadeware has an application that is used as a card catalog for the internal library. The librarian is the only person that uses this application. The librarian uses the application to update which books are checked out to whom. This application currently does not have any contact information except for the name of the borrower, and this is manually cross-referenced with a phone list by the librarian. The enhancement to this application is to have it automatically query Active Directory for information about the individuals who have checked out books. Several different enhancements are targeted. First, if a person were approaching a deadline, the application would create a mailing list to send a reminder. The application would also notice any users who were removed from the system, and it would create a notice for HR about the books checked out.

After determining those applications that you are prepared to integrate with Active Directory, you can create an application roadmap for your Active Directory implementation. This is important because as you scope your project, you need to expose the dependencies of your project and the impact it has on the entire organization.

With Wadeware, we have identified several applications; some are part of Phase 1, and some are not. Tables 5.1 and 5.2 document the disposition of each application for modification in Phase 1.

Wadeware has an application in each category, enterprise, workgroup, and stand-alone. Depending on the size of the organization and the policies for application maintenance, it might not be practical in every organization to get an application in each category; although it does provide an excellent footing for future applications integration. In the first phase of implementation, you need to make a decision. Is it more important to take on the additional risk of combining some application integration with the initial implementation? In some cases, you might need the application to get the sponsorship for the project. This is a scenario where the only reason you are migrating to Active Directory is the opportunity to leverage the directory's information.

In any case, the set of applications that you decide to embrace and move forward with provides the scope of the effort required and a reading of the risk involved the project. A table, like that shown in Table 5.2, helps to quantify the scope of the project.

Table 5.2   **Phase 1 Application Summary**

Application	Complexity of Application	Complexity of Using Active Directory	Effort	Phase 1	Future Features
HR Application 1	Simple: VB application with a single interface.	Moderate: Email status based on the location in the directory.	Moderate	Yes; 12 weeks effort —16 weeks duration.	
Operations	Excel spreadsheet coupled with undocumented complex processes; company resource security is managed by a variety of administrators.	Moderate: Use of directory-supplied roles; apply to predetermined directory scheme.	Undetermined	Partial implementation; 8 weeks effort; 10 weeks duration.	Further implementation
Event Tracking	Access with some processes.	Simple to moderate.	Simple to moderate	Yes; 6 weeks effort; 8 weeks duration.	
Shipping Department	None in existence.	Simple.	Simple	Yes; 4 weeks effort; 6 weeks duration.	
Library Check-out	Access.	Simple.	Simple	Yes; 4 weeks effort; 6 weeks duration.	

Administrative Structure

The administrative structure of the organization has an impact on how the Active Directory implementation takes place. A variety of administrative structures can be in place before Active Directory. The scope of the effort in the area is determined by the current administrative structure and the targeted administrative model. There are two main areas most administrative models fall into:

- Centralized administration
- Decentralized administration

In addition, there is the possibility for a hybrid model, in which some administration is done centrally and some administration is distributed to administrators in remote offices or separate divisions. With Active Directory, there is also the capability to permit end users to provide administrative support.

The administrative model that you choose and how you intend to implement the administrative model affect the scope of the effort.

Components of an Administrative Model

To identify how an administrative model influences the scope of your efforts, you must first have a clear understanding of the components in an administrative model. Several components are used in developing an administrative model. They include the following:

- The design supporting the administrative model
- The roles of administration
- The tools for administration
- The process needed to apply the roles and tools

Administrative Model Design Process

Chapters 6 through 15 address the specifics of the design, but the primary components of the design that affect the scope of overall effort is determined by how much consensus is needed in developing the design. A centrally controlled design process can provide for faster results. If your organization needs consensus for the design from a broad range of organizations and/or regions, the process can take months, especially if it is in addition to members' other day-to-day responsibilities.

Looking at two polar scenarios can help to illustrate how the design process can significantly affect the scope of the effort. The first scenario is one in which you have almost total control. You have executive sponsorship to make the directory design happen, and the decisions of your team are final. You have the resources to implement the effort; therefore, funding for tools, software, hardware, and staffing is not in question. Using this scenario, you are able to come up with a design, whether it is decentralized or centralized, with relative ease. You are able to identify a small team for the design.

The consensus building process is among a smaller group and typically does not take a long time.

With a larger organization in which the effort requires justification and the administrative model is not clearly defined from the start, the design process can take time. If there are multiple groups with different interests, the consensus building process can take months. The process of coming up with a design that delivers on the administrative responsibilities, which each organization, or role-level, requires, and still realizes the potential administrative gains that Active Directory promises can be a challenge. The need for multiple reviews, detailed explicit design documentation, and an ongoing need to re-evaluate the design can spin the design process on forever.

One way to minimize the threat is to first present the process for creating the architecture. This identifies how decisions are made, how issues are resolved, the timeline for the design, and the responsibilities of each contributor. After you have described the process, you should have each member acknowledge that he or she endorses the results of the process. Giving the architecture team the roadmap for developing a design and their commitment to live with the results, usually helps the team stay on focus.

Regardless of the scenario for your organization, there is no replacement for clear and detailed documentation about your design. Although the second scenario can be painful, if documented properly, most of the pain is overcome through the initial process. Likewise, if early consensus leads to lack of documentation, problems can arise later based on a failure to have clear documentation and a false understanding of what the impacts of the design are to the real effort. This can be compounded by the fact that Active Directory is new to most of those involved in the effort.

Regardless of which scenario reflects your organization and challenge, it is important that your documentation includes the justification and rationale for the resulting architecture.

Administrative Roles

As part of the design process, you determine what type of administrative roles should exist in your organization. In the strictly centralized model, everything from schema changes, backup, disaster recover, maintenance, and rights changes to data changes is made by a central group. In larger organizations, these responsibilities are distributed among a tier of administrators. The centralized group administers the infrastructure of Active Directory including the schema, back/disaster recovery, and distribution of rights for administration. The remote locations or divisions are responsible for administration of tasks that are important to being close to the end user. The remote administrator provides, adds, moves, and changes for users in their location. A remote administrator might handle the changing of access to specific resources in an organizational unit (OU).

End user administration is also possible with Active Directory in this scenario. A user is able to update information regarding their personal data, such as address or telephone number. This can significantly reduce administrative overhead and provide real-time updates for changes.

Depending on the administrative model that you decide on, the scope of the project is affected. By choosing a centralized model, you are able to eliminate the need for multiple groups and discussions about who has what rights and capabilities. This model is easier to implement and scope. With a decentralized model, there is a need to define additional levels of rights, as well as to ensure that the model is implemented properly through a testing effort. The documentation of the effort and the testing add to the scope of the project.

Administrative Tools

The tools that you determine you need have an impact on the scope of your effort. Using the Microsoft Management Console (MMC) provides the ability to create customized consoles for specific roles within your organization. If your effort includes multiple separate responsibilities, you need to create specific tools for this. MMC enables you to do that. By taking specific modules or snap-ins from the family of MMC-available modules, you are able to create tools that enable only specific administrative responsibilities.

Each of these specific tools requires some effort for creation and testing. Although these are not your typical tools for development, they do take some time, and that impacts the scope of the effort.

Depending on your need for large administrative changes, you might need to create some scripting-based tools, using Windows Scripting Host (WSH), Active Directory Services Interface (ADSI), and C++ programs. WSH provides for the ability to run batch jobs created in Visual Basic Script or Java Script and access Active Directory objects, such as users, distribution lists, and computers.

Microsoft also provides support for the Lightweight Directory Access Protocol (LDAP) and Lightweight Data Interchange Format (LDIF). The LDIF is a draft of an Internet standard for a file format that can be used for performing batch operations on directories that conform to the LDAP standards. LDIF can be used to export and import data. If you are required to perform large changes, such as creating, deleting, or modifying users, this tool can help make the task easier. A tool called LDIFDE is included in Windows 2000 to support batch operations based on the LDIF standard.

There are also third-party tools available that help in migrating to Active Directory. These tools provide support for migration from disparate directory technologies to Active Directory. These tools can be helpful during the migration and coexistence phase that your organization might have. The Microsoft Web site has a growing list of tool vendors for Windows 2000 Active Directory. These tools support migrating to Windows 2000 and moving objects between Forests and trees.

With the large suite of tools that are available, scoping your overall effort is dependent on which tools you choose and how complex they are relative to skill set of the staff you have to support the environment. Rather than ending up with a mixed bag of tools, take the time to analyze the functionality you need for migration and Phase 1 support, and minimize the number of tools you embrace. By starting out simple, you reduce the confusion. Over time, as your organization's sophistication with Active Directory and Windows 2000 increases, you can diversify.

Scoping the Effects of the Administrative Process

The administrative process is what glues the design, the roles, and the tools together in a comprehensive environment. With multiple layers of administration and the distributed management of the environment, the administrative processes need to be detailed to avoid risky encounters during the migration, coexistence, and early adoption of Active Directory. When scoping the effort, it is important to consider the effort involved in testing the rights and privileges that are established.

Training the Active Directory team on the technology as well as the process takes time, but it provides a strong foundation for the move to Active Directory. Your decisions about the lines of responsibility and process definition affect the effort involved, but time spent here pays off in a cleaner migration and reduces confusion in the operation of the environment.

Deploying

Two basic approaches for deploying Active Directory affect the scope of the effort. One choice is to do a location-by-location migration in which each location has the autonomy to drive their own migration, as long as they adhere to the standards defined. This meets with success as long as each organization has the drive to start and complete the task. A schedule of organizations is important to provide the centralized organization with some time to stage the back end support as needed.

Another choice is to direct the entire effort centrally and stage work teams to implement the migration by workgroup, location, or geographical location. This effort is methodical and achieves the goal on a specific timeline.

Environmental Considerations

This section reviews the remaining key components of your Active Directory effort. The remaining components should serve as a checklist for scoping your Active Directory effort.

Security Environment

The security environment that you decide on affects the scope of the project. Security is a big issue, and it is covered in detail in Chapter 15, "Developing a Network Security Strategy." With your implementation of Windows 2000 and Active Directory, you can pick from three approaches for integration. The decision for integration that you pick has an impact on the effort of your implementation.

The first approach for security is to use the straightforward security implementation that is available with Windows 2000 and Active Directory. This implementation would be a homogeneous implementation of Windows 2000 and Active Directory. This approach uses Kerberos in the background for authentication and access to resources.

The second approach for security integration is to use Active Directory as the basis for single sign-on. This effort requires integration with, potentially, a variety of operating systems. The greater the number of operating systems the larger the scope your project will have. If you choose integration of Unix or Novell with Active Directory as the central repository, your efforts increase dramatically. You are moving your efforts from a homogeneous implementation to one requiring integration with multiple operating systems. This requires an understanding of the security model for the foreign environments and an understanding of how applications work with the various operating systems.

Earlier in the chapter, possible uses of Active Directory by applications were discussed. In this case, the application integration includes modifying applications to support secure access without application-based authentication.

A third approach for security is to use Active Directory in a security scheme for partners to access internal resources. Several scenarios need to be considered after you have decided to support partner authentication. The simplest choice is to create an OU for the partners and add users for each partner. Another approach is to create a separate tree for partners. A separate tree ensures isolation. If your partner is using Microsoft, you could also consider a trust relationship between a partner NT 4.0 environment and your new Active Directory environment. This seems clumsy because it requires your administration group to work with your partner's administration group.

A more complex effort would include creating your own Certificate Authority (CA) and distributing/maintaining certificates for all your partners. With this approach, it is also possible to map certificates to users created in a separate OU. Depending on the size of your partner community, the effort required for setting up, testing, and administering this type of an environment can be significant.

Keeping in mind that you have the option of implementing some combination of the approaches described, you begin to realize that the security approach you choose is a project in itself. However, in the case of partner integration and access, it might provide a value that defines the need for Active Directory.

Remote Access

Windows 2000 and Active Directory provide remote access solutions. How you embrace the various technologies affects the scope of your effort. Most organizations are using Virtual Private Network (VPN) solutions to obtain secure remote access to corporate resources. Microsoft provides a variety of solutions.

You can use Point to Point Tunneling Protocol (PPTP), which is widely supported and enables you to pass through a network address translation (NAT) device. This protocol has the advantage of not requiring a CA, and it provides security through user identification and password. The key design criterion is simplicity. You can also use Layer 2 Tunneling Protocol (L2TP/PPP). This encapsulates PPP in L2TP and provides for functionality similar to PPTP. With L2TP/IPSec you add security, but it does not support use with a NAT device. As an example, you would use L2TP/IPSec for a site-to-site connection across the Internet.

Regardless of the solution you choose, whether it is PPTP, L2TP, or L2TP/IPSec, you need to develop a lab, provide a pilot, and then deploy the service. This is typically a large area for dissatisfaction; therefore, you need to evaluate current RAS and define a clear message about how this affects your community. In scoping the remote access solution, devote time to make it a success.

Workstation

Migrating your workstations to support Active Directory typically means migrating them to Windows 2000 Professional Desktop to gain the full benefits of Active Directory. This is the ideal approach and one that every Microsoft shareholder advocates, but there are several approaches. A migration effort usually includes a visit to every workstation. A migration to Windows 2000 probably means an upgrade to Office 2000 and other applications. This is a large undertaking considering the training (end users, Helpdesk, and desktop technicians), planning, and physical effort. Your scope should consider the duration of such an effort. Moving to a Windows 2000 desktop, with the latest applications, provides the greatest leverage for Active Directory, but it also requires a significant "out of the blocks" investment.

Lab Environment

The lab environment that you create is the fertile testing ground for your effort. This environment should include a variety of items that are typical of your real environment. Starting at the back end, your services should include some representation of your current environment. As an example, if you are moving from an NT 4.0 environment, you should have an NT 4.0 Server environment setup as part of your lab.

The bottom line is that your test lab should mirror your actual network as much as possible. This includes domains and server types for example.

Your lab should have as many of the desktop types as are currently part of your environment to ensure that realistic performance and functionality is achieved during implementation.

In Figure 5.1, a simple lab environment is put in place for Wadeware. This figure illustrates the starting point with an NT 4.0 Primary Domain Controller (PDC). This lab environment does not represent the wide area network considerations, but it does provide a simple working environment to practice migrations, perform client-to-server testing, and evaluate functionality. Performance at the server level can be evaluated in this environment.

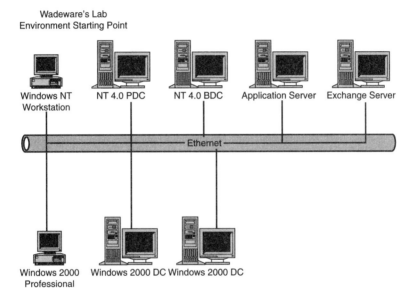

Figure 5.1   Wadeware's lab environment starting point.

Mirroring the Real Environment in a Lab

If migrating from a Windows NT Server environment, it is possible to simulate all the users into your lab. To accomplish this, first take a lab server and create it as a Backup Domain Controller (BDC) in the production environment. Remove the lab server from the production environment and promote it as the PDC in the lab environment. Now you have a replica of the production environment. Keep in mind you cannot connect the lab environment to the production environment with the PDC active.

Your lab should be isolated from the production network. With all this in mind, building this infrastructure requires time and resources. Another advantage of the lab environment is that the Active Directory schema is protected. Because changes made to the schema are permanent, if an application that you are testing makes a change to the schema that creates a problem, you will need to reinstall Active Directory. As you can imagine, you do not want to do this in a production environment.

Staff

The most important ingredient for your move to Active Directory as an integral part of your organization is the your staff. The team that takes on this challenge is the main ingredient that makes it successful. Careful planning is important; but great plans fail because of a lack of enthusiasm, and poor plans succeed through the will and determination of the staff. Making the correct assessment of your staff's ability is crucial in determining impact to the scope of the effort.

When assessing the staff's impact on the scope of effort that you are planning to commit to, consider the following list of key indicators:

- How long has your team worked together? Typically, teams that have worked together for a couple to a few years know their strengths and weaknesses.

- Has your team migrated from another technology before or performed a mission critical integration effort? A common example of a similar effort is a migration to Microsoft Exchange. This is similar in that it touches every user, has a back end component, and is mission critical for most organizations.

- Does your team view this as an opportunity and are they excited about it? Active Directory is a significant effort. Most teams should be looking at this effort as an opportunity to learn something new.

- Finally, developing a training plan for your staff should help your staff build confidence and participate in the scoping

Summary

Scoping your project is an important step in setting expectations for your Active Directory implementation. By properly identifying the scope of your effort, you are able to communicate with your organization's sponsors about the real effort and expected results for Phase 1.

The scoping effort also provides a foundation for developing an early roadmap for the project. There are many components in developing a scope and each one is important; however, the most important component is your staff.

Involve your staff early to develop a consensus on what the real undertaking is going to be. This can help to prevent resistance or surprises later.

II

Planning

6

Planning for Coexistence

O NE OF THE MOST IMPORTANT ASPECTS OF PLANNING for a deployment of
Windows 2000 and Active Directory is developing a plan for *coexistence* with the existing network operating system (NOS) and infrastructure. No matter how quickly you
are planning on integrating and migrating your existing legacy environment, it is necessary to coexist for a time. In many cases, it might be necessary to coexist for several
months and possibly years.

So, what do we mean by the term *coexistence*? Specifically, coexistence is defined as
two systems existing in the same place and having to interoperate in a cooperative
way. If considering Active Directory, we are talking about coexistence with legacy
NOS, such as NetWare, Windows NT, and UNIX. There are tools available for inter-
operating with all these environments. The keys to success in coexisting with these
environments are

- Developing a comprehensive plan for coexistence
- Understanding the limitations of the tools used during coexistence

Because of the limitations in the tools, more work is required up front in designing
scripts and secondary applications to provide the functionality required for coexistence.

This chapter, addresses coexistence with Windows NT and NetWare. To a lesser degree, we also discuss coexistence with UNIX. The reason for the limited focus on UNIX is two-fold: First, there are limited tools available for integrating the two environments, and second, it is not likely that there will be a wholesale migration from UNIX to Windows 2000. As much as Microsoft would like to believe that they are ready to displace UNIX as the operating system of choice for enterprise applications, it is not likely that it will be happening in the immediate future. Consequently, organizations that have a large UNIX infrastructure in place will most likely not be integrating a Windows 2000 environment with their UNIX environment. That said, however, it is important to note that Windows 2000 and Active Directory are based on standards, including Lightweight Directory Access Protocol (LDAP) and SMTP, which facilitates interoperability with UNIX-based systems.

Before examining some of the technical details of planning for coexistence, we discuss the methodology and process involved in planning for coexistence.

Methodology and Process

Developing a solid process and methodology for integrating two computing environments can be just as challenging as trying to solve the technical issues encountered during the integration.

The best way to plan for coexistence is to follow a standard project implementation methodology. Many organizations already have a standard methodology that they follow when implementing a new project. Although there are many methodologies, most of them follow the same basic steps. In the context of planning for coexistence, those steps would be

- Identify the stakeholders.
- Form a project team that includes stakeholders as well as individuals who will implement the plan.
- Document the existing directory environment.
- Map the existing directory data into future directory schema.
- Plan the infrastructure to support coexistence.
- Assess any risks associated with implementing the coexistence plan identified during the planning phase.

It is important to note that although planning for coexistence can be approached as a stand-alone project, it should be executed in the context of the entire Active Directory planning and deployment project. The output from this project, specifically the identification of directory data and the mapping of that data to Active Directory, is utilized by the overall Active Directory design team. In addition, many of the members of the coexistence planning team also participate on the overall Active Directory planning team.

It is extremely important that any project that involves planning, including this project for developing a coexistence plan, must be executed in the context of a larger information technology life cycle. If planning is conducted in isolation, any plan for deliverables runs the risk of being out of sync, and actually being contrary to, the Information Technology (IT) needs of the organization.

Identify the Stakeholders

The process of identifying all the stakeholders relative to your directory coexistence project can be cumbersome. However, it is an important step in planning for coexistence. As previously noted, many of the problems that can occur during project implementation can be mitigated early on by identification of and coordination with all the individuals who have a stake in the project. In the case of planning for coexistence between a legacy directory and Active Directory, there are several different types of stakeholders.

The most obvious type of stakeholder is the individual who owns the object in the directory. This individual typically has the rights to create and update the object. More than likely, this individual is part of the IT or the Information Systems (IS) groups. There might be a few exceptions, such as a directory object owned by an individual in the finance or Human Resources (HR) department.

The second type of stakeholder is either the individual whom the object effects or the individuals, or groups, who utilize the object. In the case of a user object in the directory, the stakeholders are the users themselves. It would not be practical to include every user in the planning process for directory coexistence; therefore, a single individual typically assumes proxy responsibility for representing the best interests of the users. Another example would be the case of an object in the directory that is used to support a sales-force-automation application, such as Siebel. The sales force is not the actual owner of the object, but certainly, an individual on the planning team should have the responsibility to make sure the needs of the sales force are recognized and addressed.

The third type of stakeholder is the individual, or set of individuals, who has a direct interest in making sure that the coexistence project is planned and implemented properly. This certainly includes the project manager, the IT/IS manager, and the company CIO.

Form a Project Team

After all the stakeholders are identified, it is possible to form a project team for planning the coexistence. The project team should obviously be headed up by a project manager. In smaller organizations with limited directory needs, the project manager who heads the overall Active Directory project might also be the team lead for the coexistence project. In larger organizations, coexistence might be a sub-project headed up by a different project manager than the one who is heading up the entire Active Directory project.

The team should include executive sponsorship. This might be an executive who checks on the progress of the team on a periodic basis actually participates in an active way. Whichever is the case, the executive's role should be to facilitate the removal of roadblocks to the successful completion of the project. In addition, he or she should monitor the progress of the team and report that progress to the executive committee of the company on a regular basis. Communication is one of the most important aspects of a successful project.

The project team should also include representation from all the stakeholders previously identified. This does not mean that every stakeholder should be present on the team. It is possible to identify a single individual, such as a representative from IT/IS, to represent the needs of several stakeholders.

The team should include directory experts who understand the internal workings of both Active Directory and the legacy directory environment. These individuals should also have detailed knowledge of the Microsoft Directory Synchronization (DirSync) server application.

Finally, the team must certainly include representation for all the support groups in the organization. This should include the groups that support the end users as well as central IT/IS. The implementation of any coexistence plan has an impact on the supportability of the existing environment.

Depending on the size of the organization that is planning Active Directory implementation, some of the people on this team might play several different roles. For example, the executive sponsor might also represent one of the business units.

Document Existing Environment

The process of documenting your existing environment should start by identifying the hierarchy of the legacy directory. It is important that the hierarchy is identified before the actual data is documented so that relationships between objects can be identified and understood.

After the directory hierarchy is documented, the next step is to identify all the data that exists in the legacy environment that needs to be synchronized with Active Directory. The best way to do this is to create a table that contains each object in the legacy directory and details whether there is a need to synchronize each of the object properties. See Table 6.1 for an example.

Table 6.1 **A Sample Data Identification Table**

Object Name	Properties to Synchronize	Periodic or One-time Object	Owner
User	All	Periodic	Network Administrator
File Share	Share Name	One-time	Workgroup Administrator

After you have identified all the data in the legacy directory that will be synchronized, you need to contact the object owner for each object and work with them to formulate a comprehensive coexistence strategy. Most major issues with coexistence and migration occur if the team that is planning the coexistence and migration does not identify all the individuals and organizations who have a stake in the process and work with them to mitigate any possible disruptions or problems with the process.

Map the Data to Directory Schema

After the project team has identified all the data to be included in directory synchronization, it is time to map the existing data into the new directory schema that is implemented in Active Directory. This essentially means identifying the containers in Active Directory and Novell Directory Services (NDS), which will be synchronized. Because synchronization occurs on a container basis, it is not necessary to map specific objects in one directory to specific objects in the other directory. In other words, the level of granularity needed in identifying synchronization between directories is minimal. This process varies depending on the third-party directories that are being synchronized with Active Directory.

Plan the Infrastructure

Planning the infrastructure for integrating the two directory environments is critical to the success of the implementation of your coexistence plan. When planning the infrastructure, it is important to take into account the location of the legacy directory server with which Active Directory will be coexisting. The placement of servers should be such that unnecessary load is not placed on the network when the synchronization traffic starts between the two directory environments. Much of the data about the network, its clients, and its servers, is gathered during the Active Directory design project. Most of this data is valid for the coexistence project, and it should be used where appropriate.

Publisher and Subscriber Directories

Coexistence between two directory services is typically configured in such a way that one directory is a publisher and the other directory is the subscriber. This means that one directory is the owner of the data and the second directory simply receives updates of the data. In the case of synchronizing directory data between Active Directory and NDS, the most likely configuration is for NDS to be the subscriber and Active Directory to be the publisher. The reason for this is that Active Directory will most likely be the long-term migration path and, consequently, will own the synchronization process and the data from the beginning. The relationship between the two directories is identified in Figure 6.1.

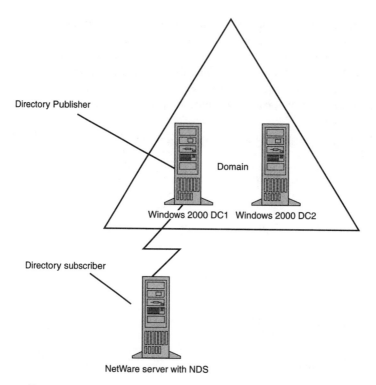

Directory Publisher

Domain

Windows 2000 DC1   Windows 2000 DC2

Directory subscriber

NetWare server with NDS

Figure 6.1   The usual configuration for the Microsoft DirSync Service
will be a one-way synchronization between Active Directory and NDS.

Establishing one-way synchronization between Active Directory and NDS prompts
many organizations to rethink their directory administration strategy. This is especially
pertinent to those organizations that are migrating from NDS to Active Directory. In
the case of an organization that is planning a limited coexistence period, the administration of the NDS environment by way of Active Directory might not be cumbersome because the NDS environment will be retired in a relatively short amount of
time. However, in the case in which there is a requirement for the NDS environment
to coexist with Active Directory for an extended period, it might be necessary to
implement a new directory administration model.

For example, in the case of Wadeware, our sample company, there is an existing
NetWare environment in Tucson (a finance application that is not going to be
migrated to Windows 2000 for at least a year.) The finance department would like to
maintain all their user data in NDS and log on to the NetWare environment, and yet,
they would like to have all their user data published to Active Directory. Before integration, administration for NDS and the NetWare environment in the finance department is conducted by the Finance NetWare Administrator, who resides in Tucson. He

or she has been granted administrative rights to the Finance container in the NDS tree. To continue as the administrator of the NDS environment for Finance, he or she must be granted administrative rights to the corresponding Finance organizational unit in Active Directory. They then must begin making all the changes to finance user data in Active Directory. That data is then synchronized with NDS periodically, based upon the timing that is configured in the Sessions settings on the DirSync Server Domain Controller (DC).

The publisher and subscriber model is not applicable to coexistence between Windows 2000 and Windows NT 4.0 environments. In the case of coexistence between Windows 2000 and Windows NT 4.0 in the same domain (rather than in two separate domains with trusts established between the domains), changes made in either environment are synchronized with the directory in the other environment. In other words, there is *bi-directional* synchronization between the two systems that share the same domain. It is important to note that this is only the case if the Windows 2000 DCs are running in mixed-mode. After they have been switched to run in Native Mode, no integration is possible between Active Directory and the Windows NT 4.0 Security Account Management (SAM).

Planning for Coexistence with NetWare

Coexistence between Active Directory and NetWare is the second most common coexistence scenario, following coexistence between Active Directory and Windows NT 4.0. Many organizations have Windows NT application servers but have maintained NetWare for their network environment, files, and printers because they needed a hierarchical directory. Now that Windows 2000 is a viable option, these organizations are beginning to implement Active Directory as well as NDS. In many cases, it is not prudent to perform a rapid migration to Windows 2000 and Active Directory. Instead, the Network Administrators in these organizations want to establish an Active Directory environment with which their Windows NT Servers can coexist, while proving that Active Directory meets the needs of the organization and is robust enough to support the needs of their enterprise. This section examines some of the issues Network Administrators need to keep in mind if planning for coexistence between Active Directory and NDS.

For the initial release of the Microsoft DirSync tool, two-way synchronization is possible between Active Directory and NDS version 4.1x or greater. The Windows 2000 DirSync Server is a Windows service that runs on a DC. The DirSync Server is managed by a DirSync MMC snap-in that can reside either on the DC that is hosting the DirSync Server or a Windows 2000 Server computer or on a Windows 2000 Professional Desktop. In the case in which the MMC snap-in is not located on the same computer as the DirSync Server, there must be RPC connectivity between the DC and the computer hosting the snap-in, as identified in Figure 6.2.

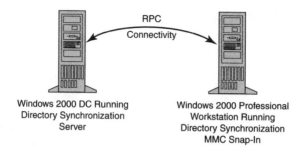

Figure 6.2 If the computer hosting the DirSync MMC snap-in is not the same as the DC hosting the DirSync Server, it is necessary to have RPC connectivity between the two computers.

In addition to planning the configuration of the DirSync service on your DC and any associated workstations, you must also plan how you are going to provide connectivity to the NDS environment. To connect to the NDS environment, you must install the Novell client for Windows 2000 on the DC that is running the DirSync Server. Running the Novell client, however, does not give you the ability to synchronize passwords between the two environments. To synchronize passwords, you need to load a third-party NetWare Core Protocol (NCP) compatible client.

One major drawback of implementing directory synchronization between Active Directory and NDS is that the DirSync Server does not support connectivity to the NetWare environment by using Transmission Control Protocol/Internet Protocol (TCP/IP). It is required that the NetWare Server be running IPX/SPX and be broadcasting SAP traffic. There are many organizations that have upgraded their NetWare environments to version 5.0 specifically to eliminate IPX from the network and, consequently, to eliminate the constant SAP traffic on the network. It is likely, then, that there might be organizations that opt to postpone integration between Active Directory and NDS until the DirSync Server supports TCP/IP connectivity between the two environments.

After you have identified all the directory data that is synchronized during the period of coexistence, the next step is to map the data from one directory schema to another, as shown in Figure 6.3. In the case of coexistence between Active Directory and NDS, the mapping process is relatively simple because it is only possible to map entire containers and sub-containers between directories, not individual objects. What this means is that a single container in NDS, such as *Users*, is mapped to a container in Active Directory. All the contents of the Users container are synchronized to Active Directory.

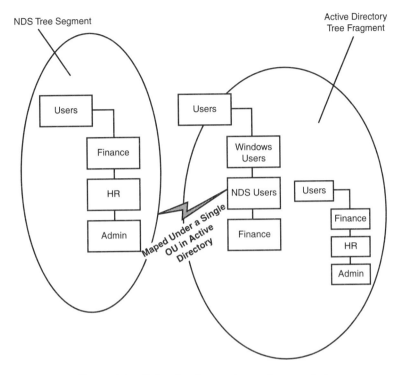

Figure 6.3   If planning for coexistence between Active
Directory and NDS, identify the object containers
that contain the objects to be synchronized.

Planning for Coexistence with Windows NT 4.0

Coexistence between Active Directory and Windows NT 4.0 is the most common
type of coexistence scenario. It is also the type of coexistence that is the briefest. If an
organization is currently deployed on Windows NT 4.0 and is able to prove that
Windows 2000 and Active Directory are viable technologies, there is little reason for
remaining on Windows NT 4.0.

The structure for coexistence between a Windows NT 4.0 environment and Active
Directory depends on the type of domain environment that exists in the Windows
NT 4.0 environment and the migration strategy that has been selected for moving
to Windows 2000. There are essentially two types of domain migration strategies from
Windows NT 4.0 to Windows 2000:

- **Domain Upgrade**—This is essentially an in-place migration to Windows
  2000.
- **Domain Restructure**—This is a domain consolidation or restructuring in
  which the complete domain structure is modified.

Domain Upgrade

A domain upgrade from Windows NT to Windows 2000 is the simplest process to achieve coexistence and migration. The domain structure that exists in the Windows NT environment is maintained during the migration to Windows 2000, as shown in Figure 6.4.

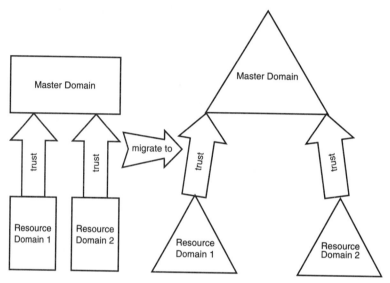

Figure 6.4   In a domain upgrade from Windows NT to Windows 2000, the domain structure is preserved.

This type of coexistence and migration path works best if the existing Windows NT domain structure is relatively simple, composed of a single domain that includes all user accounts and machine accounts, or a single user domain and a single resource domain.

Windows 2000 and Active Directory are designed to support mixed-mode environments. This means that when the Primary Domain Controller (PDC) in a Windows NT 4.0 domain is upgraded to Windows 2000, all the Windows 9x and Windows NT 4.0 clients in the domain are still able to operate as if they are authenticating to a Windows NT DC. They are not, however, able to take any advantage of the extended features of Active Directory, such as directory browsing for printer location or user information.

Because of the mixed-mode support built in to Windows 2000 and Active Directory, coexistence in a simple domain structure is relatively straightforward. A few issues that you need to contend with are:

- Administrative changes should be made on a Windows 2000 DC. As a best practice, all administration in a mixed-mode environment should be conducted on a Windows 2000 DC. This helps to assure that all new objects are created within the context of the Active Directory schema. Although it is possible to utilize the Windows NT 4.0 administration tools to manipulate objects in Active Directory, it is not advisable.

- Explicit trusts need to be established with resource domains. If you have a multi-domain environment, you need to establish explicit trusts between the master domain, which has been migrated to Windows 2000, and any down-level domains, which have not yet been migrated.

Domain Restructure

In a domain restructuring, the migration to Windows 2000 is used as a catalyst for examining the existing domain design and restructuring the design to better meet the needs of the organization. This might mean that a multi-master domain model, which includes multiple user domains and multiple resource domains, is consolidated into a single large domain, or it might be that multiple user domains are consolidated and the resource domains are maintained. Figure 6.5 is an example of a domain consolidation.

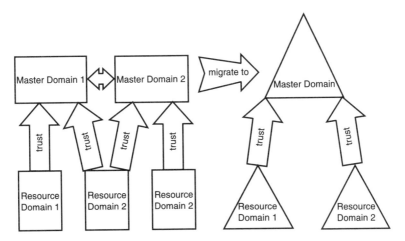

Figure 6.5   During a domain restructuring, the migration to Windows 2000 is used as an opportunity to re-examine the existing domain structure and to consolidate domains where appropriate.

Whatever the case, during a domain restructuring, there are coexistence issues that need to be addressed. These include

- **Explicit trusts**—As in the case of the simple domain migration, all domains that have not yet been migrated to Windows 2000 need to maintain an explicit trust with the master domain, or domains. These trusts need to be maintained until the resource domains have been migrated to Windows 2000.

- **Service accounts**—Service accounts, such as service accounts for Exchange Server and SQL Server, need to be granted the proper rights across domains. If the service accounts are maintained in a user account domain that has been migrated and the server machine accounts are in a resource domain that has not been migrated, make sure that an explicit trust is in place between the domains so that the service accounts can log on as a service in the resource domain.

Planning for Coexistence with UNIX

Coexistence with UNIX is not likely to be an important aspect of the initial deployment of Windows 2000. Nevertheless, it is important that we address some of the issues that might be encountered when implementing Windows 2000 and Active Directory in a network environment that includes UNIX workstations or servers.

With the Microsoft Services for UNIX, it is possible to integrate Active Directory with directories based on Network Information Service (NIS). Services for UNIX provides one-way synchronization between Active Directory and NIS. This means that passwords established in Active Directory overwrite passwords in the NIS directory. Only accounts with membership in the Windows 2000 group `PasswordPropAllow` are synchronized. This group should be created as a local group on the Windows 2000 DC that is running the Services for UNIX service. Services for UNIX also supports password changes for individual users from NIS clients by using the `yppasswd` application.

Summary

Planning for coexistence between Active Directory and the other directory services in your environment is one of the important first steps in designing your Active Directory implementation. If planning for coexistence, be sure to give enough focus to the first step discussed in this chapter: identifying the stakeholders and addressing their issues with the current directory systems they have in place and what they want to get out of Active Directory after it is implemented. The major stakeholders can just as easily promote a project to success or drive it to failure.

Also, be sure to spend an adequate amount of time mapping the data from your existing directory into Active Directory. A few more hours or days spent on designing the data map the correct way the first time can save you significant time later in the project, or even after the project is completed.

The next chapter, examines the steps involved in designing the Active Directory namespace. You map and transfer the data from your existing directory structure to this hierarchy.

7

Designing the Windows 2000 Domain Structure

A MOTORCYCLE HAS TWO WHEELS, A MOTOR, A FUEL TANK, user controls, and all the components necessary for a motorcycle to be a motorcycle. Active Directory is like the drive train of Windows 2000. It links the components that provide power to the machine with the components that make the machine move or useful. How well your motorcycle runs and distance between unplanned overhauls is determined by the quality of your drive train. Nobody wants a motorcycle that only has one gear, or one whose chain breaks in the middle of a mountain pass.

Active Directory is a domain structure built upon one or more namespaces that are within an Active Directory Forest. How you define this domain structure, and the organizational units (OUs) within, determines to what extent your Windows 2000 and Active Directory implementation meets the business requirements defined at the beginning of the project.

Determining the Scope of Active Directory

One of the most important steps in any project is to define a project scope. The project scope helps to define at what point the project is complete, and it helps to define if the project is successful.

A project scope should be static. Sure, there are changes to technology and requirements that can force project scope change, but to keep the project on course and on budget, the project scope should not change much without a change to the overall focus of the project.

For these reasons, determining the scope of the Active Directory phase of a Windows 2000 project is important. What's more, it is important to choose a scope for which there is a good chance of success. Depending on the size of the organization, there can be several phases in which Active Directory is deployed across the organization. However, in smaller to medium-sized organizations, deploying Active Directory might be completed in one step. Which approach you should take is a function of time, budget, and resources.

Determining the Initial Scope of Active Directory

When determining the initial scope of your Active Directory project, remember the following points:

- If possible, create a design that includes the entire organization.
- Use project management techniques to budget resources within your desired timeline. If you do not have enough resources, change the timeline, increase resources, or reduce the project scope.
- Make sure your team's areas of influence, or political leverage, have clout in each area of the organization included in the project scope. If possible, recruit sponsors from each area of the organization to represent you and your project's interests.

To illustrate this topic consider our imaginary company, Wadeware, which has chosen to migrate from Windows NT 4.0 to Windows 2000. They hope to be done with their migration by the end of the year. Wadeware has built a project team with a dozen members, each representing an area of the company or a department within Information Systems (IS). Wadeware also has selected several contractors that they plan to use for the deployment.

The Wadeware organizational structure can be seen in Figure 7.1.

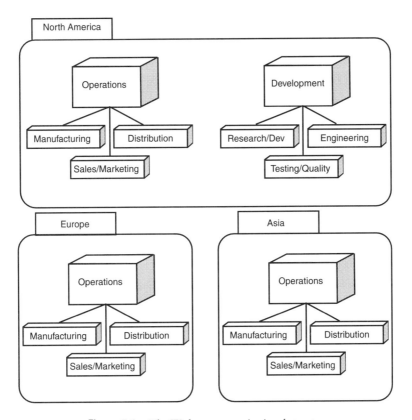

Figure 7.1 The Wadeware organizational structure.

Based on this organizational structure, the number of resources Wadeware has, and the timeline they have chosen, Wadeware has decided to focus on the following areas of the organization during the initial design and rollout of Windows 2000 and Active Directory (see Figure 7.2).

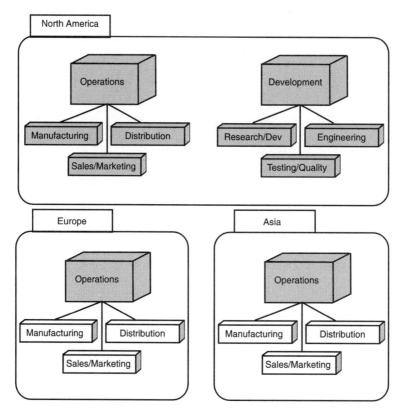

Figure 7.2   Portions of Wadeware's organizational structure
that are within the scope of the Active Directory project.

It is important to reiterate that despite the scope of the Active Directory project being
limited to only a portion of the organization, the design decisions should be based on
the entire enterprise.

Determining Which Portions of the Organization Participate in Active Directory

Which portions of the organization should participate in Active Directory is really a
two-part question. First, which portions of the organization should initially participate
in Active Directory? Second, are there any portions of the organization that will not
eventually participate in Active Directory, and if so, why?

If you choose to do a staggered, multi-phase rollout of Active Directory, you
should, if possible, first choose those groups or departments in the organization that
are sympathetic to your project. By working with cooperative groups or departments
first, the project starts on the right foot.

Unfortunately, it might not always be possible to start with cooperative groups or departments. For those portions of the organization that participate in the initial roll-out of Active Directory, another starting point is to choose a Windows NT domain that has limited user and computer objects.

If there are areas of your organization that you do not plan to include in your Active Directory, there should be a good reason. Try to include all parts of your organization in your Active Directory namespace design.

Delegating Administrative Functions

One of the reasons for implementing Windows 2000 and Active Directory is the directory's capability to delegate administrative tasks. Part of defining the scope of your Active Directory, and therefore its namespace, is to identify which administrative tasks are delegated to which groups. Identifying the amount of delegation goes a long way toward determining the complexity of the Active Directory domain and OU structure.

A good example of where administrative tasks can be delegated is the Helpdesk. When users dial the Helpdesk on the phone and the automated operator answers, they might be presented with a menu that allows them to navigate to the type of support they need. In the same way, specific administrative permissions can be delegated to the groups that perform these support tasks:

- **Change or Reset Password**—This group of Helpdesk support can be granted permissions to change passwords without having permissions on other attributes of the user object.

- **Create or Remove Network Accounts**—This Helpdesk group can create and delete users, but they cannot change preexisting user object attributes.

- **Enable RAS Access**—This group of Helpdesk can guide users through setting up their RAS services and enabling their Active Directory account for RAS access.

- **Change User Name**—Perhaps an administrative assistant for every group is granted the ability to change user names.

- **Change Directory Information**—Users can be granted the right to maintain their own Active Directory object information.

Human Resources (HR) is a department in many organizations that could assume much of the maintenance responsibility for the network account. HR manages user benefits, payroll, and personnel files—why not their network accounts too? When users are added to the HR system, a process or script could start that would create an Active Directory account in an OU and domain that is appropriate for the user as well as an Exchange mailbox on the appropriate Exchange server. This would go a long way toward alleviating IS from these day-to-day administrative tasks and freeing up resources for head-count to improve the IS infrastructure, not just maintain it.

Determining Which Applications Depend on Active Directory

Many directory-enabled applications depend on the directory for their functionality. It is important to know the requirements for the directory-enabled applications in your environment.

It is just as important to ensure that current applications with their own directory will have the same functionality after they rely on Active Directory. For example, an organization might use Microsoft Exchange on Windows NT 4.0. Microsoft Exchange versions 5.5 and earlier has its own directory service that users can access for directory information. After the next version of Exchange (which no longer has its own directory but uses Active Directory) is released, it is important that Active Directory provides users the same look and feel as they had with the Exchange directory. This might not be as easy as it sounds. With Exchange, each Exchange server hosts a complete copy of the Exchange directory. With Active Directory, each Active Directory Domain Controller (DC) only hosts object information for the objects that are in its domain. A Global Catalog (GC) server is the only server that contains partial object information for every object in Active Directory. Therefore, a user looking up detailed information from the Exchange directory might have a different experience when looking up the same data from Active Directory, especially for a user who exists in a different domain.

One of the primary reasons for implementing Windows 2000 is Active Directory's capability to interact with applications. Active Directory provides a solid foundation of organizational data from which many applications draw. Therefore, it is important that the namespace is designed so that applications can take full advantage of this Active Directory feature.

Applications that store directory data within Active Directory are also able to change the Active Directory schema. If an application is installed and makes modifications to the schema, those definitions describe the classes of objects being used by the application, thus enabling other applications can use that information.

Determining the Future Scope of Active Directory

Although in small, and even medium-sized, organizations the scope of the initial Windows 2000 deployment might encompass the entire organization, in larger organizations there will probably be a staged rollout that might take several months or even years. Whatever scenario fits your organization, it is important to remember that although the initial rollout of Windows 2000 might only be to a portion of the organization, the Active Directory design should consider the entire organization, because you don't know what the future might hold.

Determining Which Portions of the Organization Should Eventually Participate in Active Directory

Your organization might choose to only include North American locations in its first Windows 2000 design and deployment. You have taken the initiative and are designing a namespace and Active Directory that will eventually meet the needs of the entire organization. You might not know all the requirements of your European and Asian locations, but you have built in enough flexibility so that what ever their requirements turn out to be, you are going to be able to accommodate them. However, unbeknownst to you, the networking services group is implementing Active Directory-enabled network routers. These routers provide a Quality of Service (QoS) based on Active Directory users and groups. These routers can also restrict access to areas of the network depending on the user. Not knowing these new requirements has tested the flexibility of your namespace and directory. What you have learned is that there are not only vertical areas of the organization, such as line-of-business, departments, regions, and groups, that need to be considered, but that there are horizontal areas of the organization, such as networking services, data services, and telecom, which also might eventually participate in your Active Directory. Hence, if possible, look at the organization from 20,000 feet, speculating on the future direction of both the vertical and horizontal areas of your organization.

Determining Which Administrative Functions Will Eventually Be Delegated

One of the other primary reasons organizations implement Windows 2000 and Active Directory is the capability to delegate the management of resources out from IS to the departments where they belong. For example, many organizations reorganize frequently. Other organizations frequently move people and resources from office to office or building to building. Other organizations do both, by constantly reorganizing and moving. In the middle of this chaos, the IS group has trouble keeping up with new office numbers, printer locations, and even telephone numbers. Most IS groups quit managing this directory information because of the overhead involved with keeping up with the organization. If, however, the management of this data could be delegated out to the groups or departments that move, part of the move process could be for a group or department administrator to update the directory information. By delegating administrative authority for specific object attributes to departmental administrators, IS no longer needs to spend resources managing this ever-changing information.

Determining Which Applications Will Eventually Depend on Active Directory

It is a valuable exercise to try to determine which applications will eventually depend on Active Directory. The reasons for this are twofold: to be proactive in your namespace and Active Directory design (taking into consideration an application that will rely on Active Directory), and to help further legitimize the project as having benefit now and in the future. Chapter 18, "Windows 2000 and Exchange Server," describes the design considerations placed on Active Directory by Exchange 2000, (an Active Directory-enabled and dependent application). By acknowledging both current and future applications that are supported by Active Directory, those applications are more easily implemented, and Active Directory is more justified.

Assessing Your Environment

Now that you have spent time considering the scope of Active Directory and all the areas of the organization that it affects, the next step is to assess your organization's computing environment. Next you will look at the areas of IS that the Active Directory design affects or is affected by.

Network Assessment

Active Directory is a distributed service, meaning that few functions are provided by only one DC. Most Active Directory services are provided by most, if not all, the DCs. The nature of this type of service is that clients need to communicate with DCs for Active Directory services, and DCs need to communicate with other DCs for changes to Active Directory database or environment. Therefore, the network is a critical component to a functioning Active Directory. If client access to a DC, domain name system (DNS) server, or GC server is hindered, Active Directory services can fail. If DCs are unable to replicate domain information between them, domain services can become unpredictable. In either case, for Active Directory to provide full functionality as expected, the network that supports Active Directory must be understood so that your Active Directory can be designed to accommodate its limitations.

The networking services representative on the Active Directory team should be able to provide a WAN topology as well as LAN topologies where appropriate. The WAN topology should be translated into the available bandwidth and throughput between physical locations.

For example, Wadeware utilizes a frame relay network to connect all their North American locations (see Figure 7.3).

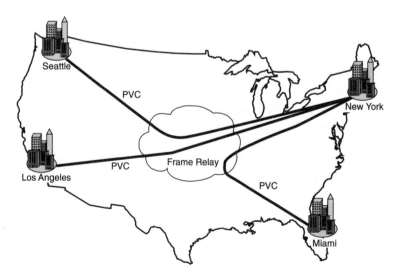

Figure 7.3 The Wadeware North American frame relay network.

In this example, you can see that each location in North America is connected to the frame relay network, but that Permanent Virtual Circuits (PVCs) are defined between each location and New York. This means that if a person in Miami sends a message to a user in Los Angeles, the bits must travel from Miami through the frame relay network to New York, and then they are routed back through the frame relay network in Los Angeles. This is not necessarily a bad design, but it should be understood when designing your Active Directory architecture. This is because clients communicate with DCs, and DCs communicate with other DCs. How these hosts communicate is dependent on the Active Directory design. Understanding the route that bits take between hosts helps to design the optimal Active Directory site design.

Wadeware's European division has outsourced their European network, as seen in Figure 7.4.

In this example, each location has an access rate and a committed information rate (CIR). Although the access rate to each location is 128Kbps, the CIR is only 64Kbps. The networking services representative should know that the frame relay rules in Europe are different from those in the United States and that supporting speeds over the CIR in Europe is not only costly, it is undependable because the carrier regularly drops packets over the CIR. This causes the router to resend the packet, just adding to the problem. Armed with this information, Active Directory can be designed in Europe with this limitation in mind. Moreover, the Active Directory team can also use this knowledge to lobby for a higher CIR in Europe.

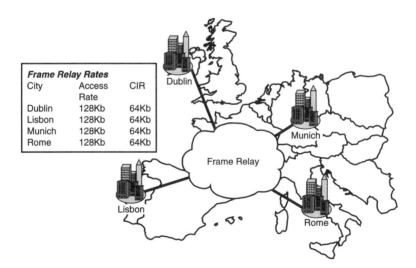

Figure 7.4 The Wadeware European frame relay network.

Therefore, when assessing your network, you should be armed with the following information:

- WAN topology map, including logical circuits, access rates, and CIRs if appropriate
- List of physical locations, the number of users, the number of workstations, and LAN and WAN usage characteristics
- Available bandwidth between physical locations during both business and non-business hours
- Internet connectivity, including firewall information, DNS authority, and usage statistics
- Future WAN/LAN enhancements, such as Asynchronous Transfer Mode (ATM)
- Remote user connectivity strategy
- Common communication paths, such as routine messaging paths and work-groups that span physical locations
- Directory enabled devices, such as routers, switches, PBXs, Voice gateways, or IP phones

This information is used to determine where Active Directory site lines are drawn, where DC and other Active Directory services are located in relation to clients, whether there are any areas of the WAN that could increase bandwidth, and possibly how many domains are necessary.

Workstation Assessment

Workstation assessment is part of the Windows 2000 deployment, especially if Windows 2000 is to be deployed on the desktop. It's also important for the Active Directory planning process to know how many and where, desktops exist the applications they run, their attrition schedule, and their construction (how much RAM they have, what class and speed CPU they use, the amount of available disk space, and what operating system they are running).

This information is used to assess the number and placement of domain services. It is also used to assess how well Group Policy Objects (GPOs) can be applied to individual workstations.

User Assessment

One of the most difficult assessments required is the assessment of your users. Many projects that implement services to be used by users avoid asking the question: What type of users do you have? This is because, typically, there is no easy answer. To simplify this task, it becomes necessary to look at the organization as a whole. Is yours a high-tech company or a call-center outsourcing company? Each has a different typical-user profile. Each of these users has different requirements and expectations.

If your organization is not so easily generalized, try to break it down by department. Is there a research and development department full of engineers? Is there a sales and order-entry department? Each of these departments also has different expectations and requirements. That's not to say that the order-entry department would automatically have fewer expectations than the research and development department. On the contrary, order-entry users who work with their computers constantly throughout the day might have more rigorous demands than those of research and development users.

Evaluate your organization and categorize users in one of three classes: heavy, medium, or light users. After these categories are defined, group users at each location into one of these three classes. With this information, you are better able to determine the amount of domain resources required at each location.

Politics and Religion

The final analysis is at a more pragmatic level. What is the political climate surrounding the Windows 2000 and Active Directory project? Active Directory is beginning to approach the turf of other legacy system, especially UNIX. As Windows NT grew up in the enterprise from a simple workgroup file-server to what it is now, providing full-fledged enterprise services, other congregations of operating system loyalists have drawn lines in the sand, stating "Windows NT, knock yourself out providing file services to your workgroups, but don't cross the line into the enterprise arena." For many organizations, the first battle was fought and won by Microsoft Exchange, which became the first client/server system to achieve true enterprise-level presence with high levels of functionality and a low cost of ownership. However, this just backed the legacy system loyalists further into their corner, re-enforcing their resolve. They didn't see Exchange coming, but this time they are ready. The expected beachhead will be over which system hosts DNS, but that will just be the first battle of the war.

Anyway, make sure you're aware of how your Windows 2000 and Active Directory project is being received throughout the organization. Arm yourself with knowledge of the issues surrounding coexistence, such as the dependencies of Active Directory on DNS and why one implementation is better than another, before you go into battle. Make sure that you placate if necessary; choose your battles wisely.

Assessing the Administrative Structure

Microsoft has really used the increase in administrative capabilities provided by Windows 2000 and Active Directory as a spearhead for its marketing campaign. Rightfully so, Active Directory does provide much more administrative functionality than Windows NT 4.0. As one of the co-authors of this book likes to state, "The pendulum has swung from minimum administrative flexibility in NT 4.0 to maximum flexibility in Active Directory."

Hence, organizations now have the ability to reevaluate their administrative structure and implement an Active Directory design based on business processes not technical limitations.

Current Administrative Responsibility

The first step in assessing your administrative structure is to figure out how things are currently being administered. What is the structure of your IS group? Define what administrative tasks are preformed and by whom. Examples of such tasks include

- Creating and deleting users
- Creating computer accounts
- Changing and resetting passwords
- Changing user information
- Creating mailboxes
- Managing IP addresses
- Managing user policies
- Managing application rollout
- Managing Helpdesk services
- Managing inventory control

Current Grouping of Administrators

Based on the preceding list, determine how your administrators are grouped. For example, an organization might have a multi-master NT 4.0 domain topology, each with its own set of administrators. For each domain, the administrators might bear the responsibility of all the previously listed tasks. Groups of administrators, such as the NT operators group, in each domain might perform specific tasks. How administrators are grouped, whether by domain, responsibility, or both, needs to be documented and considered during the administrative model design process.

Current Permissions of Administrative Groups

After the administrative groups have been documented, it is important to identify what permissions they have, on which resources, and for what purpose. This data should provide a matrix of administrative groups and responsibilities that represents your organization's administrative structure.

Documenting the Administrative Structure

The administrative structure information should be compared to the existing administrative model documentation to make sure there aren't any glaring differences in approach. If an administrative model does not exist, this information should be used to create a short outline of what currently exists. This document might become part of the Active Directory architecture.

Assessing the Application Structure

If easing administrative burdens is not the driving force behind implementing Active Directory, perhaps it is the functionality of directory-enabled applications or the control of applications through policies.

Certainly, with the next generation of BackOffice products, Active Directory is a requirement. You can also expect that other hardware and software vendors will enable functionality that is dependent on a directory, such as Active Directory.

Directory-Enabled Applications

The easiest way to determine which applications depend on Active Directory is to identify which applications have Lightweight Directory Access Protocol (LDAP) capabilities. There are a number of ways that applications can use a directory. One of the most obvious ways is as a source for user and resource information. Applications can benefit from directory information in countless ways. Take voice over IP (VoIP) for an example. An application could be written that would use Active Directory as a method for company employees to communicate in real-time, using VoIP. Let's say that Bill wants to talk to Doug. Bill right-clicks on Doug's object in Active Directory and selects the Communicate option. The VoIP application checks to see if Doug is logged onto the network. If Doug is not logged on, a blank email message is spawned and Bill sends Doug an email. If Doug is logged on, the VoIP application determines which computer Doug is logged on and what type of communication peripherals that computer has. If both Bill's and Doug's computers have video and audio capabilities, Bill is prompted to choose which method he would like to try. If Doug's computer only has audio capabilities, a VoIP session is established, and Bill has his conversation with Doug. If the computer Doug is logged onto does not have audio capabilities, or if Doug is on the other side of a slow link, an email message is sent by Bill to Doug.

Applications can also store data in Active Directory. However, it is not designed for typical data storage. The data application's store in the directory should be specific and relative to Active Directory. It is important to understand the impact that an application has on Active Directory. Modifications made to the schema and the nature of the data being stored should go through a change-control process and lab testing. Microsoft's Active Directory development guide is a good source of information about how and what information should be stored in the directory.

Controlling Applications with Group Policy Objects

One of the methods of reducing the cost of desktop ownership is to lock the desktop down and to assign applications to users based on their location in the domain/OU structure. Although this is contrary to some corporate cultures, this method should be evaluated to determine the impact it would have on the bottom line. Although the inspiration for the OU design in many organizations is to delegate administration, others have another driving force behind their OU structure, limiting users to only the applications they need. As discussed in Chapter 4, "Defining and Meeting Your Directory Requirements," by assigning users applications that are based on their location in the OU hierarchy, and by only allowing those users to run those applications, the workstation is better managed by IS. This reduces Helpdesk maintenance costs, potentially reduces licensing costs, and increases user productivity.

Let's say, for example, that Wadeware has three departments that each use specialized applications as shown in Table 7.1, and the entire organization uses Microsoft Office and Microsoft Project.

Table 7.1   **Example of Departments and Necessary Applications**

Department	Applications
Engineering	AutoC, Active Directory, Visio
Accounts Receivable	VisiCalc, ARsoft+
Accounts Payable	VisiCalc, APsoft+

With your group and application matrix (which you built earlier in the chapter), you can build an OU structure that uses inheritance to enforce group policies throughout your OU tree.

Active Directory OU structures can be used for purposes other than applying group policy, such as administrative delegation. It is important to look at your Active Directory design from a business prospective and make sure it reflects your organization's needs.

Documenting the Application Structure

After grouping users together and identifying the applications that they use and the applications they need, an inventory should be constructed. Most organizations have a software inventory of some kind. Use this inventory to determine how you would publish or assign applications using the Active Directory OU structure.

Assessing the Organizational Structure

Another possible design consideration in your Active Directory domain and OU designs is the organizational structure. The organizational structure is not likely to be the primary consideration when designing your OU structure. Its only advantage is that users are presented with a directory that is organized in a way that they are accustomed. As users browse Active Directory (Yes, you can browse Active Directory using My Network Places.), it is segmented into OUs based on division, physical location, or both. This allows a user visiting Houston to locate a printer or a conference room based on familiar criteria.

Therefore, although it is not recommended that you design your domain or OU structure to mirror your organizational structure *just* for ease of browsing, it is recommended that the organization's structure be considered as an influence in the OU design.

Weighing the Requirements

After the assessment phase of the Active Directory project is complete, you should have a solid grasp of the current computing environment. Information should be gathered and contained in a series of documents:

- **Environment Assessment**—This document includes three important sections. Network, workstation, and user assessments are used for the design and implementation of Active Directory. The network, in particular, transcends user and business requirements to put technical limitations on the Active Directory domain topology. Understanding the infrastructure of an organization, including the hardware and software being used, provides useful information necessary to build your Active Directory architecture.

- **Administration Assessment**—This document illustrates how the current environment is managed. Grouping administrators by the tasks they perform gives you a view of the administrative environment as it is now. Many organizations base their Active Directory design heavily on the administrative requirements of their organization.

- **Application Assessment**—This document inventories the applications that are currently in use and identifies the users of each. Active Directory gives you the ability to better manage the workstation by restricting the applications that users can access. It also gives you the ability to publish or assign applications to specific groups of users, based on OUs, sites, or domains.

- **Directory Integration Assessment**—This document is meant to determine what role Active Directory plays in the organization's overall directory services strategy. There are usually multiple directories in an organization. Determining what role Active Directory plays, and how it is integrated with the other directories, helps to scope the project.

- **Organizational Structure Assessment**—This document is made to expose the project team to the entire enterprise and to give context to the far-reaching ramifications that the Active Directory design has. The Organizational Structure Assessment can also be used to compare how an OU structure built based on administrative or application business requirements compares to how the organization is actually structured.

Documenting the Organizational Structure

This document can exist on paper or electronically, but it should exist. Locating an up-to-date organizational structure to a level of detail that is practical to this project will assist in designing Active Directory.

Defining Active Directory Namespace Candidates

Now that we have gathered a great deal of information about your organization relevant to the Active Directory domain design, we need to take that information and put it to use. After a brief review of Active Directory domains and trees, we will look at some of the design decisions necessary to construct a sound domain topology.

A Few Active Directory Basics

Active Directory is a distributed system that is made up of a directory *database*, which includes a schema, transaction logs, and all the other necessities that come with a database, and a directory *service*. The directory service is the process (or processes) that makes use of the information stored in the directory database.

Active Directory provides directory services geared toward the enterprise. This means that Active Directory services need to provide additional functionality and availability, such as

- **Scalability**—Active Directory domains are logical security boundaries around a set of objects. A domain can contain a varying number of objects ranging from the hundreds to the millions. Domains can be added and deleted as necessary.

- **Extensibility**—As previously mentioned, the Active Directory database uses a schema. The schema is the definition of all the objects that can be created in Active Directory, along with their attributes. The schema can be modified, allowing for new objects or modified attributes on existing objects. In addition, new object classes can be added to the schema to support directory-enabled applications.

- **Internet Standards**—Microsoft is starting to move away from proprietary protocols and methods. They would rather sponsor RFC drafts, which support naming that adds their desired functionality (which is good for us all). Subsequently, name resolution and the directory access and security protocols are basic Internet standard protocols.

- **Single Seat Administration**—Administrators can administer any portion of the directory from a single location in the organization (with the right permissions, of course).

- **Fault Tolerance**—Each DC in the domain has a complete copy of that domain's directory, making Active Directory a multi-master directory. Each DC has a writable copy of the domain partition. If one DC fails, the other DCs are still able to satisfy requests for Active Directory services.

- **Security**—The access control lists (ACLs) control who has permission to access directory data.

- **Interoperability**—Active Directory, being based on an X.500 directory and using Internet standard protocols, is able to interact with other X.500 based directory services.

Naming and Name Resolution

Every object that represents information or resources in Active Directory must have a name unique to Active Directory. Additionally, Active Directory must support several of the common naming conventions that clients might use. The name is a X.500 style distinguished name (DN) that describes the object's location in the directory. The relative distinguished name (RDN) is the portion of the DN that makes the object unique. If you have two Ed Brovicks in your organization, as long as they are in different OUs, or have different RDNs, they will have unique DNs. For example, there could be two Ed Brovicks in two different OUs because the OU made the DN unique. If there are two Ed Brovicks in the same OU, they would have to have different RDNs, such as `CN=ebrovick` and `CN=ebrovick1`, so that they are unique DNs.

- **Name resolution**—is the process that takes the DN and translates it into an object or into information that the DN represents.
- **Active Directory**—is a collection of objects. What these objects are and their definitions are as follows:
  - **Object classes**—are the types of objects that can be created in the directory. Object classes have attributes associated to them, which compose the object class. Users, for example, are a class of objects. *First Name* and *Last Name* are examples of attributes associated with the Users object class.
  - **Objects**—are the instances of the object classes that you create. When you create a user object, it is based on the object class.
  - **Attributes**—are the characteristics, or fields, that make up the object class. The attributes that each object has, as well as the values that they can contain, are defined in the object classes. Attributes can be mandatory or not. Again, when a user object is created, there are attributes on that object that are populated. Examples of such attributes are *First Name*, *Last Name*, and *Display Name*.
  - **Schema**—contains all the Active Directory object classes and attributes. The dictionary defines what is in the Active Directory database.

Active Directory Logical Structure

Objects in Active Directory are organized in containers. A container itself is a directory object that holds other objects. The types of containers Active Directory uses to organize objects are:

- **Organizational Units (OUs)**—contain objects for organizing those objects. Objects within an OU can be treated as a collection of objects when Group Policy Objects are associated with an OU.
- **Containers**—are different from OUs in that although they are built into Active Directory, they can't have GPOs associated with them. The Users container is an example of a container.

- **Domains**—are containers that also define a security context. This means that Active Directory is written to treat all objects within a domain by the same rules.

- **Trees**—are a collection of one or more domains that share a common namespace. Although all domains trust one another, the tree relationship is defined by the namespace that is necessary to support the domain structure. The root domain of `wadeware.net` can have two sub-domains named `backoffice.wadeware.net` and `office.wadeware.net`. This relationship between the root domain and the two child domains is what forms a tree.

- **Forest**—is a collection of one or more trees. Trees within the Forest share the same Active Directory but do not need to share the same namespace. Therefore, you can have two organizations, such as `wadeware.net` and `wadeco.net`, which are contained in a single Active Directory; they share the same configuration, GC, and schema partitions; but they have different namespaces.

- **Global Catalog (GC)**—is a central source for all directory objects. Not all the attributes from each object is stored in the GC but just enough to make it useful for searching the entire Active Directory. This is because objects replicate among the other DCs within their domain only. That means that a user looking for an object in another domain is not be able to find that user's object from his or her DC. Therefore, the user would query the GC server and find the DN for the object. The user could then locate the object in Active Directory.

- **Trust relationships**—are logical links that combine two or more domains into one administrative unit. This allows permissions to be associated from one domain to another, because one domain *trusts* that the other domain has authenticated its users, and they are who they say they are.

- **Namespace**—is the DNS type namespace that represents domains. Active Directory is dependent on DNS and the DNS namespace. This makes it important to design your domain topology in a DNS-friendly way and to provide clients with reliable DNS services.

Physical Structure

If the logical components aren't difficult enough to keep straight, the physical components only add to the mix:

- **Sites**—are groupings of computers (or subnets) that share high-speed, high-bandwidth, and connectivity. A subnet can only be associated with a single site. Sites only contain resource objects, such as computers. A site definition is stored as a site object in Active Directory. Multiple site objects construct a site topology, which is different from the logical topology of the network. This means that you can have one domain across more than one site, and you can have one site that contains multiple domains. Therefore, sites ignore domains and namespaces.

They define how and, perhaps, when replication between DCs occurs and which DC a user's computer contacts for authentication. A site can also have a group policy imposed upon it. Lastly, clients are associated with a site based on the subnet that the client is on. Clients should first try to contact DCs within their site.

- **Domain Controllers (DCs)**—are servers that provide Active Directory services to clients and users. The DC stores a complete copy of the domain's objects, along with the Active Directory schema and configuration in what are called *partitions* or *naming contexts*. Remember, the DC only stores domain partition information for the domain to which it belongs, but it stores schema and configuration partition information for the entire Active Directory. Each DC can write to Active Directory. Active Directory uses a multi-master replication model where every DC is equal. There are DCs within the Forest that play an additional role in Active Directory. *Flexible Single Master of Operations (FSMO)* is a role that some DCs play, which must be performed by a single DC in the domain or Forest. The Primary Domain Controller (PDC) emulator is an example of a FSMO. Each domain, when running in mixed-mode, can only have a single PDC emulator. By default, the first DC in the domain assumes this role.

- **Global Catalog (GC)**—a DC that also hosts a partial replica of every other domain in the Forest. That is, a GC server contains all the objects and their attributes for the domain which it is a member, in addition to all the objects for the other domains in the Forest. However, these objects from other domains in the Forest do not include all their attributes. This way, a GC server in a domain can provide basic object information about users and computers in other domains. The GC is only replicated to DCs that have been designated as GC servers.

Active Directory Operations

Now that we've reviewed the basics of what is what in Active Directory, we'll review how it works. Understanding the relationships between DCs is important when designing an Active Directory topology.

Information Is Replicated to DCs

If a change is written to Active Directory, the DC has to replicate the change to all other DCs in the domain. Also, if a new DC joins the domain, the Active Directory partitions are replicated to the new server. This might seem like a lot of replication every time a change is made to Active Directory, but the benefits of fault tolerance and end user performance are worth the added traffic. Also, remember that the domain partition is only replicated between DCs in the same domain, and that replication can be scheduled with sites.

GC Server in the Physical Structure

As mentioned earlier, the GC is a partition that is only replicated to DCs that are configured as GC servers. The location of GC servers in your organization is an important design decision because clients require access to GC servers when they log on. Universal group membership is stored in the GC. Because universal groups can deny access to resources, a user's membership to the universal groups must be discovered during logon to build the logon access token. In addition, the GC server provides clients to view objects outside their own domain.

Partitions

Partitions are physical storage containers that contain a specific type of data for Active Directory. For each Active Directory, there is a schema partition, a configuration partition, and a domain partition for each domain. The Active Directory domain partitions segment each domain's directory information. The objects in each domain partition are identified by their DN. The GC hosts all objects within the Forest but not all their attributes. The GC has the DN of each object, and therefore, it has enough information to locate a replica of the partition that holds the object.

Naming Context

The *naming context,* not to be confused with the namespace, represents a contiguous subtree of the directory and is a *unit of replication.* A partition is a naming context and is therefore replicated. In Active Directory, a single server always holds at least three naming contexts:

- **Configuration**—This naming context contains physical data for sites, services, and partitions.
- **Domain**—This naming context is the default unit of replication and contains domain directory data.
- **Schema**—This naming context contains the schema for the entire Active Directory.

When DCs replicate, each of these naming contexts is replicated between the appropriate DCs.

Naming Context Replication

Naming contexts replicate between DCs so that each DC has up-to-date directory information for its clients. It is important to remember, however, that not all naming contexts replicate between all DCs. Remember that the domain naming context only replicates between DCs within a domain, and the GC only replicates between GC servers.

Intra-Site Replication

Naming context replication within a site uses RPC replication (referred to as IP in the user interface). All DCs within a site replicate using RPCs and are unschedulable. The RPCs used during replication require a certain level of available network bandwidth. This means that the DCs within a site must be well connected to the network. If the available bandwidth between DCs becomes limited, the RPCs might fail causing replication failures. Hence, it is important to define a site architecture that groups DCs together on a network with adequate available network bandwidth.

Inter-Site Replication

After a domain structure is divided into sites, those sites must be connected using site link connectors. There are two transports that site link connectors can use: SMTP and RPC.

The IP (RPC) site link connector suffers from the same limitations as RPCs within a site, which is that RPCs are not reliable across unstable links. Therefore, sites with limited or unstable network connections between them should use SMTP as the transport for the site link connector. Site link connectors also use compression, which makes inter-site replication more efficient. One important caveat in choosing a protocol for your site link connector is that the domain naming context cannot be replicated between sites using the SMTP transport. Therefore, sites and domains need to be defined so that all DCs within a site have adequate available network bandwidth. A domain can still be divided up into multiple sites, for purposes of client connectivity, but those sites must use the RPC transport between sites. This means that domain boundaries have to be evaluated depending on the available bandwidth between sites.

The SMTP transport, which is asynchronous and streams data between DCs, is more stable and reliable across networks with unreliable network connections.

Security

Active Directory is a secure directory. Four security features provide a secure application that serves as the security subsystem for the Windows 2000 operating system.

- **Discretionary ACL**—determines the type of access an authenticated user or group of users has on an object.

- **Delegation**—allows administrative authority to be delegated to groups of administrators to manage a specific container or subtree.

- **Access rights**—can be granted or denied to authenticated users or groups of users on containers, objects, or classes of objects.

- **Trust relationships**—allow users in one domain to gain access to resources and information throughout the Forest. Transitive trusts are created by default between a new domain and the root domain, regardless of the location of the domain within a domain tree. A transitive trust means that the new domain trusts all other domains trusted by the root domain. Explicit trusts can be manually created between two domains. Explicit trusts can be created to improve LDAP referrals between two domains that are in different domain trees.

GC Services

The GC is a service that provides an efficient way for clients to locate objects beyond the local domain. The GC hosts a portion of each domain partition—enough for the client to locate domain objects not found in the local domain. This means that if the data contained in the GC changes, those changes must be replicated to all the GC servers in Active Directory. GC servers are DCs that not only host the domain, schema, and configure partitions, but the GC partition as well.

.As previously mentioned, each client must have access to a GC server for a logon access token to be created. This means that the placement of GC servers in the organization is important. It is recommended that each site has at least one GC server. Those sites that are split between two or more physical locations might need a GC server at each physical location in case the WAN connection between the physical location fails. With a GC server at each physical location within a site, clients would still have access to it, even if a WAN connection were to fail.

Why not make all DCs GC servers? Making all DCs GC servers increases the amount of GC server replication and requires additional resources on all DCs. To reduce the amount of replication and resources required for DCs, strategically place GC servers throughout the organization so that all clients and servers have a GC server available on the LAN.

Number of Forests

If possible, you should have only one Forest. Multiple Forests are not something that you should build to accommodate a single organization. Multiple Forests limit Active Directory's functionality at the enterprise level, and this can make administration difficult.

Multiple Forests typically arise if two organizations merge or participate in a joint venture. This might be necessary if the two organizations do not trust one another or cannot agree on a change-control policy. There is one Enterprise Administration and Schema Administration group within a Forest. Both organizations must agree on a central group of users who are members of these groups. If they cannot, multiple Forests might be warranted.

To allow access between Forests, the simplest method is to create explicit one-way trusts between the domains that must trust one another. Explicit trusts are not transitive. Therefore, in a multi-tree, multi-domain Forest, the creation of explicit trusts can be complex. For this reason, it is important to keep it simple by limiting the domains that trust one another.

Number of Trees

Although multiple Forests in an organization are usually not feasible, multiple trees are. Trees provide an additional level of separation between domains that must still share resources. Multiple trees also allow multiple namespaces to coexist in a single directory.

If you have multiple trees in a Forest, each tree has its own root domain name.

In Figure 7.5, you can see that each organization can maintain their identity while still benefiting from having a unified directory service across the entire organization.

Does having multiple trees reduce replication? No, the schema, GC, and configuration partitions are replicated to all DCs in the Forest. The domain partitions are only replicated within the domain.

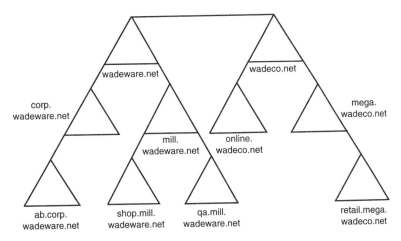

Figure 7.5   Multiple trees in the same Active Directory Forest.

Does having multiple trees require explicit trusts? No, a logical transitive trust exists between root domains. This means that each domain in the Forest trusts the others.

You should only use one tree, unless you have specific reasons for multiple namespaces in your organization.

If you are planning for multiple trees in a Forest, identify the areas of the organization that are included in each namespace, confirming that every area falls into one namespace or another. After the organization has been divided up into separate namespaces, the next step is to design the domain structure of each tree.

Defining the Domain Hierarchy

In a tree, domains represent an administrative boundary, a replication boundary, a security boundary, and a namespace boundary. Domains are also a way to organize objects and apply GPOs. It is important to note, however, that OUs are also a means of object organization and GPO application. So, when should you use domains, and when should you use OUs? Well, there are some specific reasons for creating multiple domains. Such reasons include

- **Administrative Model**—This model might require an administrative boundary between various parts of the organization. There might be departments within an organization that require individual control over the security for that organization. Unlike two organizations that don't have a trust with each other, these departments are part of a unified organization that can decide on a change control policy and a group of administrators that have enterprise-wide permissions. By having multiple domains in an organization, you can draw distinct lines between groups and users and the permissions they have. Furthermore, if your administrative model is decentralized to the departmental or physical location level, multiple domains are a way of providing this decentralized administration.

- **International Model**—This model usually influences the administrative model. Traditionally, international organizations are managed and administered by a separate group of administrators from that of the North American organization. This organizational model might call for separate domains. International organizations might also have language, currency, and other localization requirements that require multiple domains.

- **Network Limitations**—These limitations could also be overcome using multiple domains. Make no mistake, the first means of solving network bandwidth limitations is to purchase additional bandwidth. The second means of managing bandwidth limitations is to use Active Directory sites. Remember , that whether you have one site or many, the domain partition is replicated between all the DCs in the domain. Designing an Active Directory domain topology based on available network bandwidth might diminish the return on investment for Active Directory because the design is not defined by business requirements but rather network requirements. However, if the network bandwidth between physical locations is limited, creating domain boundaries can keep the domain partitions from replicating between those physical locations. It is important to remember that the configuration, schema, and GC still replicate to all DCs in the Forest, regardless of domain boundaries despite domain and site boundaries.

- **Independent OU Structures**—These can be created in each domain. If different portions of an organization require different OU structures, domains provide for varying OU organization.

- **Security Policies**—Different policies for various parts of the organization might also require different domains. Separate password policies and group definitions are examples of security policies that might cause multiple domains.

The First Domain

The first domain in Active Directory is special. The Active Directory Forest is established with the first domain. This domain contains two Forest-wide groups, the Enterprise Administration and the Schema Administration group. The first domain, or root domain, must always exist, because these groups cannot be recreated in another domain. Hence, it is important to choose this domain wisely.

If your Active Directory has only a few domains in a single namespace, the first domain is considered a permanent domain. However, if your Active Directory has multiple namespaces, you want to make sure the domain you install first, which contains these critical groups, is one that is permanent and one in which these groups can be managed. This means that if there are different entities within one organization, each with individual namespaces, one entity will host these enterprise-wide groups.

In cases where organizations support more than one namespace in Active Directory, it might be prudent to create an empty root domain. As seen in Figure 7.6, the root domain would not be part of an entity's namespace; membership and management of the root domain could be done at the enterprise level, and the replication of this domain to DCs spread across the enterprise would then be possible because of its limited number of objects.

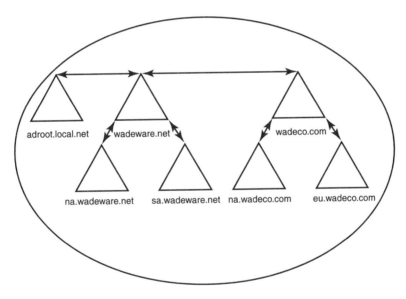

Figure 7.6 An empty root domain in a multi-tree Active Directory Forest.

Defining the OU Hierarchy

For many, the OU design is where the rubber meets the road. OUs are object containers that host Active Directory objects. Administrative tasks can be delegated to various groups of administrators based on OUs. Furthermore, group policies can be applied to OUs.

What this means is that a compromise between administrative requirements and group policy requirements might need to be struck. If delegation of the administration of computers, users, printers, groups, and other resources is a paramount requirement, steer your OU design toward meeting your administrative requirements. On the other hand, if your group policy delegation requirements are paramount, steer your OU design toward an OU structure that best meets your group policy delegation requirements.

As previously mentioned, each domain can have its own OU structure. This does not mean that they must be different. For ease in administration, it might be wise to make them the same, but it is possible to vary which set of requirements is satisfied in the same way that they vary across your organization.

Some tips for designing your OU structure are

- Layout your administrative and group policy requirements, and decide which leads the way in designing your OU structure.

- Review your administrative model, mapping the requirements of the administrative model to the OU structure, where appropriate.

- Create multiple OU structures that can be tested in the lab. Create some that satisfy all the requirements of your administrative model, others that satisfy all requirements of your group policy strategy, and still others that compromise between administrative and group policy requirements. Take these OU structures into the lab, test them out, and see for yourself how they work and whether they provide the level of functionality you need.

- Choose OU names relevant to your organization. In addition, it is important to remember that users *are* able to see the OU structure if they browse the directory. Microsoft believes that the searching mechanism built into Windows 2000 clients is used to locate objects more than to browse; however, it is important to remember that LDAP is not the only method of accessing the directory.

OUs can be nested within other OUs. If an OU is nested, it inherits the properties of the parent OU by default. It is best to limit the number of OU levels. Many levels of OUs might increase the administrative burden and confuse both administrators and users. Another reasons for limiting the level of OUs is performance. When a user logs on, the policies that user is subjected to have to be built by interrogating the OU hierarchy. Therefore, the number of OU levels and the number of policies a user is subjected to might impact logon performance.

Top Level OU

It might be that you only have one level of OUs, which is simple and easy to manage. However, if you are going to nest OUs, choose names for your top level OUs that are general and static in nature. This minimizes the need to have to rename these OUs because of reorganizations within your organization.

Lower Level OUs

The remaining OU levels should have distinct purposes, and they should have been created for the sake of creating multiple levels of OUs. Some considerations when creating multiple levels of OUs include

- How do you delegate administrative responsibility? Based on departments, administrative function, or types of administration?

- Does the parent OU host objects that can be divided into child OUs? For example, if you create an OU for your engineers, are there different types of engineers that could be further segregated into child OUs? Say you have civil engineers, mechanical engineers, and apprentice engineers. If each type of engineer requires a different group policy or if each is administered by different administrative groups, segregating the engineering OU into child OUs, one for each type of engineer, might make sense.

- Remember that group policies can also be applied to domains. If you have a GPO that you want to apply to everyone in the domain, apply the GPO to the domain rather than one or all OUs.

- Remember that group policies can also be applied to sites. If you have defined each physical location as a site and have a group policy that you want to vary based on physical location, apply that GPO to the site rather than creating an OU for each physical location.

- Remember that OUs inherit the group policies of their parent OU by default. This means that a hierarchy of OUs, built to satisfy group policy requirements, should have the most global group policies applied near the top of the hierarchy. This way a group policy that is meant for all engineers would be applied on the engineers' OU, and group policies meant for civil engineers only would be applied to the civil engineers' OU only. Therefore, civil engineers would have both the engineers' and civil engineers' group policy applied to them when they logged on.

The Administrative Delegation Model

An example of an OU hierarchy that primarily satisfies administrative delegation requirements has two levels of OUs. The first level categorizes resources in the organizations. As new types of resources are added to the directory, new OUs can be added to this top-level hierarchy. The second level of OUs is based on geographic location, as seen in Figure 7.7.

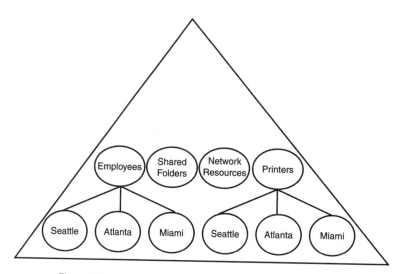

Figure 7.7   OU structures by resources then locations.

With this OU structure, it is possible to grant the centralized IS group permissions on the top level OUs while granting local IS groups limited permissions on the objects in their respective OUs. Because permissions are inherited down the OU hierarchy, the centralized IS group's permissions located on the top level OUs are inherited down to each location's OU, as seen in Figure 7.8.

It would also be possible to swap these OU levels. The OU structure in Figure 7.8 is less centralized than in Figure 7.7. With this OU structure, each local IS group has permissions on their own OU. It is then possible to grant administrative permissions on specific second-level OUs to specific groups within each local IS group. For example, the Seattle IS group could have a group of administrators that can only reset passwords for users in the users OU.

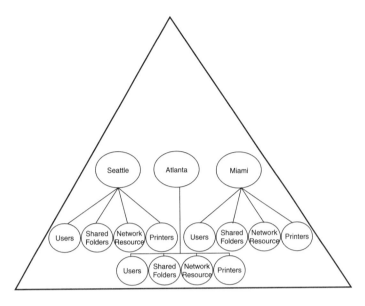

Figure 7.8 A three-tier OU structure.

The Group Policy Model

An example of an OU hierarchy that primarily satisfies the group policy application requirements is one that again has two levels of OUs, as seen in Figure 7.9. The first level categorizes objects by departments. The second level categorizes objects by roles within each department.

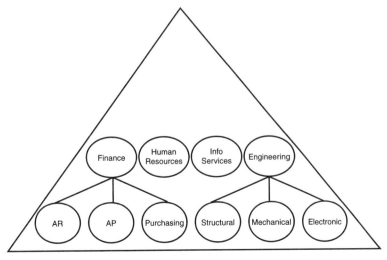

Figure 7.9 OUs structured by group policy requirements.

With this structure, objects in each department can have GPOs applied that provide applications or enforce policy based on department. Policies can be further applied based on job function in the second tier of OUs. All users might have a core set of applications they have permissions to run. This group policy would be set at the domain level. Then, because additional applications are necessary, those applications could be added to GPOs on specific OUs. Engineers have application requirements beyond the core applications. These applications would be added to a GPO on the engineers' OU. Structural engineers might have application requirements that could be added to a GPO on the structural engineers' OU. By locking down the workstation and providing applications to users based on the OU they are in, an organization decreases maintenance and increases user efficiency.

This model could also be applied with a geographic level of OUs, as seen in Figure 7.10.

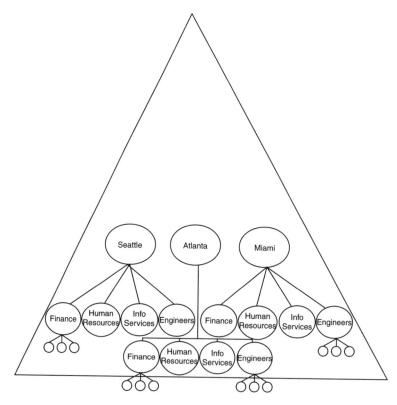

Figure 7.10 OUs structured primarily by geographic location.

This would support a decentralized administrative model while still allowing Group Policy Objects to be applied at the department model. This model might be stretching the limits of complexity that you want to design in an OU model. However, as with any design, you would want to take this design and others into the lab and test for functionality and performance.

It is also important to note that sites can have GPOs applied to them. Therefore, if site lines were drawn around geographic locations, it might not be necessary to create an OU level dedicated to geographic location. Rather, geographic group policies could be applied to each geographic location's site.

Physical Sites and the Network Affect Domain Structure

When designing your domain and OU model, you must also define sites. The best way to design a site structure is discussed in Chapter 10, "The Physical Topology: Sites and Replication," but it is an important component to the domain structure. Sites are a physical representation of the domain structure. They mitigate domain replication traffic within a domain and the preferred DCs for clients within the same site. The domain and OU hierarchy should not be affected by the site design, but the site design should consider the domain hierarchy.

Defining DCs and GC Servers

Another important part of the site design is the location of DCs, GC servers, and domain name servers. A client must have access to each of these services to logon. Therefore, at least one (and probably two) of each of these services should be available to clients in each location. To eliminate WAN outages as a potential point of failure, it might be prudent to locate these services at each physical location.

Namespace in Domain Structure

The namespace is represented in the domain structure. Top-level domain names, especially if there are multiple domain names being used in an organization, affect the domain design. However, if an organization has a single domain name and the domain design calls for multiple Active Directory domains, the namespaces are built below the top-level domain.

Summary

The domain structure of your Active Directory Forest needs to be carefully considered. Keeping your domain structure as simple as possible, and only creating multiple domains when necessary, is the prudent approach. Its also prudent not to assume your current Windows NT domain topology is the best Active Directory domain topology. To fully benefit from this powerful, enterprise-wide directory, a well thought-out design is required.

8

Designing the DNS Namespace

ACTIVE DIRECTORY IS ONLY AS RELIABLE AND EFFICIENT AS THE domain name system (DNS) service. Today DNS is the foundation for name resolution for the Internet and many corporate resources. Web browsers use DNS to translate Transmission Control Protocol/Internet Protocol (TCP/IP) fully qualified domain names to IP addresses. Mail systems use DNS to resolve mail address domains to specific host names and IP addresses. All over the world, Internet and enterprise applications are dependent on correctly-configured DNS entries for their applications to work properly—now add Microsoft's Active Directory.

DNS is the name master for the world. As one of the services that helps to maintain peace and order in the Internet, Microsoft has made the decision to resolve names by using DNS. Microsoft's Active Directory is dependent on DNS for name resolution in finding resources.

There are several reasons for using the reliance on DNS for Active Directory. The first and most obvious reason is the need to use a service that has demonstrated scalability. Although Microsoft has used the Windows Internet Naming Service (WINS) not only as a NetBIOS name resolver but also as a hostname resolver for many of today's needs, it can be difficult to administer in large environments. DNS has demonstrated its scalability with its widespread use on the Internet as well as in corporate America.

A second reason for using DNS is that it has the capability to integrate with other existing namespaces, namely existing DNS environments. Rather than building a new and improved naming service, Microsoft has embraced the Internet standard and is working to expand its functionality through the standards bodies. Embracing the pre-existing DNS infrastructure leverages the current investment of organizations. This provides total cost of ownership (TCO) benefits.

Finally, DNS has a ready place in the computer community. Although DNS might seem outdated in its early forms, you likely already have a trained staff that knows how to create, modify, and administer DNS.

Windows 2000 DNS: With Active Directory and Without Active Directory

With Windows 2000 DNS, can be utilized as a traditional DNS server. You are able to use similar configuration files and directly interface with non-Microsoft DNS servers and Windows NT 4.0 DNS servers. This use of Windows 2000 DNS provides for integration with an existing DNS implementation as either a secondary or a primary DNS server. If you bring a Windows 2000 DNS into an existing DNS environment, it is typically as a secondary server that uses the typical full-zone file transfers.

You can also integrate the DNS databases into Active Directory. If you decide to use Windows 2000 DNS and Active Directory integration, you are able to take advantage of Active Directory's replication scheme and multi-master approach. Windows 2000 DNS supports RFC1995, which enables zones to be transferred (or replicated) incrementally. In addition, if the Windows 2000 DNS zones are integrated into Active Directory, they become full participants in the multi-master database. This eliminates the single point of failure associated with the traditional DNS strategy. With traditional DNS implementations, the primary DNS server is a single point of failure. If the primary goes down, there is no server to update the secondary servers. With the Microsoft implementation and the integration with Active Directory, each server acts as a primary master.

There is a potential risk with the multi-master replication. With multiple masters, a dynamic DNS (DDNS) update to different DNS servers provides the possible risk that queries to the two different DNS servers could provide different results. This can happen if a system that is registered with DNS is moved. The machine registers with a DNS server, and until it propagates the new address, the remaining DNS servers return the wrong result for the system that is moved.

Dynamic Host Configuration Protocol (DHCP) and DNS

DHCP works closely with DNS in Microsoft's Windows 2000 and Active Directory. DHCP assigns addresses dynamically to any DHCP client, including Microsoft Windows 2000 clients. After the address is assigned, the DHCP client and/or the DHCP server can update DNS resource record and the PTR resource record in your DNS zone with an Alias (A). This is supported through the dynamic update as defined in RFC2136.

This provides for an accurate DDNS environment without human intervention. When a client computer starts, it requests an IP address and corresponding TCP/IP configuration parameters from the local DHCP server. You can configure the server and clients so that one of three scenarios takes place. The three scenarios are

1. The client updates both the A and PTR records.

2. The DHCP server updates both the A and PTR records.

3. The DHCP server updates the A record and the client updates the PTR record.

By default, the client (host) updates the A record and the DHCP server updates the PTR record.

The capability to configure whether the server or the client updates DNS is important for coexistence phases. If you are supporting down-level clients, such as Windows 95, you need to have the DHCP server update the records because the client does not support this. If you are running with Windows NT 4.0 as your DHCP server and you have migrated the clients to Windows 2000, your DHCP client needs to make both updates to DNS because Windows NT 4.0 DHCP does not support updating DNS.

Microsoft's DNS implementation also has a unique feature that is available if DNS uses Active Directory as the replication agent. In this scenario, each instance of the DNS database on a Windows 2000 server is a primary master that can be updated. Changes to DNS are then replicated using Active Directory. Figure 8.1 depicts the typical scenario in which the primary master DNS server must be updated directly. This can create a bottleneck if many systems are coming online at the same time. With the Microsoft DNS sequence that is depicted in Figure 8.2, the changes are made to a local DNS and those changes are replicated using Active Directory.

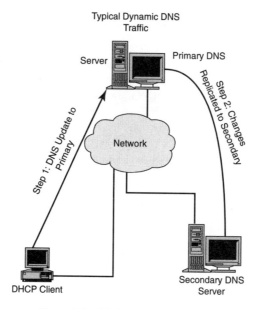

Figure 8.1   Typical DNS traffic patterns.

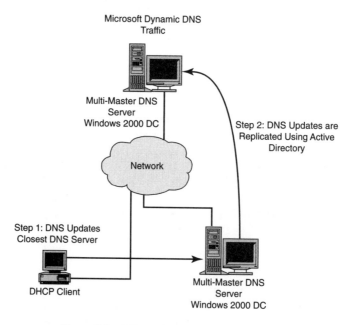

Figure 8.2   Microsoft DNS traffic patterns.

DNS Standards that Support Active Directory

Active Directory can work without implementing Window 2000 DNS. The must-have requirement for Active Directory is support for service records (SRVs). This is supported in implementation of BIND 4.9.6. The nice-to-have requirement is support for dynamic update. This is supported by BIND 8.X., BIND 8.2.1, and later releases, which are the preferred DNS implementations.

Microsoft DNS

Microsoft DNS for Windows 2000 provides a rich set of new features. Although most of us may think that an Internet service that has been around as long as DNS has little room for improvement, Microsoft has worked with the organizations and standards bodies to create a product that is an improvement for DNS users, especially for those that are using Active Directory.

Microsoft's DNS provides for several new features beyond the DNS that is available with Windows NT 4.0. These features include the following:

- Incremental zone transfers—RFC1995
- Dynamic updates to DNS—RFC2136
- Draft standard: A DNS RR for Specifying the Location of Services—RFC2052
- The capability to use Active Directory as a replication vehicle and to support a multi-master implementation of DNS. Each of these features is described in the following section.

Incremental Zone Transfers

Incremental zone transfers provide the organization with better utilization of available network bandwidth. Rather than sending all the zone-file's contents, only the incremental changes are transferred. This reduces the impact of DNS on network traffic. This feature becomes particularly important if you consider all the traffic that might be generated with the next feature, which is dynamic updates to DNS. If incremental zone transfers were not implemented in Windows 2000, every time a new client logged on to the network and registered with DNS, the entire zone file would be transferred between DNS servers. This would have a significant impact on available bandwidth.

Microsoft's Use of Underscore

Another fascinating aspect to Microsoft's DNS is its use of the underscore in the default sub-domain names. This is Microsoft's way of assuring that the names are unique. There's a RFC draft allowing any character, including underscores, to be used in domain names. Microsoft has also tested this with all the leading UNIX operating systems (recent versions) and has encountered no problems. In addition, BIND DNS servers implement the "check-names ignore" parameter in the `named.conf` file. This permits the use of underscore in names.

Dynamic Update to DNS

Support for dynamic updates to DNS is provided in the Windows 2000 release of DNS. This feature works with DHCP. The client and/or the server updates DNS with the relevant resource records based on the TCP/IP address allocated by the DHCP server.

This feature reduces administration overhead and provides for a higher level of accuracy in the DNS tables.

With the use of dynamic updates to DNS by systems, there is the possibility for stale records in the DNS environment. This can happen if a client who has registered an entry with the DNS server is then removed from the network before the lease expiring.

Support for the Draft Standard: A DNS RR for Specifying the Location of Services

SRVs simply identify (within DNS) the IP address of computers capable of providing a service. Specifically, the SRV identifies the IP address and the port for the specific service. This is used by clients to find servers that can meet their service requests. For example, when a user attempts to log into a domain, the user's computer queries DNS for a list of servers that are able to authenticate the user's credentials. Kerberos, the authentication protocol, uses port 88. Through the SRVs, the client is returned the IP address and port 88 to identify which system and which port to use for authentication.

Active Directory as a Replication Vehicle

Active Directory works as a replication vehicle for DNS. Rather than using the clumsy full-zone transfers method and primary and secondary roles of DNS servers, Active Directory can replicate changes to multiple Domain Controllers (DCs), each acting as its own master. This master functions as a DNS primary master, and changes are made to this master and replicated to each master.

This provides the benefit of eliminating a single point of failure. With older DNS systems, the zone's primary server acts as the writable master. In the advent of a failure, the secondary DNS servers do not receive updates after the update interval designated in the Start of Authority (SOA) record for the zone.

Wadeware's DNS Implementation

Now that you know that DNS is a name resolution system for Active Directory, it is important to identify how to create, modify, and administer DNS to support Active Directory. Given that the objective is to create a system that best supports Active Directory, you need to identify the type of environment in which your Active Directory installation is going to be implemented.

Your organization can be faced with three main scenarios. The first is that there is a pre-existing DNS implementation and the pre-existing system remains the sole DNS. This is where a majority of the systems probably will start in the near term. The second scenario is that there is an existing DNS implementation, and the existing DNS implementation is integrated with Microsoft's DNS. The third scenario is that there is no DNS implementation and you have decided to use Microsoft's DDNS.

Wadeware Uses Existing DNS

Wadeware has determined that it is going to use an existing DNS installation for the integration with Active Directory. The current installation is a UNIX-based installation that is supported by a group of UNIX Administrators. They are the team that created the initial installation. They are knowledgeable about DNS, and they have kept the software version for DNS within a couple of point releases of the latest version.

You are already familiar with the main requirement for Active Directory (that is, incremental to the typical functionality of DNS). The incremental requirement for DNS is support of the service record (SRV) resource record.

There is a preferred feature of late DNS versions that is a "nice-to-have" feature. This feature is incremental zone transfers. Microsoft's DNS supports this feature. Incremental zone transfers provide for a more efficient use of network bandwidth. Rather than sending the entire zone file across the network to all the secondaries each time a change is made, only the records that are changed are sent between the DNS servers. This can reduce network traffic.

Design Considerations

There are several design considerations in implementing DNS for Active Directory. When designing DNS for Active Directory, consider the following list:

1. With Internet connectivity, the root of your DNS space should be unique to the entire Internet. If possible, pick a name that is unique on the Internet, and register the name. If your access to Active Directory is for internal use, you can also take your external DNS name and convert it to a `.local` address. Therefore, for `Wadeware.net`, you would create an internal domain name of `Wadeware.local`.

2. You should consider your namespace as either contiguous or disparate. If your namespace is not contiguous, a multiple-tree Forest implementation is required, and each tree name should be registered for an Internet registered name.

3. The root domain cannot be changed or renamed without reinstalling Active Directory.

Long Term Goal

With Wadeware, you have determined that your long-term goal is to have a single DNS technology. You do not have a mandate for this, but you suspect that a single technology will reduce administration, ongoing support, and training costs in the long run. Your hope is to also consolidate DNS administration and Active Directory administration.

Now that you have determined that you would like to have a single focus for DNS administration, you want to make sure that your DNS design does not preclude you from using the Microsoft DNS as the primary server. You are aware that in the short run you need to coexist with the current environment. You have determined that you will handle the migration in two phases.

The first phase is for you to start Active Directory implementation while keeping Wadeware's existing DNS implementation active for most of the users. This first phase is used by a pilot group of users and administrators. The final phase is to supplant the current DNS with the Microsoft DNS.

A second consideration is how you are going to treat your integration with the Wadeware's Internet presence. There are two options here as well.

First, you could have a single DNS namespace both for your internal name resolution and external name resolution. Another approach is to have an external presence, such as Wadeware.net, and a separate internal presence, such as Wadeware.local. No .local resources can be accessed from outside the firewall or the proxy of Wadeware.

You decide on using a single DNS namespace. You decide on this for two reasons. Your existing implementation has a single namespace, and this has provided the security that you needed. You have hosts that relay external connections to hosts internally that provide the requested service. These are called *bastion* hosts. The bastion hosts are on an isolated LAN coming off your existing firewall router as part of the implementation. Although this has required some additional configuration between firewall rules and server software configuration, you are convinced that this provides the security you need. The original thinking is that this should largely remain a static configuration after it is configured to meet your security requirements.

Your current implementation provides for two primary DNS configurations, one for the external name resolution, and one for the internal resolution. The internal DNS server provides name resolution for all the internal and external resources. This is depicted in Figure 8.3.

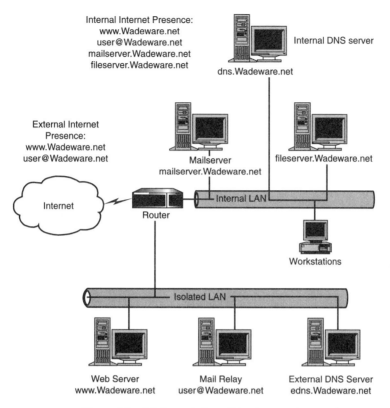

Figure 8.3 Wadeware's firewall implementation.

There is a network segment that is exposed to the Internet. This segment only exposes the mail server and the Web server. A single external DNS server has redundancy support from a server at your Internet service provider (ISP). The internal DNS server provides resolution of all name resolution requests for internal resources and forwards requests for external resources. These two servers represent the two network segments. In this example, there are three externally exposed servers, each providing support for a single application. The three servers are for mail, DNS, and Web support.

With this approach, resources (such as Web servers or email exchangers) can be located in a separate subnet or isolated LAN also referred to as the demilitarized zone (DMZ), which reduces the possibility of a security breach.

There are two DNS configurations for Wadeware. The external DNS configuration is relatively simple. This configuration contains the information for address resolution of Web services and the mail server. The internal DNS server provides name resolution for all the servers in the organization that provide services for internal use (for example, `fileserver.Wadeware.net`. The internal DNS server also provides name resolution for the mail server and Web servers. These entries are for the internal and direct address, not the same address that is given out on the external DNS server. Finally, the internal DNS provides forwarding for addresses that do not reside internally. An example of this functionality would be a user who needs resolution on a www.microsoft.com. The address is resolved by the ISP's name server. The configuration for Wadeware's external view is as follows:

```
;
;   File:     db.wadeware
;
Wadeware.net.    IN SOA server1.Wadeware.net. postmaster.Wadeware.net. (
                    1999020777   ; serial  [yyyyMMddNN]
                    21600    ; refresh [6h]
                    3600   ; retry   [1h]
                    691200    ; expire  [8d]
                    86400)  ; minimum [1d]

;
;  Nameservers
Wadeware.net          IN NS    server1.Wadeware.net.
Wadeware.net            IN NS     server.someISPout-there.com

localhost.Wadeware.net  IN      A        127.0.0.1
mailpo.Wadeware.net     IN      A        149.55.44.32
ftp.Wadeware.net                IN      A       149.55.44.32
www.Wadeware.net                IN      A       149.55.44.41
mailpo2.Wadeware.net    IN      A        149.65.44.32

Wadeware.net.           IN      MX       0        mailpo.Wadeware.net.
Wadeware.net.           IN      MX       10       mailpo2.Wadeware.net.
```

The internal DNS table for internal name resolution looks like the following:

```
;
;   File:     db.wadewareinternal
;
Wadeware.net.    IN SOA server1.Wadeware.net. postmaster.Wadeware.net. (
                    1999020777    ; serial  [yyyyMMddNN]
                    21600    ; refresh [6h]
                    3600   ; retry   [1h]
                    691200    ; expire  [8d]
                    86400)  ; minimum [1d]

Wadeware.net          IN NS    server1.Wadeware.net.
Wadeware.net            IN NS     server.someISPout-there.com

localhost.Wadeware.net  IN      A        127.0.0.1
server1.Wadeware.net    IN      A        149.55.44.31
mailpo.Wadeware.net     IN      A        149.55.44.32
ftp.Wadeware.net                IN      A       149.55.44.32
www.Wadeware.net                IN      A       149.55.44.41
mailpo2.Wadeware.net    IN      A        149.65.44.32
```

```
server2.Wadeware.net     IN     A     149.55.44.52
server3.Wadeware.net     IN     A     149.55.44.53
server4.Wadeware.net     IN     A     149.55.44.54
server5.Wadeware.net     IN     A     149.55.44.55
server6.Wadeware.net     IN     A     149.55.44.56
server7.Wadeware.net     IN     A     149.55.44.57
server8.Wadeware.net     IN     A     149.55.44.58
server9.Wadeware.net     IN     A     149.55.44.59
server10.Wadeware.net    IN     A     149.55.44.510

Wadeware.net.            IN     MX    0      mailpo.Wadeware.net.
Wadeware.net.            IN     MX    10     mailpo2.Wadeware.net.

kerberos.tcp.Wadeware.net       600    SRV    0 100 88 server2.Wadeware.net
ldap.tcp.Wadeware.net    600    SRV    0 100 389        server2.Wadeware.net
```

You should note that the internal configuration provides information about additional servers (servers 2 through 10). The SRVs are also in use for pointing to the server that provides the Kerberos and Lightweight Directory Access Protocol (LDAP) services. These files do not represent a complete set of DNS configuration files, but they give an idea of how Wadeware's DNS configuration starts out.

Phase 1

In Phase 1, you have a pilot group and a segmented network infrastructure so that DHCP is supported by Microsoft DHCP. Now you are going to add Windows 2000 with Active Directory. You want Active Directory to rely on this DNS, and the DNS needs to be changed so that Active Directory servers are able to provide resolution by using DNS. This presents an important question. What is going to be the root domain name for your Active Directory tree? You cannot use Wadeware.net because the existing DNS is the SOA for Wadeware.net.

If you decide to create a sub-domain under Wadeware.net, such as usa.Wadeware.net, you need to modify the DNS to support this, and more importantly you are not able to have Wadeware.net as the root.

Another option is to rebrand your identity with the eventual movement to Active Directory and Windows 2000 DNS. This would enable you to create a new tree with the new domain name. Instead of Wadeware.net, you would create a tree with the new name, Wadeware.local. Externally, your identity can remain Wadeware.net.

The other question that is implied is whether you are going to create a Forest or a tree. For Wadeware, the answer is a Forest. This gives you the capability to have a non-contiguous namespace. The best solution for the name is to start out with Wadeware.local and then add sub-domains or additional trees as the need arises.

Phase 2

During Phase 1, you demonstrated that Microsoft's DNS performs well as a DNS server. You have demonstrated that it can function as a primary server and interoperate with the existing DNS. You have also demonstrated, in production use, the advantages of DHCP and DDNS using these features in the new domain that you created for a pilot group in your organization.

Now is the time to transition your environment to a strictly Microsoft DNS. This can take two tracks. The first is to completely eliminate the existing DNS structure and migrate it fully in the Windows 2000 DNS. You can do this by creating a new tree for the Wadeware.net namespace. The second track is to leave the internal namespace based on the Windows 2000 DNS and the external namespace on the UNIX-based DNS for the Wadeware.net domain. This is a modest compromise although it does reduce some of the benefits of the single point of administration.

Summary

DNS is the name server for Active Directory. By integrating DNS with Active Directory, Microsoft provides us with a solution that overcomes many of the deficiencies found in many DNS products available today. Including the capability to accept dynamic updates from DNS clients, incrementally update zone files, and provide for a fault-tolerant zone master.

Microsoft DNS provides several advantages for use with Active Directory. Incremental zone transfers improve network performance. The multi-master DNS server improves availability by eliminating the primary DNS server as a single point of failure. The multi-master DNS server also improves performance by enabling updates to DNS for a specific zone in more than one location.

DNS is an important service in support of implementing an Active Directory system. There is the capability to use non-Microsoft implementations, but the best solution is Microsoft's for integration, performance, and reliability. Most organizations are faced with the politics of migrating from traditional UNIX-based environments, but a strong push toward Microsoft's DNS will prove well worth the effort.

9

Group Policies

ACTIVE DIRECTORY IS A DELIVERY COMPONENT for group policy. Group policy provides the system administrator and architect with the ability to manage the desktop environment. With the growing requirement for different, yet standard desktop environments, organizations are able to create a system that provides a controlled desktop customization and a level of redundancy that eliminates the need for a time-consuming rebuild of the desktop. With proper planning and some insight into your future growth plans, architects and administrators are able to design an environment that balances the needs of a variety of users and yet permits administrative control and supportability for the administrator. The tools that can affect the organization most are group policies. Some questions about group policy we will answer in this chapter include: How are group policies implemented through the organizational unit (OU) structure? How can implementing group policies affect total cost of ownership (TCO)?

Windows NT 4.0 System Policy Capabilities

With Windows NT 4.0, administrators are able to develop some control of the desktop through careful planning and execution. For the most part this is limited to restricting the capabilities in the Windows NT 4.0 product. The current capabilities of a Windows NT 4.0 System Policy implementation include the ability to control the items that show up on the desktop and which applications are available to the user. Administrators are also able to have user-specific desktop configuration information follow users.

With Windows NT 4.0 and Service Pack 4 or later, administrators are able to control the size of the user profile. This capability adds some additional complexity to administration and the end user. If the user profile size is limited, the user is not able to log off until they reduce the size of the user profile to under the defined limit. This can be tricky and frustrating to the user.

If the user exceeds the user profile limit, an error icon appears on the system tray. If the user opens the error icon, it shows a list of files that are in the profile. This can be used by the end user to delete files that are in the profile so that they can reduce the size and then log off properly. The tricky part is that it only shows the files that are greater than 2KB in size. Files that are smaller than 2KB do not show up, and therefore, might be tricky to find. For example, when using Internet Explorer 4.0, the user can have many small files, the user might become frustrated if the profile file list shows no fields and they continue to receive a message saying the profile is too large for them to log off. These capabilities were implemented in a few basic ways. The administrator could implement mandatory profiles by creating a profile and requiring that this profile be implemented if the user logs into the domain. This type of implementation is employed in environments that require a consistent look and feel or strict control of the desktop to prevent unauthorized use of the system. An example of a mandatory profile implementation is a kiosk based on Windows NT 4.0.

Roaming profiles is another implementation of the capabilities enabled by Windows NT 4.0 profiles. Roaming profiles give the user the ability to keep their personal desktop from a variety of workstations. For example, if a user keeps their working documents on their desktop when they log off, the configuration information including the documents is saved to a network share. This becomes extremely valuable if the user works from a variety of machines or if a desktop machine has a critical malfunction.

A typical use of roaming profiles is to increase availability. With roaming profiles, if a desktop system becomes disabled, the user's profile can be recovered. With roaming profiles, a base desktop system is built; and when the user logs into the network, the profile information is applied to the new system. Business examples of this are a roaming supervisor, or any individual that travels from site to site or shares a PC with others.

Another example of using roaming profiles is in a student computer lab on a university campus. In this example, users do not have a workstation permanently assigned to them. They must use whatever machine is available.

Policies in Windows NT 4.0 also play a role with profiles in specifying which features of a desktop environment are enabled or disabled. Using the System Policy Editor, a Windows NT 4.0 administrator is able to specify exactly what applications and files a user can access. An administrator might want to eliminate whether a group of users has the ability to run applications using the Run selection from the Start menu. This can prevent use of unauthorized applications.

The typical experience with Windows NT 4.0 system policies and profiles is that it provides control of the desktop environment. There are tools available to help control the computing environment, but administrators were crying out for additional functionality that included enabling and managing the desktop rather than the more draconian desktop lockdown capabilities of the Windows NT 4.0 policies and profiles.

Windows 2000 group policies provide similar functionality to Windows NT 4.0's capabilities. In addition, Windows 2000 group policies provide the user with the ability to apply policies on more than a domain basis. With Active Directory, the administrator is able to apply group policies to sites, domains, and OUs. OUs can have multiple levels permitting additional levels to apply group policies.

Group Policies

The pieces and parts of group policy are composed of several components. This section focuses on identifying the key components and how they work together for a basic understanding of group policy.

Group Policy Editor

The Group Policy Editor (GPE) is a MMC snap-in that provides you with the capability to add, modify, and delete components of the Group Policy Object (GPO). Figure 9.1 is a view of a GPO that is discussed in this chapter.

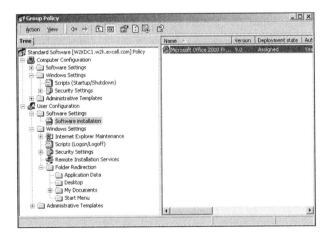

Figure 9.1   MMC view of a sample GPO.

The GPE can be started by right-clicking an Active Directory container, selecting Properties, followed by selecting the Group Policy tab, and right-clicking on a GPO. In addition, you can start the MMC, add the GPE snap-in, and select a specific GPO for editing.

GPO

A GPO is collection of settings to be applied to a computer, which are based on the computer or user. This sounds confusing—look at Figure 9.1, which is a GPE view of a GPO called *Standard Software*, for an illustration.

The Standard Software policy provides several setting options. There is the Computer Configuration. Looking at the object, you see there are software settings, windows settings, and administrative templates. The software settings are for how the software should be configured for all computers that use this GPO. This is in contrast to the software settings for the user configuration, which are applied to all users that are assigned to this GPO. You might ask when each is used. You would use the computer settings if you were applying this GPO to a particular group that needs a specific application. In this example, the Finance department needs access to an invoicing application, and this can only be run from specific machines that are on the third floor where the Finance department is located. In this scenario, if a Finance staff member went to another floor and used their user ID to log into a workstation, the Finance user would not be able to run the application because the software setting only permits the application to be available from those machines on the third floor.

With the user setting/software setting scenario, the user would be able to use the application regardless of which machine is used. In contrast, although a non-Finance user uses a workstation that is located in the Finance department, they would not have access to the application.

Figure 9.1 also shows a few other configurable items that are part of a GPO. They include the window settings that are part of the computer. One that can be used to further control the desktop and a user's interaction with the configuration of the desktop is the `Computer Configuration|Windows Settings|Scripts`. This provides the capability to write custom scripts using Windows Scripting Host (WSH) to configure items or clean up a workstation. You can control whether the scripts run at startup or shutdown.

Also, notice that under the `User Configuration|Software Settings|Software Installation` tab, Microsoft Office 2000 Premium has been assigned for installation. This GPO provides for dynamic installation of Office 2000 for all users that have the Standard Software policy configured in the hierarchy of the container that the user object is located.

The administrator can also decide to assign or publish software based on GPOs. Assigning software to a computer pushes software to the computer. Publishing software is providing the capability for users to install software if they need to use it. Assigning software to a user also provides the software for use by a user. Typically, software that is used by most users, such as Microsoft Office, would be assigned to desktop computers. These are mostly static. The software that is used, for example, might be an application that is only used by the Financial Analyst in the organization. The difference between publishing and assigning software to a user is subtle, but the main difference is in the typical use. Software assigned to a user is typically installed by clicking the icon for the application on the Start menu. Published software is not an installed application on the start menu. Published software is installed when the user uses the Add/Remove Programs in the Control Panel.

The GPO is the component that groups settings together for a particular purpose. As is the case with many of the features of Windows 2000 and Active Directory, a good starting point is a few general GPOs, rather than many granular GPOs. One approach is to migrate parallel functionality to Active Directory from your Windows NT 4.0 environment. So rather than trying to invent a new approach from the start, start by translating current NT 4.0 functionality into a simple group policy approach.

Group Policy Container (GPC) and Group Policy Template (GPT)

The GPO exists in two parts as it is implemented. There is the GPC and the GPT. The GPC contains information about the GPO. The GPC contains information on the GPO status, what version of the GPO, and the components that are contained in the GPO. This is analogous to the directory information for the GPO. Guess where this information is stored—yes, in Active Directory. The GPT contains the setting information for the GPO. This information includes the script files, security settings, and application installation information that are depicted in the view of the GPO seen in Figure 9.1.

You can find GPT information in the System Volume. With a standard installation, this puts you at `c:\winnt\SYSVOL\sysvol\w2k.com\Policies\{29xxxx..xxx}\`, where w2k.com is the domain name for the directory and `{29xxxx..xxx}` is the Globally Unique Identifier (GUID) for the GPO. If you look at the directory `\user\scripts\`, you will see a directory logon and logoff. This is where the logon and logoff scripts for the GPO are contained.

Group Policy Processing

Group policies can be applied at several levels. They can be applied at the Site, Domain, or Organizational Unit (SDOU) level. The order of application to a computer or user is starting from the site, then to the domain, and finally to the OU. There can be multiple OU levels, and group policies are applied from the top level OU on down.

Using Figure 9.2 as an example of a SDOU structure, for users in the Dover OU, site level group policies would be applied first, then domain level, and finally OU level group policies. The OU policies are applied from the Europe OU, then the England OU, and finally from the Dover OU. Therefore, if there was a user group policy at each level, there would be five group policies applied to the user. In summary, they are applied from the site, then to the domain, then to Europe OU, England OU, and finally to Dover OU.

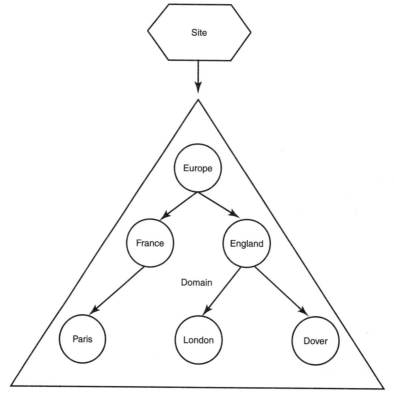

Figure 9.2   Sample SDOU structure.

How to Administer Group Policies

Group policy administration represents a task of potentially great complexity. With careful design and some initial simplicity, using Active Directory and group policies to administer your enterprise environment provides a manageable environment. Creating a multi-level OU structure and a variety of GPOs can lead to a complex login and startup structure that can increase administration and make problem resolution almost impossible. The upcoming example depicted later in this chapter suggests that complexity increases rapidly. Although this example has a GPO for each feature that is implemented for demonstration purposes, one can imagine a number of GPOs for different profile users. A well thought-out design is critical in developing a functional environment. In our experience, is is best to start with a simple group policy approach.

Creating GPOs

After you have decided on the GPOs needed for your organization, you need to create them. GPOs are typically associated with SDOUs. It is also possible to create a local GPO for standalone machines. If you are creating a GPO, you need to associate the GPO with one of these objects. There are two main ways to start to create a GPO for domains and OUs. The first way is to start with the MMC and add the group policy snap-in. A wizard comes up that asks you to identify the SDOU in which you want the GPO to reside. The other way is to start the Active Directory Users and Computers administration tool. With this tool, you traverse the OU structure to where you want the GPO to reside. By right-clicking on the object (an OU, for example) you are given a list of the tasks you can perform. By selecting properties, you receive all the properties for the OU object. A group policy tab appears, providing you with all the tasks for a single GPO administration. You are able to create a new GPO; edit a GPO; and review, delete, or modify the properties of a specific GPO.

For a GPO at the site, you use the Active Directory Sites and Services snap-in. With this tool, you select the site for which you want to create a GPO, and then right-click and select Properties. The Properties page appears and at the top, there are tabs. You select the group policy tab. From this dialog box, you are able to create, edit, and remove GPOs for the site.

When you are starting out, you select the New button to create the GPO. After you have named the object, you are ready to edit the object. This is accomplished by selecting the Edit button. The Edit button triggers another MMC tool that contains the defaults for a GPO. You can then traverse the GPO and modify the entries. This establishes a GPO.

Now that you have a GPO established with the specific setting required for your computer and user settings the next level of execution of a GPO is to implement whom and what receives the GPO assigned to it. By default, all users and computers receive group policies based on the OU in which they reside. A GPO applied to an OU is applied to the objects within that OU (subject to access control list [ACL] settings) and to the objects within all child OUs located within the OU.

Controlling the Way That GPOs Are Applied

You now have a GPO created. This GPO has impacts on computer settings and user settings. After some experience using the GPO you determine that a specific OU could need different user-based GPOs. Each user-based GPO permits a different set of applications to be distributed to the workstation.

To control which GPO is applied to a user or group, you select the GPO and click the Properties button. Under the Security tab, you can configure a list of users and groups. For each user or group added, you can apply permissions. The permissions that affect whether a GPO is applied to a set of users are the Apply Group Policy permissions (Apply) and the Read Group Policy permissions (Read). If Allow is selected for both the Apply and Read permissions, it is applied. A sample is depicted in Figure 9.3. In this case, all users in the Authenticated Users group have the GPO applied.

There are other possible scenarios using these settings. If the Apply and Read permissions are set to Deny (regardless of the participation the members have in other security groups), this GPO is not applied. If the permissions for Apply and Read are not both set, nothing happens for the users of the security group. The GPO is neither applied nor explicitly denied.

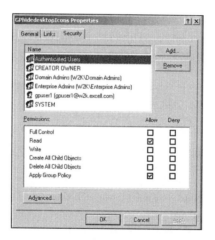

Figure 9.3 The group policy security tab.

Also note in Figure 9.3 that the permissions, such as read, write, create all child objects, and full control, are used to control who has the ability to administer the GPO itself.

GPOs: Order of Application

In a single container, there can be multiple GPOs. The GPOs are implemented based on the order they appear in the group policy tab for that container, from the bottom up (lowest to highest priority). The lowest GPO in the list is applied first. The implication here is that if every GPO has a policy setting to enable and the top GPO has the setting to disable, the final GPO—the top one—is applied and the policy is disabled. A view of this list is in Figure 9.4.

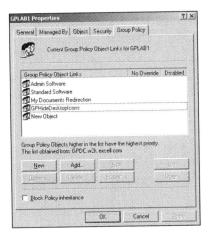

Figure 9.4 The group policy tab for the GPLAB1 OU.

Special Case Application of GPOs

At this point in the application of group policies, there is functionality that is capable of handling most every scenario. You have group policies that can be applied at multiple levels in your Active Directory. You also have the ability to restrict application of a group policy. There is also a straightforward, top-down approach to applying group policies.

However, as is the case with the rest of Active Directory, Microsoft is providing a broad range of options and features. In the case of group policy, there is no difference. There are ways to create controlled exceptions to the standard rules for the application of a GPO.

No Override

A No Override button can be selected for a GPO. No Override provides the administrator with the ability to prevent other GPOs from overriding the settings in a selected GPO.

Block

The Block configuration setting blocks inheritance from parent-level OU settings from affecting an OU. As an example, a regional OU might want to prevent the distribution of an application to their OU until the users in their region have been trained on the new products. However, the GPO has been applied at a parent OU, and it would normally be distributed to the users in that group. The Block configuration setting would accomplish the object of this example.

Enforce

It is also possible to enforce a group policy. The Enforce option prevents a GPO's policies from being blocked. The Enforce option overrides the Block and forces the GPO to be applied on child OUs.

Asynchronous or Synchronous

The GPO's area is applied synchronously to your system by default. With the computer policies, all the applications are complete before a user is able to log on to the system, specifically before the CTL+ALT+DEL prompt is present. The user policies are applied before the Windows desktop is up and available for use. More specifically, the user policies are applied before the user is allowed to interact with the shell.

It is possible to change the GPO setting to "asynchronous." The results for asynchronous GPO process are unpredictable, and this approach is not recommended by Microsoft.

Debugging Group Policies

After you have implemented the design for your GPOs, you need to start testing and evaluating the adherence of your implementation to your design. This can identify problems in your implementation. In some cases, even your design can be exposed for what it really is, but assuming your design is correct, fixing your implementation requires some strategy for debugging your GPOs.

Before we describe the strategies, the first step is to use a resource kit tool that is available. This tool is GPResult.exe. GPResult provides you with a list of the GPOs that were applied to your computer. You run GPResult from the command line. There are four options. They are

- /V for verbose mode
- /S for super verbose
- /C for computer settings only
- /U for user settings only

The following sample output for GPResult was run on a Windows 2000 system with no options selected. The sample output has the information that you need to concisely identify what is happening to your environment. This includes the OS Type and Version, User group policy results, Domain, Domain type, Site name, Security Group memberships, and the User and Computer GPOs. In this case, two User GPOs were applied. They were GPOUSF and GPOU1.

```
Microsoft (R) Windows (R) 2000 Operating System Group Policy Result tool
Copyright (C) Microsoft Corp. 1981-1999


Created on Thursday, November 11, 1999 at 10:58:04 PM


Operating System Information:

Operating System Type:        Domain Controller
Operating System Version:     5.0.2128
Terminal Server Mode:         None


############################################################

   User Group Policy results for:

   CN=Ed Brovick,OU=Western Division,DC=wadeware,DC=net

   Domain Name:          WADEWARE
   Domain Type:          Windows 2000
   Site Name:            Default-First-Site-Name

   Roaming profile:      (None)
   Local profile:        C:\Documents and Settings\ebrovi

   The user is a member of the following security groups:

         WADEWARE\Domain Users
         \Everyone
         BUILTIN\Users
         BUILTIN\Administrators
         WADEWARE\Domain Admins
         WADEWARE\Seattle Users
         \LOCAL
         NT AUTHORITY\INTERACTIVE
         NT AUTHORITY\Authenticated Users


############################################################

   Last time Group Policy was applied: Thursday, November 11, 1999 at 10:54:30 PM


   ============================================================
```

```
The user received "Registry" settings from these GPOs:

    GPOUSF
    GPOU1



################################################################

Computer Group Policy results for:

CN=WADEWARE-XH3MRH,OU=Western Division,DC=wadeware,DC=net

Domain Name:        WADEWARE
Domain Type:        Windows 2000
Site Name:          Default-First-Site-Name

################################################################

Last time Group Policy was applied: Thursday, November 11, 1999 at 10:53:53 PM


================================================================


The computer received "Registry" settings from these GPOs:

    Local Group Policy
    Default Domain Policy


================================================================
The computer received "Security" settings from these GPOs:

    Default Domain Policy
    Default Domain Controllers Policy


================================================================
The computer received "EFS recovery" settings from these GPOs:

    Local Group Policy
    Default Domain Policy
```

There are strategies you can use to debug your policies. The first is to start peeling back your GPOs by disabling each GPO. As an administrator, you can disable a GPO so that it is eliminated from the processing and evaluate the effect. This approach is time-consuming if you have many GPOs; therefore, keeping the design simple helps here as well. Also, remember that you need to restart your system to receive computer policy changes.

The second strategy is to establish the logging of group policy events. This can fill up your event log; so, when enabling a group policy event, you should plan carefully and create a set of policies that only affect a select group. If you start logging production GPOs and if you have thousands of users logging in all the time, your ability to review the log might be difficult.

Improving Performance on GPOs

To improve performance, you are able to specify whether the computer configuration or the user configuration should be acted upon. This prevents the system from parsing the entire GPO and improves performance. As an example, if you deploy a new application using a GPO, you would only use the user portion of the GPO. In this case, you should block the computer configuration portion to prevent it from being unnecessarily parsed.

How to Use Group Policy

Group policy provides the capability to control a wide variety of desktop configurations. In addition, through group policy, selective and dynamic application deployment is possible. This section provides an overview of what can be done with group policy.

Now that you have been introduced to the components that make up group policy and understand how to create a GPO, the next level of planning and capability is to discuss how to use group policies.

A straight forward way to look at implementing group policies is to look at the various desktop types that you are interested in supporting. This is a simple first step. Based on your organization and the size of your staff, you need to decide on the number of supportable desktop configurations and how best to design the OU structure to support it.

The trade-off that you are evaluating is the benefit of the multiple desktop types and their impact on the complexity of the administrative environment. If you have single OUs and no child OUs to work with, and if each department in your organization would like to have a unique desktop standard, you can imagine a GPO nightmare in a large organization. The impact on performance, administration, and troubleshooting becomes too costly to justify the unique desktop standards. As the Active Directory designer and administrator, you might need to make compromises and to combine requirements into a single GPO. As an example, the Finance department users might have similar application requirements to the sales staff. Both need access to quantitative tools and database access tools. One approach would be to combine the requirements of these users into a single GPO.

Another approach would be to have unique OUs for each one of the unique desktop standards. This would result in an OU structure that was wide and flat. A flat OU structure provides for a decentralized administration, and the GPO processing time is better than deep OU structure with many GPOs to process.

Another approach is to create a layering of GPOs. How does this work? Group policies can be applied to SDOUs, as was mentioned before. The interesting part is that GPOs are applied to users and computers based on where they are located in the OU structure. The GPOs are applied from the top down, and they are cumulative. If we take Figure 9.5 as a sample environment, Site A has two users and two computer GPOs, Domain Windows 2000 has two users and computer GPOs, and OU1 has a single user and computer GPO. If a user, George, logs in, all the GPOs are applied to his computer and his user ID. Depending on if George's account is located in Domain Windows 2000, OU1, or Site A, he receives a different set of GPOs applied to his working environment.

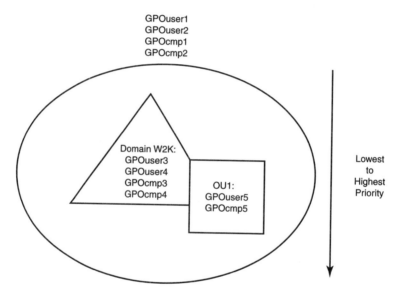

Figure 9.5 Example SDOU group policy locations.

Let's take a few scenarios to demonstrate how the GPOs are applied. If George's account is in Domain W2K, George and the workstation he is logging in to receive GPOcmp1 through GPOcmp4 when the computer starts up. User GPOs (GPOuser1 through GPOuser4) are applied when the user logs in. In addition, the administrator should note that the order of application is GPOcmp1, GPOcmp2, GPOcmp3, GPOcmp4, GPOuser1, GPOuser2, GPOuser3, and GPOuser4. This describes the simplest application of group policies. This example demonstrates how Active Directory hierarchy affects the application of GPOs.

With Active Directory, the administrator can block a policy from a specific OU or domain. In the example, the administrator could specify that the GPOuser3 be blocked from OU1. If a user in container OU1 logs into the directory, GPOuser3 is not inherited. A GPO that specifies Enforce is applied to all the objects in that container and to those below it. The Enforce takes precedence over a Block.

The next level of control for GPOs is the use of security groups. The administrator of each GPO has the ability to prevent the GPO from being applied to a specific group of users. By default the Apply Group Policy access control entity (ACE) is turned on. In other words, by default, GPOs apply to users and groups within the hierarchy. This can be explicitly turned off by disabling the Apply Group Policy ACE (see Figure 9.3).

Application of GPOs

The application of GPOs and user settings to your computer is important to understand when configuring a series of GPOs for managing your desktop. By understanding how GPOs are applied to your system when you start up and log in to your domain, you are better prepared to create a solid design that works as planned. In the case that your design is not operating the way you expected, the order in which the GPOs are applied and the interleafed events help debug and resolve unexplained occurrences.

If a Windows 2000 system starts up, the system applies the computer settings from the group policies. The Startup scripts are the executed. If the user logs into the computer, the user settings from the group polices are applied, and then the logon scripts are run.

There is also a tool for evaluating security settings without logging in and out of the system. You can use `secedit`. The syntax is: `secedit /refresh policy {machine policy ¦ user policy} [/enforce]`. The machine policy is for the local machine. The user policy is for the user currently running `secedit`. The enforce option refreshes the security settings, even if there have been no changes to the security policy.

To cement the understanding of the application of GPOs on a user or computer, please examine the following scenarios. There are two security groups, Finance and Sales. The Finance and Sales groups have users at the domain level and at the OU level. The domain and GPOs are as depicted in Figure 9.4. Table 9.1 describes the additional features that have been applied to the specific GPOs and security groups.

Table 9.1 **GPO and Security Group Features**

GPO	Enforce	Block	Apply Group Policy	Policy
GPOcmp1				Enable disk quotas
GPOcmp2				Enable disk quota of 100MB; warning at 75MB
GPOuser1	Yes			Enable hide IE 5.0 icon on desktop

continues

Table 9.1 **Continued**

GPO	Enforce	Block	Apply Group Policy	Policy
GPOuser2		Finance		Enable hide MyDocuments icon on desktop
GPOcmp3				Enable disk quota of 75MB; warning at 50MB
GPOcmp4			Deny Finance	Enable disk quota of 75MB; warning at 25MB
GPOuser3			Deny Finance	Disable hide IE 5.0 icon on desktop
GPOuser4				Screensaver enabled using specific screensaver
GPOcmp5		Sales		Enable disk quota of 50MB; warning at 25MB
GPOuser5			Deny Sales	Remove all desktop icons

Using Table 9.1 and Figure 9.4, we will demonstrate the impact of the GPOs on users logging into Active Directory. For this example, we'll consider a user that is located at the domain level and is a member of the Finance group.

1. The GPOcmp1 policy results in disk quotas being enabled.
2. GPMcmp2 establishes a quota of 75MB.
3. GPOcmp3 establishes a warning level of 50MB.
4. GPOcmp4 is not applied because the user is in the Finance group, and the setting for Apply Group Policy is denied.
5. The GPOuser1, GPOuser2, GPOuser3, and GPOuser4 policies are applied.
6. The GPOuser1 policy hides the IE 5.0 icon.
7. The GPOuser2 policy is not applied because the user is part of the Finance group.
8. The GPOuser3 policy is not applied because the user is in the Finance group.
9. The GPOuser4 policy is applied, resulting in the screensaver being enabled. This results in hiding the IE 5.0 icon, and the screensaver is enabled with the specified screensaver.

Keep in mind that this is an example, and in the real world, the GPO would contain multiple configuration options, and the impact of an Enforce, Deny, or restriction based on user or group can be significant.

Applying or not applying a GPO affects a variety of options. If you start layering GPOs on top of each other and if each GPO has multiple features enabled with a variety of different configuration settings, predicting the outcome can be difficult.

Delegation Group Policy Administration

Group policy administration can be distributed based on groups. As an example, enterprise administrators have the ability to read, write, create all child objects, and delete child objects for a specific GPO. You are able to create a group of administrators and give them rights for administering a GPO. The list of permissions is long and granular. Administrators can identify individuals for specific tasks and give them the permissions to perform them on specific GPOs.

A scenario in which you might use delegation of the group policy administration is one with a set of GPOs that are used by a specific set of users. As an example, the Finance group might need to have a GPO, or a series of GPOs, modified while a new application is in beta. Rather than have a centralized administrator work with this while the standards for use are being developed, it is appropriate to give it to an individual that working on the specific application installation.

Group policy administration can be delegated to individuals and groups through security groups. There are six different parameters to set as part of the group policy. These options can be set to an individual level. They are as follows:

- Full Control
- Read
- Write
- Create all child objects
- Delete all child objects
- Apply group policy

Full Control permits the user, or group, the ability to change any of the settings for the GPO. The owner of the object should have this capability. The Read and Write are available for applying changes. The Apply option needs to be coupled with Read for the Apply option to be "Applied." The Create and Delete all child objects provide the permissions for deleting or creating child objects for the objects selected. The Apply Group Policy is to identify that a policy is applied to those users identified in the Security Group window.

These permissions are applied to some of the standard security group when GPOs are created. The Domain and Enterprise Admins group has the ability to read, write, create child objects, and delete child objects when the object is created. Authenticated Users have the GPO applied by default. They have the read and apply group policy permissions.

If you need to create a new GPO, you need to have access to the MMC snap-in Active Directory Users and Computers. From there, you need administrative access to the OU and the object. Most everyone has access to the OU. By default, all those in the domain have the read and apply permissions. These permit them to read the GPO, but you are not permitted to make any changes without specific access to the system.

If you create a GPO but you want someone else to maintain it, you are able to give him or her the tools and set their permissions on the object to read, write, create, and delete child object permissions. If you want to test the result of your changes, you should build a lab. This prevents any unwanted GPO application.

Migrating Group Policy from Windows NT 4.0

With the migration to group policies in Windows 2000, several scenarios can arise. This section addresses the impact of the various scenarios on your Windows 2000 and Windows NT 4.0 workstations.

With Windows NT 4.0 clients logging into Windows 2000 or Windows NT 4.0 Domain Controller (DC), the Windows NT 4.0 clients receive Windows NT 4.0 policies. For Windows 2000 clients, there is a variety of scenarios. First, if the Windows 2000 client logs into a Windows NT 4.0 domain, the Windows 2000 client receives the Windows NT 4.0 System Policy and the local group policy. If the Windows 2000 client logs into a Windows 2000 domain, the client receives the local group policy for the local site, domain, and organizational unit (LSDOU). If the Windows 2000 client logs into a domain in which all the Windows 2000 DCs are down and the Windows NT 4.0 DCs are up, the Windows 2000 client receives the LSDOU with the cached credentials.

Now if the computer account and the user account are straddle the Windows NT 4.0 domain and the Windows 2000 domain, there are two different results based on the Windows 2000 client logging in. If the computer account is in the Windows 2000 domain and the user account is in the Windows NT 4.0 domain, the computer receives the group policy and the user receives no policy. If the computer account is in the Windows NT 4.0 domain and the user is in the Windows 2000 domain, neither the computer nor the user policy is applied to the Windows 2000 client.

Summary

GPOs are powerful tools for controlling desktop environments. In Windows NT 4.0, policies and profiles were limited to locking down your desktop. With GPOs, you are able to lockdown, as well as extend, the desktop. With GPOs and Active Directory, the customization options are limitless. However, initially start out simple. This helps you evaluate the impact to your organization and establish an easier environment to modify and support.

The Physical Topology: Sites and Replication

I T IS EASY TO FOCUS EXCLUSIVELY ON THE logical Active Directory design. After all, the logical design is the new and challenging aspect of Active Directory, and so we tend to spend a lot of time getting it right. However, the physical design of Active Directory is also important, and it requires close consideration to ensure that Active Directory is custom fit to the network that supports it.

Active Directory services are provided to clients and applications through Active Directory Domain Controllers (DCs). Each Active Directory DC hosts at least three different database partitions (also known as naming contexts as mentioned in Chapter 7, "Designing the Windows 2000 Domain Structure") that make up these services. These partitions include the domain partition, the configuration partition, and the schema partition. Each DC in an Active Directory Forest has a complete copy of each partition with the domain partition belonging to the DCs domain. Each DC can read and write to the domain partition, making Active Directory a multi-master directory. This means that each DC can write changes to its domain database. These changes then have to be replicated to all other DCs in the domain so that they too reflect that change and can provide consistent information to the client computers and users.

Replication is a tricky business. The more changes made to the directory, the more it is necessary to replicate. The more DCs replicate, the more network bandwidth is consumed with replication. Replication intervals can be configured. For example, if 100 changes are made to a DC in an hour, you can replicate those 100 changes incrementally throughout that hour or all at the end of the hour. Either way, all 100 changes to the directory are going to replicate, and they will consume the same amount of network bandwidth. To help mitigate replication traffic, it is important to consider domain and site design. The physical design is built with sites and site link connectors. Sites, and how they are connected, help to determine the performance, and possibly the reliability of your Windows 2000 Active Directory. This chapter looks closely at Active Directory sites and the Active Directory replication that occurs within them.

Physical versus Logical Structure

The logical structure of Active Directory design is represented by the domains, their relationships with one another, along with the organizational units (OUs). These relationships are represented in domain and OU topologies, as seen in Figure 10.1

Figure 10.1 A domain tree with parent and child domains.

Sites represent the physical network within Active Directory. DCs communicating within a site behave differently than DCs communicating across sites. Furthermore, because we want clients to communicate with DCs located on the network near them, clients are also site aware.

The network topology and the desired domain topology are the basis for site design, as shown in Figure 10.2. It is important to understand the network, as well as the business, requirements driving your domain topology when constructing your site design. Therefore, understand your current and future network design before designing your site topology.

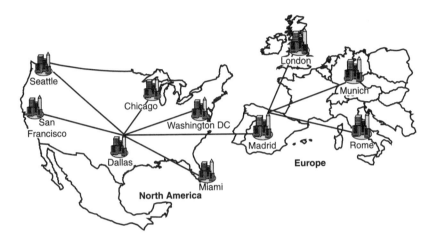

Figure 10.2 Documented physical network topology.

Properly mapping the physical topology to the logical topology increases the efficiency of client access, increases the efficiency and availability of resources, reduces replication latency, and helps to ensure that Active Directory provides the return on investment promised. See Figure 10.3 for an example domain topology.

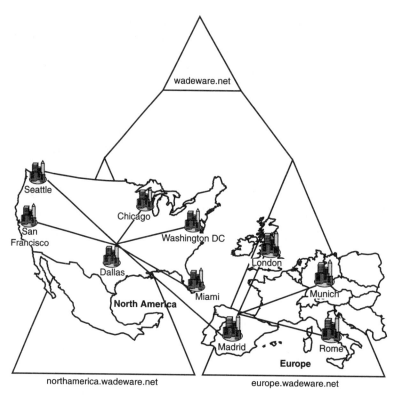

Figure 10.3 Domain topology over physical topology.

Replication

To provide quick and efficient directory services to clients across the enterprise, clients should have the data that they require most frequently within close proximity. For example, to provide the same local directory services to clients in London as those needed locally by clients in Taipei, it is necessary to replicate the directory data between the DCs that provide those services. Understanding replication leads to a site and domain design that replicates efficiently enough to support the enterprise.

Multi-Master Theory

Multi-master means just that; no one master source manages directory data. Unlike Windows NT 4.0, where the Primary DC is that master of the domain database and the Backup DCs cannot write to the directory, Active Directory enables each DC to write to its local copy of the directory. This removes the "single point of failure" limitation of Windows NT because although one DC can fail, the other DCs continue to provide read/write domain services to clients. These changes are then replicated to all the other DCs in the domain.

As shown in Figure 10.4, each DC hosts at least three Active Directory partitions that all replicate. In this model, it is possible, and likely, that at times different DCs will not have the same domain data because changes have occurred and replication has not taken place. This is the nature of a distributed, multi-master directory. This means that reality might be a bit different across the organization at various times because not all the objects in the directory are constant. This theory of *loose consistency* stipulates that not all DCs in the domain are guaranteed to be a perfect copy of one another at all times and that this is OK. However, the DCs become consistent after all changes have converged upon each DC. *Convergence* stipulates that despite possible inconsistencies at any given time, the final state of the data in the directory is consistent because each attribute's current value exists somewhere in the directory and will be replicated across the enterprise.

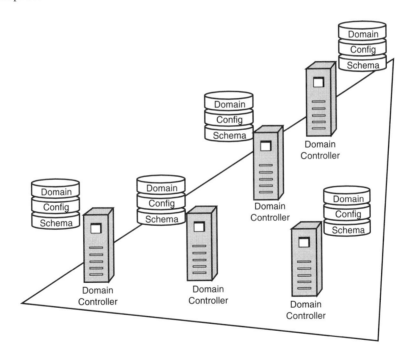

Figure 10.4 A single domain with multi-master DCs.

The Replication Process

The replication process is a complicated one. Reason being that objects, which exist on multiple servers, are assets of an organization and their integrity must be maintained. To maintain this integrity, it is important to assure that as objects change in the directory, the value that survives replication is the value intended to survive.

The replication process establishes and maintains a series of values on each attribute (as well as on the object) that are incremented as changes are made. As a DC receives replicated data, it uses these values to assure the data being replicated to the server is newer than the data contained on the server. The majority of the time changes replicate among the DCs without incident. It is not common for replication conflicts to occur, especially when replication occurs at the attribute level. However, when they do occur, they must be dealt with.

Imagine, for example, an administrator in London changes the value of a user's phone extension to 72164. A few minutes later, an administrator in Los Angeles changes the same phone extension to 71963. Both of these changes need to replicate, but which change is correct? Look at an example that is a bit more complex. Imagine that an application in London makes 10 changes to an attribute in the directory. *After* which, another application in Los Angeles makes one change to the same attribute in the directory. Which change is most valid? The 10th change made in London or the only change made in Los Angeles? Look which values are maintained during replication and how they are used during conflict resolution to see if we can figure it out.

Replication Partners

First, it is important to understand the relationships between DCs. As you will see in a few pages, the DCs in your Active Directory have a special relationship with at least two (when available) other DCs in their site. These other servers are designated as the DCs replication partners. By having more than one replication partner, each DC can receive replicated data from more than one path, providing fault tolerance. On the other hand, by not having each DC replicate with every other DC in the site, replication traffic is mitigated. The replication partner strategy provides a happy medium between fault-tolerance and minimal replication traffic.

Keeping Track

Next, it's important to understand the type of changes made by a DC to the directory and to the values used to keep track of them. There are two types of updates to Active Directory: *originating* updates and *replicated* updates. As the name applies, originating updates are changes made to the directory by a user or administrator, whereas replicated updates are changes made to a DC database that have been replicated by another DC in the organization.

If originating updates are made to a DC, a counter on the DC is incremented. This counter, the *update sequence number (USN)*, is what is used by other DCs to determine which updates need to be replicated. Each attribute, object, and server has an individual USN. These USNs are incremented when changes take place to the attribute, object, or server.

For example, imagine a change is made to the directory on Server A. Server A's USN is incremented to 595, as shown in Figure 10.5. Five minutes later, (default) Server A notifies Server B that updates are available. Server B requests all updates greater than the USN it has for Server A, which is 594. Server A sees that Server B needs the directory update represented by USN 595 and sends Server B that update. Server B receives the replicated update, commits it to the directory, and updates Server A's USN to 595. All is well.

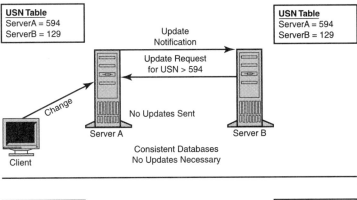

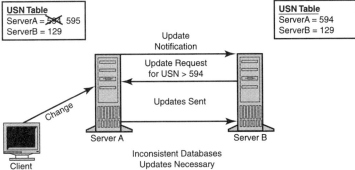

Figure 10.5 The DC replication process.

Exchange 5.5 (and earlier) also uses this directory replication process. The major difference is that Exchange servers in a site do not have directory replication partners. Rather, if a change is made on an Exchange server, that server replicates the change to all other Exchange servers in the site. Because Active Directory uses replication partners to improve performance, it is possible that a DC could receive the same replication data from different DCs. To prevent this, Active Directory has implemented what is called *propagation dampening*. Propagation dampening is the process of only requesting replication changes that have not been replicated.

To facilitate propagation dampening, each DC maintains an *up-to-date vector*. The up-to-date vector is a set of USNs that represents the highest *originating update* for each server. Each DC also maintains a *high watermark vector*, which is the highest USN for all the objects of a server in the directory.

The best way to understand how these values are used in propagation dampening is with the example illustrated in Figure 10.6 and explained in the following steps.

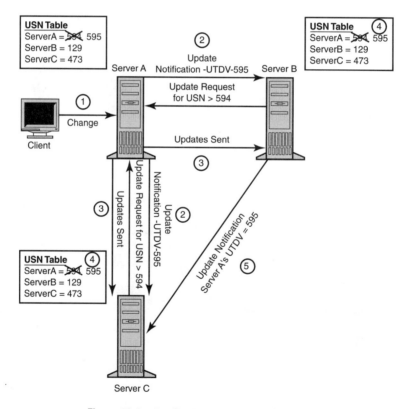

Figure 10.6   Replication propagation dampening.

1. A change is made to Server A.

2. Server A sends Server B and Server C a notice that an update has been made, *along with Server A's up-to-date vectors.*

3. Server B and Server C independently compare the up-to-date vectors sent by Server A to confirm that they require the update, which they do. They then request the updates from Server A.

4. Server B and Server C commit the changes to their directories.

5. Then, they notify their replication partners of the change. In this case, Server B's other replication partner is Server C. Server B sends Server C a notification that a change has been made, *along with Server A's up-to-date vectors.*

6. Server C receives this notification and Server B's up-to-date vectors and sees that it has already received the update from Server A. Server C does not request the update from Server B, and the replication propagation is dampened.

Conflict Resolution

If a single attribute is changed on two different DCs and between replication intervals, the directory becomes inconsistent and must determine which value should represent the attribute. *Conflict resolution* is the process of choosing one of the attribute changes as the value that represents the attribute.

DCs only replicate object properties at the attributes level, not the whole object. Not only does this increase efficiency, but it also helps to minimize conflicts. If the name of an object is changed on one DC and the address of the same object is changed on another DC, no conflict arises because of attribute level replication.

However, to resolve any attribute conflicts that do occur, Active Directory maintains version numbers and timestamps for each attribute as metadata. Unlike USNs, the version numbers and timestamps are not specific to the DC. Rather, these values are specific to the attribute.

When an attribute of an object is first populated with data, the attribute is given a version number of one. All additional originating updates (not replicated updates) increment the attribute's version number.

If a replicated attribute is received from a replication partner and if the replicated attribute's version number is the same as the local attribute's version number, then the attribute with the latest timestamp wins. In the rare case in which the version numbers and the timestamps are the same on the replicated attribute and the local attribute, then the attribute whose database has the highest Globally Unique Identifier (GUID) value wins. This assures that in all cases only one attribute wins.

Therefore, in the example at the beginning of this section, in which two phone extensions where changed on two DCs between replication intervals, the phone extension that was changed last would have the latest timestamp and would represent the phone number attribute for that object. In the more complicated example, in which ten changes were made to an attribute in London *after* which one change was made to the same attribute in Los Angeles (all happening in between replication intervals) the tenth change made in London would win despite the change occurring earlier than the one change made in Los Angeles. This is because the London change would have the greater version number.

Intra-Site Replication

Intra-site replication is replication between DCs in the same site. One of the aspects of a site that makes up the definition of a site is that all DCs share a high-bandwidth network. Rather than consume additional CPU cycles making network communications more efficient, DCs within the same site communicate freely with one another.

Within a site, DCs do not poll one another to see if changes need to be replicated. Rather, when a change is made on a DC, the DC waits about 300 seconds (or 5 minutes) before sending a *change notification* to its replication partners in the site. When the replication partners receive this change notification, they pull the change from the DC and update their databases through the replication process previously explained. The originating DC waits 5 minutes because it is probable that additional changes will be made, and it is more efficient to replicate multiple changes at once. Furthermore, if a DC receives no change notifications for six hours, then the DC initiates a replication request with its replication partners.

Now, some types of directory changes need to be replicated immediately. Specifically, changes to Active Directory that concern security, such as password changes, DC role changes, and user account lockouts. These changes will not wait the 5-minute change interval, but rather the change notification will be sent out immediately.

Inter-Site Replication

Because sites themselves are defined as having high bandwidth, the parts of the network that connect sites generally have limited bandwidth. Therefore, more effort goes into conserving network bandwidth between sites. Data is compressed as much as 15 percent before being sent between sites.

Unlike intra-site replication, inter-site replication does not use change notifications to initiate replication. Rather, replication is scheduled. This enables the site design to take into consideration off-peak network hours or an interval that does not constantly consume the entire network bandwidth.

With that said, remember that if a change is made to a DC, the change *will* be replicated between sites if the sites are in the same domain. Sites do not minimize network traffic, but they help mitigate it through compression and a replication schedule.

Replication Transports

There are two possible transports between Active Directory sites: *synchronous* RPCs (IP), see Figure 10.7, or *asynchronous* Simple Mail Transport Protocol (SMTP), see Figure 10.8. Asynchronous SMTP is more efficient and reliable over limited bandwidths and unreliable network connections than synchronous RPCs. Because it is likely that sites will have limited bandwidth, you would think that SMTP would be the best choice for the transport used between sites. However, there is one caveat: SMTP cannot be used to replicate domain partition information between sites.

This means that if a domain is going to contain more than one site, then synchronous RPCs are the only transport available for domain replication traffic between those sites.

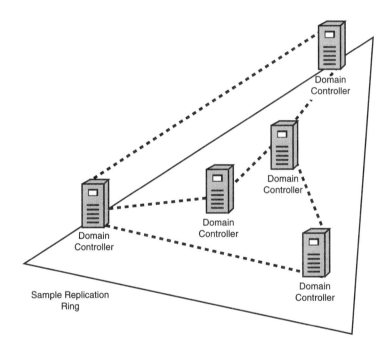

Figure 10.7 RPC site link connector between sites within domain.

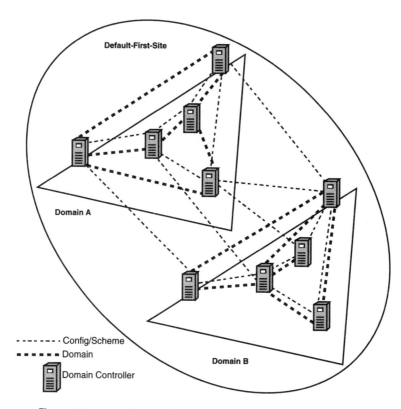

Figure 10.8   A SMTP site link connector between sites across domains.

If you have two domains, each with their own site, then asynchronous SMTP can be used to replicate the configuration and schema partitions between the two domains/sites.

What does this mean for site design? It means that the limitations of synchronous RPCs make the amount of reliable network bandwidth between physical locations a consideration when designing your domain topology. If you are designing domains to span multiple sites, consider the limitations of RPCs because it is going to be used to replicate the domain partition information between sites.

Tools for Monitoring Replication

Tools for replication should not be used only in production; they should also be used in the lab to validate that your domain and site design performs as expected.

Replication Monitor

Replication Monitor (ReplMon) can be run on any Windows 2000 computer, and it gives a detailed graphical representation of Active Directory partitions that exist on every DC in a domain. It shows each DC's replication partners, their USN values, errors, and attributes waiting to replicate.

ReplMon also enables administrators to "kick start" the Knowledge Consistency Checker (KCC) to recalculate the replication topology. This tool is a must for any Active Directory administrator with more than one DC.

Network Monitor

Network Monitor (NetMon) can be used to measure replication traffic and to analyze replication packets going between DCs. There are two flavors of NetMons. The generic version, which comes with Windows 2000, is a non-promiscuous network sniffer. This means that the generic version of NetMon only sniffs packets to and from the computer it is running on. The other version of NetMon, available with Microsoft System Management Server (SMS), is a promiscuous sniffer and captures packets between any two hosts on your network.

Therefore, if you are going to use NetMon to monitor Active Directory replication traffic, make sure that you use the version of NetMon that meets your needs. If you want one workstation to monitor Active Directory replication traffic among multiple servers, then you must use the SMS version of NetMon.

System Performance Monitor

System Performance Monitor (PerfMon) is a longtime friend of the Windows NT family of products. As with other applications and services, PerfMon counters are included with Active Directory, which enables PerfMon to track the performance of Active Directory. The counters for Active Directory include

- **DRA Inbound Bytes Total**—This is the total number of inbound bytes replicated. During inter-site replication, this is the number of bytes after compression.
- **DRA Inbound Bytes Not Compressed**—This usually represents the number of bytes inbound from other DCs in the Active Directory site.
- **DRA Inbound Bytes Compressed (before compression)**—This represents the original number of bytes that were sent before compression.
- **DRA Inbound Bytes (after compression)**—These are the compressed bytes received by the DC.
- **DRA Outbound Bytes Not Compressed**—This counts the number of bytes sent from the DC to other DCs in the site.
- **DRA Outbound Bytes Total**—This is the total number of outbound bytes replicated. During inter-site replication, this is the number of bytes after compression.

- **DRA Outbound Bytes Compressed (before compression)**—This represents the original number of bytes that were sent before compression.

- **DRA Outbound Bytes Compressed (after compression)**—These compressed bytes were sent by the DC.

Event Log

Another ally of the Windows NT administrator, the event log, is a way to monitor directory replication. The event log can be used for troubleshooting and for monitoring the success of certain functions, such as startup, shutdown, backup, and system maintenance. The Windows NT resource kit also contains utilities that notify administrators if a particular event ID is logged.

Sites Explained

Sites define areas within an organization that have high network bandwidths. It is necessary to define these high bandwidth areas of the network so that DCs can take advantage of this high bandwidth when communicating with other DCs in the same site. Likewise, by defining sites, DCs can conserve network bandwidth when communicating between sites. Sites do not define what is replicated, domains do that, but sites do define how the directory data is replicated and how much effort is put forth by the DCs to conserve network bandwidth.

Sites also define where clients access domain resources. When a client logs on, the client contacts a DC in its site. If a DC is not available in the client's site, the client attempts to contact a DC outside its site. In the first scenario, client logon traffic is centralized to the client's own high bandwidth site—increasing performance and utilizing cheap local-area bandwidth rather than expensive and limited wide-area bandwidth.

Group Policy Objects (GPOs) can also be assigned to a site. As was discussed in Chapter 8, "Designing the DNS Namespace," clients who exist in a site have the site's GPOs applied to them. This is the one area where the physical topology can be used to manage users and workstations.

Sites can also affect the *Distributed File System (DFS)* topology. The DFS uses sites to determine which file share is local to a client and redirects the client to that file share.

Intra-Site Replication Topology

As previously mentioned, replication partners are established between DCs in a site. Unlike the servers in a Microsoft Exchange site, which communicate directly with one another in a full-mesh fashion, Active Directory DCs in a site build a partial-mesh topology within the site. Microsoft likes to call this a ring topology, but the topology created is not necessarily a ring. This is because each DC is on average no more than three hops away from any other DC in the site. Therefore, when you have sites with many DCs, you loose the ring as in Figure 10.9.

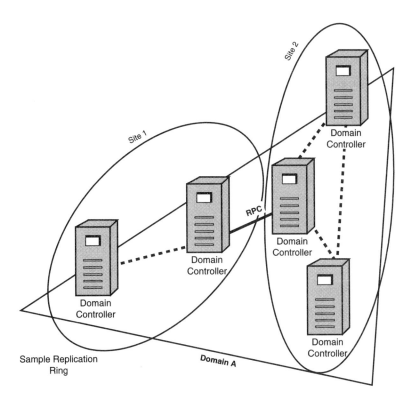

Figure 10.9   A replication ring within a site.

When thinking of replication partners and the replication topology, it's important to remember that not all Active Directory partitions are the same. Therefore, Active Directory partitions might have their *own* replication topology. Why? This is because domain partitions are independent of configuration and schema partitions and might need to replicate to different parts of the enterprise. Remember, the domain partition only replicates between DCs *in the same domain*, but the schema and configuration partitions replicate to all the DCs in the Forest. Therefore, the schema and configuration partition share a replication topology, but the domain replication topologies are likely to be different, especially in a multi-domain environment.

For example, a site with two domains has three rings (one schema/configuration and two domain rings), and a site with three domains has four rings (one schema/configuration and three domain rings). Figure 10.10 shows the replication rings for a two-domain site.

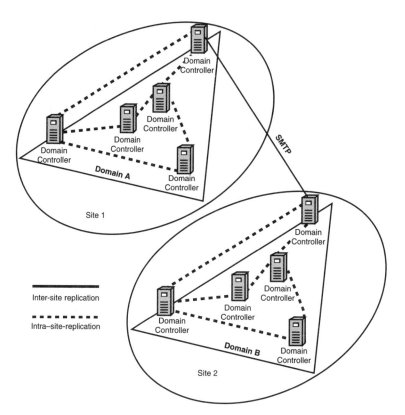

Figure 10.10 Replication rings within each domain
for domain partitions and across domains for
schema and configuration partitions.

Intra-Site Topology Generation

The intra-site replication topology is generated automatically by the KCC. The KCC builds *connection objects* within a site that represent potential *direct replication partners* between DCs. The KCC takes these connection objects and builds a replication "ring" between DCs in the site using the KCCs replication topology generator service. After direct replication partners are established by the KCC for a given DC, the other DCs in the site are considered *transitive replication partners*. Transitive replication partners are those DCs in the site that make it possible for a DC to receive replication data through an indirect replication partner.

Connection objects are unidirectional. They are created by the KCC, but they can also be manually created by the administrator using the Active Directory Sites and Services MMC snap-in. To configure bi-directional replication between two DCs, two unidirectional connection objects must be created. A connection object between two sites is all that is needed to replicate all Active Directory partitions. It is not necessary to create multiple connection objects between sites.

The ReplMon tool shows a DCs direct replication partners and transitive replication partners.

Inter-Site Topology Generation

It is important that all sites within a Forest replicate efficiently between one another. Remember, the configuration and schema Active Directory partitions are replicated to all the DCs in the Forest. Hence, consider the entire Forest and how replication data travels between them when planning sites. See Figure 10.11 for an example of a large site topology.

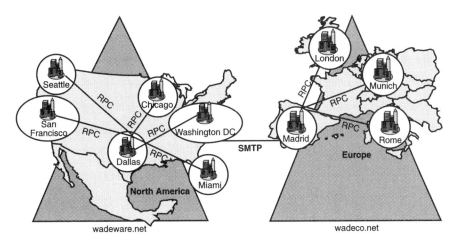

Figure 10.11 A large site topology with multiple sites within each domain.

Manually created connectors, called *site link connectors*, which are configured between sites define the inter-site replication topology that is created. The appropriate Active Directory partitions use the site link connectors to replicate data between sites. If sites are connected using site link connectors, a *bridgehead* in each site manages replication traffic to and from the other site. Because there is a potential 5-minute delay in replication between DCs, and because there is a maximum of three hops between any two DCs in a site, there is a potential 15-minute delay between when a change is made on a DC in a site, and when the bridgehead receives the replication update. Therefore, the *potential* replication latency between any two DCs in a Forest is:

(site connector replication interval * (number of sites − 1)) + (15min intersite * number of sites)

For example, imagine that an Active Directory has three domains and three sites in a tree. Each domain has 5 DCs, and the replication interval between all the sites is 30 minutes. Therefore, this Active Directory would have a potential replication latency of:

(30*(3-1))+(15*3)=135 minutes

How Sites Affect Replication

When the first DC is installed and a Forest is created, the DC is placed in a site. This site, the *default-first-site-name*, also hosts all the additional DCs until additional sites are created. As your Active Directory is built by adding DCs, sites are created and DCs are moved into those sites. The sites are connected using site link connectors, which provide a replication path between sites.

How directory replication is performed within a site is different than how replication is performed between sites. As previously outlined, intra-site replication partners are established, and replication occurs at 5-minute intervals as needed. Replication between sites is scheduled and managed by the site link connectors that have been established between sites. Some changes are immediately replicated between DCs within a site. Specifically, changes to Active Directory that has to do with security, such as password changes, DC role changes, and user account lockouts.

Site Link Connectors

Site link connectors connect sites. All sites must be connected to at least one site in the Forest. However, which sites connect to one another is a significant component to any Active Directory design. It is important to take into account the network topology when designing your sites and site link connectors. This is necessary because you want replication traffic to flow across your network in a natural path taking advantage of high bandwidth where you have it, and conserving network bandwidth where it is limited.

Site link connectors are configured with the following attributes:

- **Member Sites**—define two or more sites to be connected using the site link connector. Which sites are connected using site link connectors is established in the Active Directory design.

- **Schedule**—defines the times when replication can occur. This is something that is not configurable within a site. It is important to remember that changes replicate across sites. If you extend the interval, replication changes queue up at the bridgeheads and replicate at the next interval. If you replicate your data more frequently, latency is reduced and changes are reflected across the Forest in less time. Regardless of the schedule, changes will replicate.

- **Cost**—assigns a value to the site link connection. This value is used to determine which site link connection is used to replicate between two sites.

- **Transport**—is the protocol the site link connector uses to replicate data. When deciding which protocol to be used across the site link connector, remember to keep in mind which partitions can replicate across which protocols.

SMTP

SMTP is a legacy protocol that has been around for most of the history of modern computing, and it is only becoming more popular. Defined by RFC821, this Internet standard protocol is used to move messages between hosts. It began as the protocol used by UNIX send-mail applications, and it is now a common protocol for client-server email applications, such as Microsoft Exchange. SMTP is playing a bigger and bigger role in Microsoft products. Although Microsoft Exchange has always had an SMTP host as a transport option, Exchange 2000 uses SMTP as its primary transport between Exchange servers. Active Directory also has the capability to use SMTP to transport replication messages between sites. SMTP is an asynchronous protocol that is fast and efficient. For organizations that currently use SMTP to move email messages around an organization, using SMTP as the site link connector protocol complements the WAN that is currently configured to manage SMTP.

SMTP cannot be used to replicate domain data between sites. Therefore, if you have a domain that spans sites, the site link connector between those sites has to be configured with the IP/RPC protocol.

SMTP is a more efficient protocol over limited bandwidth or unreliable connections than RPC.

Because SMTP is a message transport, replication data using SMTP is contained in messages. These messages can be queued between Active Directory DCs and streamed across the WAN at a rate the WAN can support. SMTP is asynchronous, meaning that the sending SMTP host establishes a session with the receiving SMTP host and streams the data across without waiting for acknowledgements (see RFC821 about chunking). RPCs, on the other hand, have more overhead in the way that they communicate. Not only is establishing the session between hosts less efficient, but there is more overhead during transmission. Another difference between RPC and SMTP is that SMTP is an asynchronous protocol, whereas RPC is a synchronous protocol. This means that SMTP can send data to the receiving host without having to wait for an acknowledgement, whereas RPC waits for an acknowledgement from the receiving host before continuing the communication.

IP or RPC

The IP choice of site link transports is really using RCPs across an IP (SMTP is also an IP protocol). RPCs are a standard Windows mechanism for communication between Windows computers. Many Windows applications use RPCs for communications. Everything from earlier versions of Exchange to Windows NT tools, such as Server Manager and Users Manager, use RPC to communicate.

The IP/RPC transport can accommodate any Active Directory replication message, and as previously mentioned, it is the only choice for replication between DCs in the same domain, whether in the same site or across sites.

Rules for Replication

Therefore, with all these protocols and attributes configurable on the site link connector, take a look at each Active Directory partition and how it replicates across the Forest or domain.

Domain Partition

The domain partition is the only partition that is not common across every DC in the Forest. Instead, the domain partition is only common between DCs that are members of a particular domain. Within a Forest, a domain partition exists for each domain. The objects from each domain are brought together to form the Global Catalog (GC). The GC contains a reference to every object in all the domains of the Forest. However, the objects maintained in the GC do not contain all the attributes that make up each object, except in a few instances. This means that there are two types of domain partition:

- **Full domain replica**—DCs hold a replica that contains all the information for the entire domain.
- **Partial domain replica**—This replica contains all the objects in the domain, but it contains only a subset of each set of attributes for each object.

Most DCs host just the full domain replica for the DCs domain. GC servers host not only its full domain replica, but also a partial domain replica of all other domains in the Forest. The first DC in each domain is a GC server by default. The number and location of GC servers should be defined in your Active Directory design.

Configuration Partition

The configuration partition is made up of Forest configuration information, such as what domains make up the Forest, how they are constructed, and how many DCs are present in each domain, along with what services they host. Unlike the domain partition, the configuration partition is replicated to every DC in the Forest.

Schema Partition

The schema partition consists of the Active Directory schema, or database definitions, for all objects and attributes in Active Directory. In addition, the schema contains the rules for creating and changing Active Directory objects. As with the configuration partition, the schema partition is replicated to all DCs in the Forest.

Site Functionality Beyond Replication

Sites are primarily designed based on Active Directory replication. There are other functions that sites perform, which need to be mentioned here.

How Sites Affect Client Logon

As previously mentioned, clients and DCs are grouped together by sites to make the client-server process more efficient. For a client to function normally, it must have access to an Active Directory DC, domain name system (DNS) services, and GC services. Therefore, plan your sites so that these services are available to clients with the highest availability possible (or affordable). This entails providing these services locally, or on the same LAN as the clients, as seen in Figure 10.12. It is also prudent to provide redundant services if there are many clients dependent on a site's services. If Active Directory services are provided across a WAN connection and the WAN fails, then clients cannot function properly.

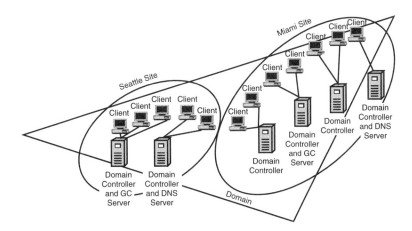

Figure 10.12   Clients connect to DCs within their own sites.

Grouping clients and Active Directory services together in sites that coexist on a LAN increases client logon performance, increases DC services availability, and focuses network traffic on the LANs.

Sites and GPOs

Another use for sites is the application of GPOs. GPOs applied to a site are applied to the users and clients in that site. This is useful for GPOs that are particular to a site and can add another dimension to your GPO strategy.

Network Bandwidth

Where should site lines be drawn? This is one of the most dynamic questions in all Active Directory design. It depends mostly on the amount of available network bandwidth exists between locations.

Many factors go into measuring the amount of network bandwidth that is consumed by Active Directory and its clients. Whether or not adequate network bandwidth is available to support multiple physical locations within the same site depends on these factors.

Start your site design by considering all the subnets, which have fast and reliable bandwidths between them, as sites. Then, expand your sites as warranted.

Site Design

Having a clear picture of your LANs and WAN is paramount to site design. The networking services group within your organization should be able to supply you with statistics showing the amount of available network bandwidth between sites at specific times of the day. This data is usually collected on routers, using network management tools. It is also collected by the carrier that provides the network connectivity between locations. Most carriers can provide reports on network traffic between locations. These statistics, whether supplied by your networking services group or the carrier, should be explained. Have them explain the results and how they were gathered. As with most statistics, the results can be made to show anything the gatherer wishes; therefore, use your common sense when deciphering these statistics.

Another important consideration, especially for locations outside the United States, is how the WAN carriers manage network traffic. For example, frame relay networks consist of an access rate and a committed information rate (CIR). The access rate is the speed at which a location connects to the carrier's frame relay cloud. The CIR is a defined amount of bandwidth under the access rate that the carrier guarantees packets will be delivered to their destination. You have the ability to burst over your CIR up to your access rate; however, for this, you sometimes pay a premium and the carrier does not guarantee that packets over the CIR reach their destination. Ideally, an organization should subscribe to a CIR that is just over their normal use but has the capability to burst over that if necessary. A flat rate is paid for the CIR, and a premium is paid for bursting over the CIR.

With that said, the rules for the frame relay can differ depending on the country you are in. In the United States, for example, some carriers rarely drop frame relay packets that exceed the CIR. In addition, the cost of exceeding the CIR is not much greater than the bandwidth within the CIR. Therefore, many organizations subscribe with a CIR of zero, not having to pay a fixed fee for the CIR, and only pay for the bandwidth that they use, be it at the premium price. In Europe, however, most frame relay carriers frequently drop packets that exceed the CIR. Therefore, in Europe, it is much more important to consider the CIR as the bandwidth ceiling, whereas in the United States it is common to consider the access rate as the bandwidth ceiling. This is just an example of the differences in WAN rules between countries and carriers. Your network services group should be aware of these differences and fully debrief you on them so that Active Directory site design can consider them.

Along with gathering the available network bandwidth between each physical location, other considerations to account for when drawing site lines include

- **Future plans**—For WAN expansion and increases in bandwidth.
- **Growth of the organization**—Both in number of users and in number of workstations.
- **Applications that use Active Directory**—How frequently these applications make changes to Active Directory.
- **Domain topology**—If a domain spans multiple sites, then is IP/RPC adequate as a site link connector to support domain replication between sites?
- **DC location**—Is there enough bandwidth to support clients accessing Active Directory services across WAN connections that are contained within a site.

Now that we are armed with how DCs behave within sites and between sites, we can start to design a site topology.

Drawing Site Lines

Site lines can be drawn to mitigate DC replication traffic and manage client logon traffic. However, the ideal site design based on replication traffic might not be the ideal site design to manage client logon traffic. Often a balance must be struck between client logon requirements and replication traffic requirements. If you understand both functions within Active Directory, then drawing site lines that meet your organization's needs is simplified.

Mirroring the Network Topology

Most site designs closely follow the network topology. Sites encircle the physical locations and site link connectors are established at those sites that have physical network connections between them. This is not a bad approach. However, it might be possible to couple together physical locations that have either high WAN bandwidth between them or limited numbers of users in one of the physical locations (see Figure 10.13).

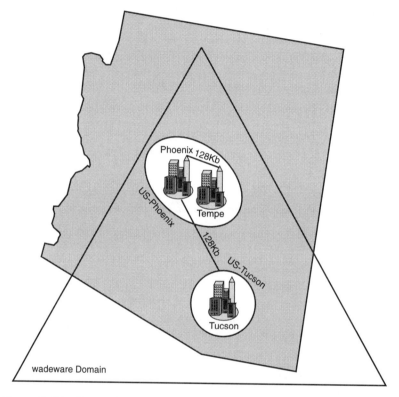

Figure 10.13   Sites include locations with adequate available network bandwidth.

For example, Wadeware has offices in Phoenix, Tempe, and Tucson. The Tempe and Tucson offices have 128K frame relay connections between them and the Phoenix office. Phoenix hosts the data center for the region and has 300 users. Tempe has limited users, 20, with only a small file and print server in the local office. All other services, such as email and Internet, come from Phoenix over the 128K connection. Tucson has 75 users with most services provided locally. In this instance, it might not make sense to put a DC in Tempe. Without a DC in Tempe, there is no replication traffic to Tempe. By making Tempe part of the Phoenix site (named US-Phoenix), users in Tempe receive Active Directory services from the Phoenix location. Tucson has its own site, which hosts Active Directory and DNS services.

What Services to Include in Each Site

Because clients require Active Directory services from a DC, GC services from a GC server, and domain name services from a DNS server, it is prudent to provide these services in each site. There might be sites that are just too small to justify providing all three services locally. In this case, remember that if the WAN connection fails between the clients and these services, the clients might not be able to logon with anything but cached credentials, which are only valid for a short time.

With DNS services, as described in Chapter 8, "Designing the DNS Namespace," Active Directory has the capability to integrate DNS zones into Active Directory, which means that the DNS database is replicated around the domain via Active Directory. This can help to satisfy the requirement of having DNS services available at in all sites.

For GC services, there might be other applications (such as Exchange) that utilize GC services for normal functionality, adding to the importance of providing these services at all times.

Flexible Single Master of Operations (FSMO) Service Locations

There are certain services provided by Active Directory that do not work well in a multi-master model. The PDC emulator service, which acts like a PDC for down level NT 4.0 DCs and clients, is a good example of a service provided by Active Directory that cannot exist on more than one server. These services, known as FMSOs, do not replicate. Therefore, it is important to know which DC hosts these services and to consider if their location should be changed.

- **Primary DC Emulator**—This service exists only in mixed-mode on the first server installed in the domain. A DC near the old NT 4.0 PDC should host this service. There is one of these per domain
- **Domain Operations Master**—There is only one domain operations master per Forest, which manages the additions and deletions of domains in the Forest.
- **Relative Identifier (RID) Operations Master**—This service generates security identifiers (SIDs) for the domain. Only one exists per domain.
- **Infrastructure Operations Master**—This service manages the SIDs of objects moving in and out of the domain. There is one of these per domain.
- **Schema Operations Master**—Only the Schema operations master can update the schema. There is a single Schema operations master per Forest

For most of these services, locating them in a centralized location, such as a hub site, that has the fewest hops to all the DCs in the organization provides the greatest performance and availability.

In large domains, consider splitting the RID Operations Master and Primary Domain Controller (PDC) emulator between two DCs in the same site. During mixed-mode operations, this spreads the load across multiple DCs.

Another best practice is to place the Infrastructure Operations Master on a DC that is not a GC server, but that is on the same LAN as a GC server. Furthermore, always place the Schema Operations Master and the Domain Naming Master on the same DC.

Evaluate each FSMO's role. Define them as per-domain services and per-Forest services. Plan the placement of per-domain services based on the sites and DCs that make up the domain. Plan the placement of per-Forest services based on the overall domain topology.

Another part of Active Directory design should be planning for FSMO outages. If a DC that is hosting one of these services fails, another DC should be designated as the service's backup. In most cases, the failed DC is brought back online before the change needs to be made. However, in the case in which the DC is unavailable for an extended period, you can use the MMC snap-in to change the role of the designated backup DC to take over providing the FSMO services.

Building Sites

After you have moved from the design phase to the implementation phase of the project, sites are built in the following manner.

- Create the sites, as defined in the Active Directory design.
- Create the subnets that are contained in each site.
- Group the subnets in their appropriate sites.
- Move DCs to their appropriate sites. This site also contains the subnet that the DC is on. As DCs are created using DCpromo, they need to be moved to their appropriate site.
- Create site link connectors between sites, as defined in the Active Directory design. Define the transport, schedule, and cost for each site link connector.

Designing the components of Active Directory's physical topology is as important to how it meets your organization's needs as the logical, or domain, topology. Where sites are placed, how they are connected, and the services provided by the DCs within them, all contribute to the efficiency and reliability of Active Directory.

Summary

The site design is built to support the Forest and domain design. The distinction between the physical and logical portions of the Active Directory design are important because they are designed based on two distinct sets of requirements. The logical design is driven by business requirements. The physical design is driven by the network infrastructure and the performance of Active Directory services.

Active Directory and Scalability

S CALABILITY IS ONE OF THE FIRST ISSUES DISCUSSED WHEN large enterprises are examining a new technology for deployment. However, scalability is seldom a deciding factor in technology evaluation for smaller organizations. This chapter focuses on the scalability of Active Directory and discusses the impact on performance if more objects are added to Active Directory.

There are three different growth aspects to consider when planning for Active Directory scalability: growing a domain, growing a tree, and growing a Forest.

Growing a Domain

Planning for domain growth should focus primarily on the way in which new organizational units (OUs) are added to the domain, as well as on which objects reside in which OUs. A mismatch between the way in which the real organization functions and the way in which Active Directory OUs are configured can result not only in poor performance for users, applications, and active network components that use the directory, but it might also result in the directory not being able to function.

Planning the correct configuration for domains and OUs is critical to the successful deployment of any Active Directory plan. Tree structure needs should not only take in to account the existing requirements of the organization but must also anticipate and account for possible changes and growth in the future.

There are two basic approaches to segmenting OUs within a domain. OUs can either be segmented by business function, or by geography. Both of these segmentations, however, are influenced significantly by the way in which the organization plans to administer Active Directory and the degree to which administration of OUs will be delegated and decentralized.

Segmentation by Business Function

Many organizations segment IT infrastructure and administration by business function. For example, every sales unit in every geography is part of a unified sales group that has a single set of access rights for network resources, a unified naming structure for file shares, and centralized, or distributed but unified, administration of the IT environment.

An OU structure designed to map to this segmentation model includes OUs that map to business units of the company. For example, in the case of Wadeware, the following organization issues affect OU configuration:

- Manufacturing is broken into business line units.

- The sales force is organized into a division that sell to large enterprises, a division that sells to small enterprises, and a division that sells specific widgets from each manufacturing line.

- There is a significant focus on acquisitions as a method of expansion for the company. All the information in the acquisitions group must be kept confidential from the rest of the company.

The previously listed organizational issues result in a corporate organizational structure that includes three major divisions: manufacturing, sales, and acquisitions. The manufacturing division is divided in to three groups: design and development, implementation, and distribution. The sales division is also divided into three groups: large enterprise sales, regional sales, and product sales. Acquisitions is a single division. In addition to these three large divisions, there is a fourth division comprising all the back office functions, such as finance, human resources, administration, facilities, and IT. The organizational structure for the organization is represented in Figure 11.1.

What does this type of corporate organizational structure mean as to how the OUs within Active Directory domains should be configured? If the OUs are segmented by business function, the tree structure mirrors the organizational structure of the business. However, it is important to bear in mind that when the OU structure is designed, the OU administration model follows the same design. For that reason, it might be necessary to modify the OU structure to incorporate administration needs, as well as organizational requirements.

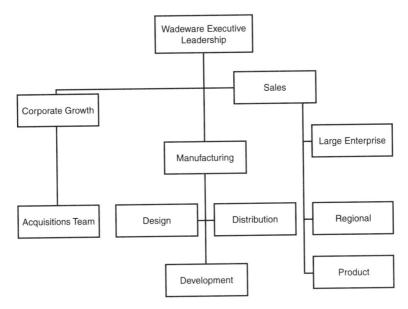

Figure 11.1   The corporate organizational structure of Wadeware
reflects the way the company does business: the sales force is
unified in selling products to large enterprise and to regions.

The administrative model for an organization essentially defines who is responsible for
managing resources across the organization. These resources can include users, printers,
workstations, and servers. A complex OU structure that mirrors a complex organizational structure lead to a complicated administrative model. In addition, as the OU
structure is scaled to meet the growing needs of the organization, the administration of
the environment becomes more complicated if the OU structure has not been
planned well from the beginning.

For example, in the case of Wadeware, the most obvious OU structure would be to
have a three-tiered structure with several OUs. There would be a root OU, for OUs in
the primary divisions, and multiple OUs for the divisional groups. If configured this
way, the structure would appear as represented in Figure 11.2. This would lead to a
complicated administration model as the company grows over time with new company acquisitions and new product development.

Instead of configuring a single OU for every divisional group, a more logical configuration that would result in a simpler administration model as the company grows
would be to create a single root OU and four secondary OUs, one for each division
(see Figure 11.3). This would provide a structure that would enable the application of
group policies and the distribution of administration responsibilities by division, but
would also be simple enough that future growth could be absorbed into the existing
OUs. New OUs would not have to be created to accommodate company acquisitions
or new product developments.

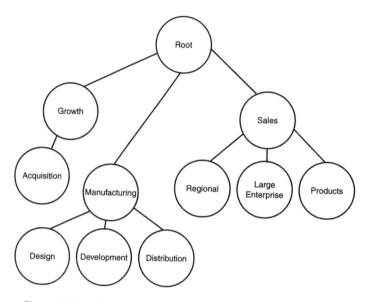

Figure 11.2 This is the OU structure, which would result if OUs were created for each division and each divisional group in Wadeware.

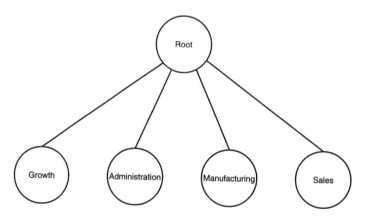

Figure 11.3 A logical OU structure that maps to the organization, and yet provides a simple, centralized administration model.

A simple OU structure, such as the previous one, is easy to plan, implement, configure, and administer. There are times, however, when simplicity is not possible. This might be because of security needs, organizational politics, or simple organization intransigence. Whatever the reason, a more complicated OU structure can certainly be accommodated by Active Directory. However, the planning team should make sure that the project executive sponsor clearly understands that the more complicated the administration model the more costly the administration is.

Segmentation by Geography

The second way to segment the OU structure is by geography. For organizations that have Microsoft Exchange or Microsoft Systems Management Server (SMS) installed, segmentation by geography might appear to be the most logical segmentation. This is because both Exchange and SMS use sites configured by geographic and network segmentation.

In the case of Wadeware, segmentation by geography might also make sense if the IT infrastructure is segmented by geography (see Figure 11.4). However, it is important to remember that segmenting a domain in to multiple OUs does not help to minimize network traffic. All the Domain Controllers (DCs) in the domain have copies of the directory schema and participate in directory replication regardless of the OU structure. Only segmentation of the domain into multiple sites results in a reduction of network traffic or, more accurately, the capability to control network traffic.

Because the configuration of OUs does not directly affect network traffic, it is important to configure the organizational structure with business needs in mind and not with performance as the main goal.

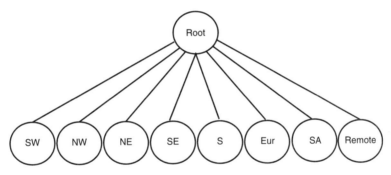

Figure 11.4   This is a representation of the segmentation of OUs based on geography. This might not be the most efficient way to configure the OU tree.

Delegation of Administration

Delegation of administration should not be considered as a primary design goal when designing your OU and domain structure. An OU structure designed only to accommodate specific administration requirements might not scale if a legitimate business need prompts modification. The administrative model for Active Directory should always be secondary to business needs.

However, after business needs are satisfied in the directory design, delegation of administration should be the second requirement considered when designing the OU structure. Delegation might be required for several reasons:

- Specific business units in the organization require control of their own user and resource administration. This might be for security reasons or other reasons.

- Administration of the IT infrastructure has always been delegated and corporate culture dictates that it remains that way.

- Move administration closer to the actual point at which the administrative task originates. This promotes both efficiency and accuracy. It is more efficient to have the team in the organization that manages the phone system actually enter the phone numbers.

- Distribute administrative tasks to the least cost resource in the organization. Rather than pay an IT architect or engineer to maintain and modify data in the directory, it is less expensive to have administrative staff migrating data. This can be accomplished by developing specialized administration tools that use Active Directory services interface to manipulate the directory.

- Consolidation of administrative tasks. Administrative tasks can be consolidated and then delegated along organizational lines rather than segmented along task lines. For example, the organization might today have individuals who administer the Microsoft Exchange environment and a different set of individuals who administer the Windows networking environment. With delegation of authority across OUs, it would be possible to consolidate all the administrative tasks for both the mail environment and the operating system environment, and then to delegate them by OU.

Growing a Tree

As organizations grow, they might outgrow the boundaries of a single domain configuration. They might outgrow this for several reasons:

- The number of objects in the domain exceeds the practical maximum for the domain. A result would be that directory searches take significant amounts of time to complete.

- The security requirements of the organization might outgrow the limits of a single domain.

- Network boundaries make a single domain environment impractical.

If this occurs, it is necessary to add domains to the tree to accommodate the growth.

Growing a Forest

The definition of a Forest is a set of domain trees that shares a common schema and Global Catalog (GC) but does not share a common namespace. For example, the root domain of one tree might be `Wadeware.net` and the root of another tree might be `wadewarewidgets.net`. The two trees share a common schema and GC as long as the second tree was initially created by joining the `Wadeware.net` Forest (see Figure 11.5).

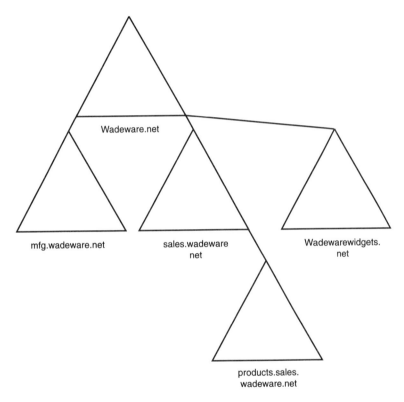

Figure 11.5   A Forest consists of two separate domain trees, which share a common schema, GC, and security context. The two trees do not share a common namespace. In the preceding example, `Wadeware.net` and `wadewarewidgets.net` are separate trees that are part of the same Forest.

Keeping in mind the definition of a Forest, it is a straightforward process to identify whether you should grow a Forest rather than a domain tree. You grow a Forest if you have a requirement to add a discontiguous namespace and yet you want to maintain a contiguous and continuous security context. If there is no need for a unified security context, it is possible to build new Forests when developing new namespaces. There is no transitive trust security between trees in different Forests.

Growing with Your Organization

As your organization grows, you need to contend with an expanding Active Directory in different ways, including adding additional geographic locations, additional demand from applications, and from more sophisticated users.

Growing with Your Applications

An important aspect of planning for scalability is taking in to account the impact of any applications that will eventually be taking advantage of Active Directory functionality. Some enterprise software vendors, such as Baan and SAP, have released product roadmaps that include leveraging Active Directory for profile management and other functionality. You should plan for additional capacity in Active Directory if your organization has these applications deployed.

If you are planning for integrating applications with Active Directory, it is important to focus on the strengths and weaknesses of Active Directory. Active Directory is a highly distributed and replicated directory and, as such, is ideal for storing information critical to distributed applications, such as sales force automation applications and enterprise planning applications. Because it is replicated, it is not ideal for storing large blocks of information that are modified on a frequent basis. If such blocks of information are stored in the directory, a significant amount of replication traffic results from the date being modified and the being replicated between DC in the domain.

Many Microsoft applications also begin to rely on Active Directory functionality. For example, Microsoft Exchange 2000 uses Active Directory for full directory functionality. Windows 2000 and Active Directory are required for Microsoft Exchange 2000 to be deployed. What does this mean for Active Directory planning? The biggest impact is to the sizing requirements for Active Directory.

For example, in Microsoft Exchange it is possible to use the directory for storing several different type of information about an individual. There are data fields for phone numbers, addresses, organizational structures, and pager numbers, just to name a few. In addition, it is possible to configure any one, or all ten, of the custom data fields. Consequently, the result is that a large set of data can be stored in the directory for any single individual.

In Active Directory, not all the data fields associated with a single object replicate automatically to the GC. It is necessary to select which properties of which object types are replicated to the GC. This becomes significant if implementing Active Directory with Microsoft Exchange because if Outlook, the Microsoft Exchange client application, initiates a directory lookup request from Active Directory, it does not pull data from Active Directory. Instead, it pulls data from the GC. This implies significant design considerations for the way in which Active Directory is used in an Exchange implementation to store information about users. If people in your organization typically use the Outlook Address Book as a phone book as well, you need to replicate phone information from Active Directory to the GC. This could result in a significant impact to the network. This is just one example of how applications that use Active Directory can affect your computing environment.

Summary

Active Directory is a scalable directory service. However, if Active Directory is scaled, it needs to be done based on an organized plan and in conjunction with the business drivers of the organization. Domains, trees, and Forests can be segmented by business function, geographic distribution, or by administrative requirements. Whatever the driving force behind the segmentation, planning should always be the first step in the process. It is also critical for Active Directory to be leveraged for the right purpose. It makes an excellent repository for relatively static, limited-size data. It is not a good place to store rapidly changing or large blocks of data.

Implementation

12

Managing the Desktop

M AINTAINING TECHNOLOGY WITHIN AN ORGANIZATION is becoming more complex and expensive, and there is a direct correlation between the two. Several studies have shown that although systems that are more complex can offer a competitive advantage and make processes more efficient, the systems themselves can become overly expensive to run and maintain.

The client/server environment is no different and is especially vulnerable to excessive cost of ownership because the client is in the hands of the user. If a user changes the client configuration or adds software, or better yet, hardware, the predictability of the client changes. This leads to additional costs predicated by a client that requires more support and is potentially less efficient.

To manage the desktop fully and successfully, you should also manage and support those systems that support the desktop, mainly the BackOffice applications and the infrastructure that supports them.

To reduce the cost of ownership at the desktop, Windows 2000 and Active Directory provide functionality that takes the fate of the client out of the hands of the user and places it back in the hands of the administrators, where it belongs.

Subsets of Enterprise Management

Enterprise management is typically broken up into three areas of responsibility: server or data center management, network management, and desktop management.

Server or Data Center Management

Data center management encompasses the group of administrators who are responsible for managing BackOffice servers and their applications. Availability and disaster recovery are of the utmost importance for the data center, as is security. Data center management is focused on groups of users and how to provide them with the highest available service.

Windows 2000 Domain Controllers (DCs), application servers, and file and print servers are among the computers housed in the data center. Several tools are available to manage each of these servers; some are included with Windows 2000 and others are available from independent software vendors (ISV). The management of the Windows 2000 Server falls within the realm of the Data Center Manager.

Network Management

Spreading from the data center, like a spider's web, is the network. The issues surrounding network management are different from those surrounding the data center; however, many of the themes remain the same. Security, performance, and availability are among the categories of network functionality that must be managed.

Windows 2000 and Active Directory also provide tools and hooks into network management. Network Monitor (NetMon), for example, can be used to monitor and analyze the network traffic between two computers. Quality of Service (QoS) is another functionality provided by Windows 2000 that works with the network in prioritizing network traffic based on the parameters defined by the Network Administrator. These parameters can be defined based on how an organization prioritizes its network traffic. QoS can also be used in conjunction with Active Directory to provide different users with different levels of service. For example, voice traffic usually has the highest priority across a network. Untimely voice packets can greatly affect the quality of voice service; therefore, they must be on time and are given the highest priority. Message traffic can have a low priority because message traffic, relatively speaking, is not greatly affected by slow traffic or dropped and retransmitted packets. Therefore, different applications can be given different priorities across the network, just as users can. Based on Active Directory's interaction with QoS, users can be granted priority or even access based on who they are in Active Directory. Take, for example, an online brokerage. The online brokerage might want to grant their customers (users) who have portfolios over $100,000 higher priority than those customers with portfolios under $10,000. Defining QoS does have its price. After an application, or group of users, has priority on the network, it is at the cost of available bandwidth for other applications. So, before implementing QoS, make sure you understand the impact it has on your network.

Desktop Management

Desktop management, the focus of this chapter, must centralize the control of anywhere from 10 to 100,000 desktop computers—each of which can vary, from Apple
Macintosh to Sun Sparc Stations, with all the flavors of Intel in between. Next, the
desktop managers must contend with software, operating systems, and user education.
It is easy to see how desktop management could be both expensive and inefficient.

Areas of Management

Data center, network, and desktop management must all contend with similar areas of
system management.

Figure 12.1 Areas of management.

The division of each of the pieces seen in the Figure 12.1 pie varies based on the
organization, its priorities, the personalities and experience of management, and what
they think is important. For example, *change and configuration management* is a crucial
management component for how desktops are installed, configured, and maintained.

How a computer performs with its configured software, whether it is an Engineer's CAD workstation or a receptionist's word-processing workstation, is a function of *performance management*. How users move and manage data and applications, based on permissions, and the areas of the network that they have access to are functions of *security management*.

This is just a taste of the overall system management pie. There are several texts on management information systems, which outline in more detail the concepts described here.

Windows 2000 Management Services

The services available with Windows 2000 to provide desktop management are comprehensive enough to provide a level of desktop management that reduces cost and increases efficiency.

Event Notification

Windows 2000, as a management solution, reports on events recorded in the event log. Applications can detect which events are occurring and can take the appropriate action. The event log, which is viewed with the Microsoft event viewer, is the central location for logged events. This gives the administrator a single place to monitor for errors or other reported events.

COM and DCOM

One of the many uses of the COM and DCOM platforms is that object-oriented applications can be developed to support enterprise management services. COM is a collection of objects that exist on multiple servers and that can be used by distributed applications. Although COM enables applications on a server to share objects, DCOM is an extension that supports communications among those objects across multiple servers on a LAN, WAN, or even the Internet.

Windows Management Instrumentation (WMI)

WMI provides an interface for which standard management data from any source can be gathered and analyzed. Likewise, through the Windows Driver Model (WDM) extension for WMI, standard hardware management data can be gathered and analyzed by management applications. This gathered data can be used by applications, such as System Management Servers (SMS), to work closely with the desktop.

Active Directory

A distributed, secure, multi-master directory service is the subject of this book. Active Directory provides two key management services:

- A standardized locator service, Lightweight Directory Access Protocol (LDAP) 3.0, provides a standard way to locate resources within the enterprise.

- A group policy system that enables user and computer policies to be applied across the directory. This is key to the Windows 2000 change and configuration management strategy. After an application is installed on the desktop, policies can be defined as to how, and if, that application can be used.

By simplifying and automating application deployment and by managing the application after it has been deployed using Active Directory group policies, maintenance costs are reduced and user efficiency is increased, effecting an overall reduction in the cost of ownership.

Future Services

The next versions of the Windows server platform will provide additional management services. Management data will be replicated to various locations within the enterprise. Management system load balancing and scheduling will also be supported for various management applications and tasks.

IntelliMirror

IntelliMirror is a set of features within Windows 2000 that defines the Windows 2000 change and configuration management strategy. IntelliMirror takes advantage of the common Windows client and server operating systems to enable user data and applications, along with their settings, to follow them through the enterprise.

By tracking the location of user data and application settings, IntelliMirror can recover or replace user data and application settings, based on policy. The three features that enable IntelliMirror to function include

- User setting management
- Software installation and maintenance
- User data management

These IntelliMirror features can be used together or independently. Active Directory and Group Policy Objects (GPOs) are used by IntelliMirror to manage user desktops. This is accomplished through policies that are applied to organizational units (OUs), which contain groups of users who have specific business requirements.

User Data Management

User data management keeps a copy of the users' personal data at a location that makes it available wherever the user roams within the organization (as seen in Figure 12.2).

As users roam from computer to computer in the organization, their documents follow them. User data can also be configured to be available whether online or offline. This is particularly helpful for users who travel with laptops.

The key to this functionality is to locate user data on the Windows 2000 file shares on the network, which a policy points to, and to configure the share to be available offline. If the share is configured to be available offline, the files in the share are synchronized to a local store on the workstation. Therefore, if the network fails or the user takes the computer off the network, such as with a laptop, the data in the directory is available offline.

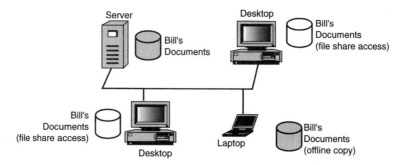

Figure 12.2 Locating Bill's data.

Software Installation and Maintenance

As user data follows a user around the organization, applications can also follow the user so that the computing environment is specific to the user not the computer. This can be an important change in the way that organizations manage hardware and software. The software license, in this scenario, becomes associated with the user instead of the computer.

Remember, one approach to designing an OU structure is to accommodate group policies so that they can be applied to a site, domain, or OU in such a way that members of those units have specific applications assigned to them. Through GPOs, applications follow the user as he or she roams around the organization. The user's Start menu and file associations are present on the computer after the user logs in. If a user starts an application that is not installed on the computer, that application is installed and starts.

This is accomplished with the help of the Windows Installer, which checks to see if the application is installed. If the application is not installed, the Windows Installer installs the application from a published installation point. This process also happens if the user attempts to open a file that requires an application that is not installed. For example, if a user was to double-click on an Excel spreadsheet file (.XLS) and Excel was not installed on the computer, the Windows Installer would install Excel from the installation point.

This mechanism also ensures that your applications are functional. If a user somehow deletes a DLL or other file that an application relies on, the Windows Installer retrieves the missing or corrupt files and copies them to the computer. This important component to the maintenance of the desktop reduces Helpdesk calls while keeping users busy.

User Settings Management

Important user settings are stored in Active Directory. A combination of group policy and Active Directory is used to enable user setting to follow the user as he or she roams about the enterprise.

There are three types of settings that follow the user: user and administrative information, temporary information, and data specific to the local computer.

- **User settings**—These include Internet Explorer (IE) favorites, quick links, cookies, the Start menu, the Outlook Express personal Web address book, and the background bitmap.

- **Administrative settings**—These include lock-down settings, such as the Hide Run command, disallowing writes to system folders, and configuring user-viewable items in Control Panel.

- **Temporary information**—These include such things as the user's personal IE cache.

- **Local computer settings**—These include such things as what folders/files are marked for offline use.

In organizations where roaming is a requirement, the local computer setting should not be configured to roam with the user. This information does not apply to the computers that the user roams to and is unnecessary.

Role of Group Policy in IntelliMirror

Change and configuration management is applied by IntelliMirror through policies. Local policy and group policy are both applied to the computer after a user logs in. Local policy is defined for the local computer. Group policy is defined for both users and computers through Active Directory. Group policy is the link between the user or computer and Active Directory. Group policy centralizes the organization's policies into Active Directory, and it is applied based on the location of the computer and the user within Active Directory.

Group policy and Active Directory enable an organization to build a set of business requirement for groups of users and computers and apply them through Active Directory. See Chapter 9, "Group Policies," for a complete explanation of group policies and how they are used.

Microsoft Installer

IntelliMirror, as previously noted, includes software installation and maintenance as a feature used to install and maintain user applications based on group policy. The Microsoft Installer plays a critical role in this process, and it's important to understand how it works. It's also important to understand the client systems to which it is applied, such as available disk space and compliance with the hardware compatibility list (HCL).

Publishing or Assigning Applications

There is a distinct difference between publishing and assigning applications. Publishing makes the application available for installation in a way that Windows 2000 operating systems can understand. Assigned applications are installed automatically and are available to the user to perform their job function.

Published applications are

- Available to users after being published.
- Installed from Control Panel, Add/Remove Programs.
- Installed if a user opens a file that requires the application.
- Removable (uninstalled) using Control Panel, Add/Remove Programs.

User assigned applications are

- Available to the user from their Start menu after they log on. The software, however, is installed if the user launches the application.
- Installed if a user opens a file that requires the application.
- Removable (uninstalled) using Control Panel, Add/Remove Programs.

Computer assigned applications are

- Installed when the computer starts.
- Can be applied using `secedit /refreshmachineposlicy` without restarting the computer.
- Not removable (uninstalled) by the user. Only the local administrator can remove the application.

The user can repair applications that have become corrupt. When assigning applications, it is important to test the application in the lab before going into production. It's also important to understand the impact assigned applications have on the network when the applications are first assigned.

Windows Installer Applications

Windows Installer is a service that is available for Windows 2000, Windows NT 4.0, Windows 98, and Windows 95. The Windows Installer service depends on a Windows Installer Package that contains specific application installation information for the Windows Installer service. Without the Windows Installer Package, the Windows Installer service has no idea how to install and configure an application.

Therefore, a prerequisite for using the Windows Installer service to install and maintain an application is for the application to have a Windows Installer Package. As Windows 2000 becomes more popular, more and more applications are released with Windows Installer Packages. Office 2000, for example, has a native Windows Installer Package. For those applications that do not come with a Windows Installer Package, you can either *author* or *repackage* the application for support by the Windows Installer service.

For authoring your own Windows Installer Packages, third-party tools are available from companies like Install Shield Software Corporation and WISE Solutions. These tools enable you to take an application and create a Windows Installer Package.

You can also repackage the application for support by the Windows Installer. Repackaging is the process of taking a clean computer, which only has the operating system installed, and installing the application. The repackaging tool compares the state of the computer, before the installation and after the installation, and records the changes made to the computer. Seagate Software's WinINSTALL LE repackages existing applications for support by the Windows Installer. This tool is available on the Windows 2000 Server CD.

Repackaging is not yet an exact science. It is recommended that packages be authored, if possible, rather than repackaged.

Publishing Non-Windows Installer Applications

It is also possible to publish, not assign, applications that do not have a Windows Installer Package. These applications are available to users through Control Panel, Add/Remove Programs, and they use the application's setup for the installation.

A .ZAP file contains a description of the application, the command line to use for setup, the setup option choices, and the entry points the application should install. The following is the .ZAP file from Microsoft for Microsoft Excel.

```
; ZAP file for Microsoft Excel 97

[Application]
; Only FriendlyName and SetupCommand are required,
; everything else is optional

; FriendlyName is the name of the application that
; will appear in the software installation snapin
; and the add/remove programs control panel.
; REQUIRED
FriendlyName = "Microsoft Excel 97"

; SetupCommand is the command line that we use to
; Run the applications setup. if it is a relative
; path, it is assumed to be relative to the
; location of the ZAP file.
; Long file name paths need to be quoted. For example:
; SetupCommand = "long folder\setup.exe" /unattend
; or
; SetupCommand = "\\server\share\long _
; folder\setup.exe" /unattend
; REQUIRED

SetupCommand = setup.exe

; Version of the application that will appear
; in the software installation snapin and the
; add/remove programs control panel.
; OPTIONAL
DisplayVersion = 8.0

; Publisher of the application that will appear
; in the software installation snapin and the
; add/remove programs control panel.
; OPTIONAL
Publisher = Microsoft

; URL for application information that will appear
; in the software installation snapin and the
; add/remove programs control panel.;
; OPTIONAL
URL = http://www.microsoft.com/office

; Language for the app, in this case US English.
; OPTIONAL
LCID = 1033
```

```
; Architecture, in this case, intel.
; OPTIONAL
Architecture = intel

; the [ext] [CLSIDs] and [progIDs] sections are
; all optional

[ext]
; File extensions that this application will
; "auto-install" for. They are not required if you
; do not want the application. This entire section
; is OPTIONAL.

; note you can put a dot in front or not, as you like
; text after the first = is optional and ignored
; but the first = is required (or the whole line
; will be ignored)
XLS=
XLA=
XLB=
XLC=
XLM=
XLV=
XLW=

[CLSIDs]
; CLSIDs that this application will "auto-install"
; for. This entire section is OPTIONAL.

; Format is CLSID with LocalServer32,
; InprocServer32, and/or InprocHandler32 (in a
; comma separated list) after the =.

{00024500-0000-0000-C000-000000000046}=LocalServer32
{00020821-0000-0000-C000-000000000046}=LocalServer32
{00020811-0000-0000-C000-000000000046}=LocalServer32
{00020810-0000-0000-C000-000000000046}=LocalServer32
{00020820-0000-0000-C000-000000000046}=LocalServer32
{00020820-0000-0000-C000-000000000046}=LocalServer32

[progIDs]
; progIDs that this application will "auto-install"
; for. This entire section is OPTIONAL.

; format is a CLSID, with the corresponding progid
; listed after the = sign
{00024500-0000-0000-C000- _
000000000046}=Excel.Application
{00024500-0000-0000-C000- _
000000000046}=Excel.Application.8
{00020821-0000-0000-C000-000000000046}=Excel.Chart
```

```
{00020811-0000-0000-C000-000000000046}=Excel.Chart.5
{00020821-0000-0000-C000-000000000046}=Excel.Chart.8
{00020810-0000-0000-C000-000000000046}=Excel.Sheet.5
{00020820-0000-0000-C000-000000000046}=Excel.Sheet.8
{00020820-0000-0000-C000-000000000046}=Excel.Sheet
{00020820-0000-0000-C000-000000000046}=Excel.Template
{00020820-0000-0000-C000-000000000046}=Excel.Workspace
```

.ZAP files are typically stored in the same network share, or software distribution point, where the application's setup is located.

Software Distribution Points

Software distribution points are strategically located file shares on your network where applications packages are stored for installation by client computers. Software distribution points should be located on one or more areas of the network, approximate to the clients that are going to require the applications that are hosted by the software distribution point.

If, for example, a GPO is applied to a domain that assigns an application to all users in that domain, it is important to provide software distribution points to the locations within that domain.

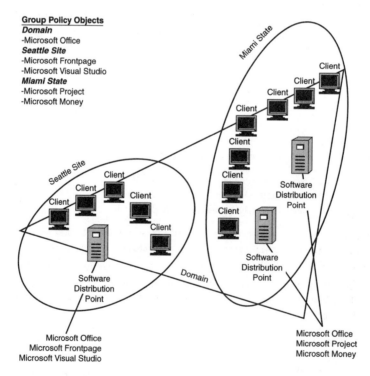

Figure 12.3 Defining group policies for the domain and for each site.

In the example shown in Figure 12.3, group policies are defined for the domain and for each site, Seattle and Miami. Objects in the Seattle site would be subject to the group policies for both the domain and the Seattle site. Likewise, objects in the Miami site would be subject to the group policies for both the domain and the Miami site. Therefore, the software distribution points for the servers in each location need to be able to provide the applications required by each site and by the domain. It would also be possible to assign policies at a more granular level within the domain's OUs.

Creating a software distribution point is as simple as creating the network share, creating the appropriate folders, copying the Windows Installer Packages and application executables to the appropriate folder, and then setting the appropriate folder permissions. The permissions should restrict everyone's read access, while enabling administrators full control, change, and read permissions. This can be made more efficient by using the Distributed File System (DFS), which redirects a common UNC path to a server within the client's site. This way, `\\fileshare\applications` could be referenced from anywhere on the network, but the actual server that a particular client connects to would be local to the client's Active Directory site.

Configuring Group Policies

After creating the package and software distribution points, all that is left is to create the GPOs. This is done using the Active Directory Users and Computers MMC snap-in. You can also configure the default software distribution points for a given group policy.

System Management Server

System Management Server (SMS) is a software distribution and management application that is part of the Microsoft BackOffice suite of products. It provides software distribution, software and hardware inventory, software metering, and remote control of users' desktops. SMS is Microsoft's application for enterprise-wide distribution of software, inventory collection, and remote desktop control and monitoring.

Hardware and Software Inventory

SMS uses the WMI and software scanners to upload hardware and software inventory information from client computers to a Microsoft SQL Server database. It is important for an organization to know the hardware and software being employed by its users, but it is also important for the SMS to have an inventory of hardware and software because other SMS components, such as software distribution, depend on the inventory for their functionality.

Software Distribution and Installation

SMS can also be used to deploy software to computers, users, and user groups. With the latest version of SMS, software distribution is rule-based. Software distribution is also integrated with software inventory to collect information about the computers, or users, to which the software is to be distributed. Based on the rules defined by the administrator, software distribution then distributes the software package to a collection of users or computers acquired from the inventory.

Software Metering

Software metering is the tracking of software use by users and computers. It can also track software use with regard to time used and license quota. Software metering can also control the use of many applications based on rules.

Diagnostics and Troubleshooting

SMS also comes with several useful tools for diagnostics and troubleshooting. NetMon, mentioned several times in this book, is a very useful network sniffer that is capable of capturing network packets traveling between two hosts on the network. Remote control, another SMS tool, enables a Helpdesk or a support person to take over a user's desktop. The support person can then diagnose and perhaps repair the problem for the user. This reduces maintenance costs because there is no visit by the Helpdesk to the user's location.

Complementing Windows 2000

SMS 2.0 and greater can be integrated into a Windows 2000 desktop management strategy. SMS complements the built-in management components of Windows 2000 by providing a software distribution infrastructure.

In Windows 2000 Server environments, SMS complements Active Directory, extending the standard change and configuration management features provided by IntelliMirror. SMS delivers an enterprise-wide change and configuration management solution for Windows environments.

Windows 2000 Remote Installation Services

The Windows 2000 remote installation service (RIS) is another component that ships with Windows 2000 Server. With RIS, it is possible to deploy Windows 2000 to the desktop. By coupling RIS with the IntelliMirror services, a complete desktop management strategy can be employed.

Deploying an operating system is no trivial task, and automating it with a software deployment application can be even more challenging. However, with the proper planning and the implementation of supporting services, remote operating system installation can greatly reduce the cost of deployment, as well as reduce the cost of desktop support.

Supporting services

RIS depends on several supporting services and prerequisites for a successful deployment. The following services must be properly deployed for RIS to function properly.

Domain Name Services (DNSs)

RIS depends on DNS, as does Active Directory, to locate directory services and clients. It is recommended that RIS use the DNS that ships with Windows 2000. If you do not use Microsoft's Windows 2000 DNS, lab testing is necessary to ensure that your DNS provides the level of service required by RIS.

Dynamic Host Configuration Protocol (DHCP) Services

Remember, RIS is installing the client operating system. Therefore, the current client operating system, if there is one, is replaced by Windows 2000. Hence, the client network interface card (NIC) must have remote start up, or Bootstrap, capabilities. This means that the client's computer starts and the NIC requests an IP address from a DHCP server. After the client has loaded the IP stack and acquired an IP address, the installation can begin. This means that DHCP must be installed and configured with IP address pools that are appropriate for your network. DHCP services can be provided by either Windows 2000 or Windows NT 4.0.

Active Directory Services

RIS is also dependent on Active Directory. Client computers and RIS servers are represented in Active Directory, and they are used during the RIS process. The RIS servers themselves are installed on Windows 2000 Servers and must have access to Active Directory DCs.

Hardware Requirements

It is also important that the RIS servers and clients meet the RIS hardware requirements. A list of hardware that is supported by RIS is available from the Microsoft Web site. This list is different from the Windows 2000 HCL. Make sure that the client and server components, such as NICs, are on the RIS HCL.

Software Distribution Points

Windows 2000 Professional needs to be copied to a file share. If you have software distribution points on your network, these might be the proper places to locate this share.

Setup and Configuration

After a Windows 2000 Server has been configured in an environment that also provides Active Directory, DNS, and DHCP services, the RIS services can be installed. A setup wizard steps you through the setup process, enabling you to choose options such as whether the RIS server responds to a client requesting service. The wizard prompts you for the Windows 2000 Professional share.

After RIS is installed, you need to authorize the RIS server to run and to define which servers will service which clients in Active Directory. This is done with the DHCP MMC snap-in.

To configure the RIS server use the Active Directory Users and Computers MMC snap-in. From here, you can configure how the RIS server responds to remote clients as well as some advanced properties.

See the Microsoft Web site or the documents that ship with Windows 2000 Server for more detailed instructions on the RIS server and client installation process.

Summary

The desktop management features included with Windows 2000 represent an exciting new dimension to the product. Never before has desktop management been so tightly integrated in a single suite of client and server operating systems. The opportunity to closely manage the desktop from an enterprise level is very achievable. With proper planning and lab testing, Windows 2000 reduces the cost of desktop ownership by managing what users can and cannot do and by simplifying application and operating system deployment.

13

Developing an Administration Strategy

DEVELOPING AN ADMINISTRATION STRATEGY IS A DIRECT product of the business requirement analysis created when putting together your Active Directory and Windows 2000 design process. The Active Directory design and the administrative strategy are closely related and possibly an iterative process.

Moving to Active Directory and Windows 2000 typically includes an effort to provide a centralized administration strategy. Does this mean that a central staff administrates and controls the entire Windows 2000 and Active Directory? This is not necessarily so. Moving to a centralized administration strategy includes defining a series of roles and responsibilities that include a variety of implementations. This chapter discusses those choices and the resulting options.

Regardless of what system or family of systems you are coming from, moving to Active Directory and Windows 2000 provides you with the opportunity to clean the slate and to create an administrative strategy and scheme that meets your needs. This chapter provides a framework for doing this with the tools that are available with Windows 2000 and Active Directory.

Typical Windows NT 4.0 Administration Models

Windows NT 4.0 Server provides for a few simple administrative models. The typical smaller organization uses the simple administrative model that includes administrators and users. This structure usually contains only a handful of administrators who have the rights for performing all the administrative functions. This includes adding users, groups, servers, hardware components, file shares, creating profiles, and changing policies.

NT 4.0 does provide some level of granularity with printer operators, backup operators, account operators, and server operators. These functions are not used unless the organization becomes so large that the special functions can organizational be divided between individuals. All these functions are subsets of the functionality that a domain administrator has.

In larger organizations with a domain structure that includes a single domain account for users and resource domain services like Microsoft Exchange, the administrator account is used within a resource domain. Having the administrator account within the resource domain, gives those administrators full control of all the servers in that domain. In this scenario, the control is divided by way of the domain.

The unfortunate reality of these scenarios is that because emergencies or short term administrative needs, the administrator password for a domain is passed around or additional special accounts with administrator privileges are created. Audits of these environments indicate that the best intentions for controlling the environment usually lead to forgotten accounts with the administrative password. Sure, you can create accounts that expire based on a given date, but it is easy to avoid this; thus, you can end up with a growing list of accounts with administrative privileges in an organization.

With Active Directory and Windows 2000, you are able to create administrative roles and tools that permit specific capabilities, which map directly to administrative strategy. This chapter investigates the options available to you as the designer of an administrative strategy.

Windows 2000 Administrative Groups

Windows 2000 and Active Directory provide groups already configured into the product. They are located in two folders: the Builtin folder and the Users folder.

Builtin Folder Groups

In the builtin folder, Windows 2000 provides built-in administrative groups. These groups are used to control the management or use of the Windows 2000 environment. The Windows 2000 environment provides the following administrative groups.

The account operators group members are able to administer domain user and group accounts. This is typically used to add and delete users, create and modify group accounts, and change passwords.

The administrators group members have full administrative capabilities in the domain. The members of this group can perform any administrative function in the domain.

Members of the backup operators group are restricted to running the backup program. The members of the backup operators group are able to backup files and folders.

The guest and users group members have the ability to use the computer they are logged into and to save documents, but these members are not able to install programs or make changes to the systems. The guest group is typically used for access to specific resources.

Members of the print operators group have privileges for administering printers within the domain. They have the ability to purge print queues and to set priorities for print jobs.

The server operators group members have the rights to administer domain servers.

User Folder

In the Users folder, there are several predefined groups. These groups include the Domain Admins, Domain Computers, Domain Guests, Domain Users, Enterprise Admins, Group Policy Admins, Schema Admins, and Cert Publishers. Each of these groups provides for users with specific access to resources in the domain or enterprise.

The domain users have specific user rights within the domain. Enterprise Admins have administrative rights within the enterprise.

Windows 2000 Administrative Strategies

There are three main strategies for Windows 2000 administration: centralized administration, moving administrative capabilities and tools out to the user, and a hybrid approach.

Administration Strategy Decision Criteria

Each organization should consciously determine an administration strategy. Most organizations have a legacy of staff and "organization" around operating their environment that is in place for reasons ranging from, "This is how we have always done it," to "We only have the budget for three staff members." The Windows NT 4.0 operations that are in place today are organized through a collection of departmental administrators, all with administrative rights. These organizations are organized through the grassroots installation of Windows NT. In contrast, some organizations have installed Windows NT from a centralized organization and have implemented a strict process that mimics their mainframe operations. Each of these existing organizations can benefit from the flexibility that Active Directory provides for administering your environment.

With Active Directory and Windows 2000, each organization should evaluate the correct model for administering their environment. There are several key criteria for evaluating how they should approach the problem. These criteria include control, demographics of the organization, security requirements, support expectations, and flexibility. These are seen as the foundations for evaluating how to build your administration strategy.

Controlling your environment is fundamental to your administration. The level of control you want over your environment dictates what you need to implement. As an example, the level of control dictates what type of Group Policy Objects (GPOs) you should create and where in the Site, Domain, and Organizational Unit (SDOU) structure the policies should be placed. Your level of control can also dictate the type of workstations you permit in your network.

The demographics of your organization also play an important part in how you need to set up your administration. If your organization has administrative staff in remote locations, you might want to distribute some of the responsibilities to them. If the end users have a high computer literacy, you might decide to distribute some of the administrative responsibilities to the end-user or you might reduce some of the control.

Security is a big factor in how you design your administration. All the requirements are related and your requirements for security have an impact on how you design your SDOU structure, what capabilities you give various administrative groups, and the processes you put in place to support the implementation.

Support expectations means the type of response and the responsiveness to problems. Depending on the sophistication and training of the user community, remote control or Web-based FAQ sheets might not meet the requirements of the community. You might need to have local technical support to meet the community's user requirements.

Flexibility in your administrative model plays an important role in defining the service you need to provide and, thus, how you define your administrative model. The requirement for flexibility has an impact on how you distribute administrative control and where you put GPOs in your SDOU hierarchy. A typical requirement for flexibility is at the desktop, where various groups require the ability to install business specific applications. Other levels of flexibility include the requirement in organizations to bring up their own servers and printers or to modify their organizational unit (OU) container.

Centralized Administration Strategy

With Windows 2000 and Active Directory, you are able to develop a multitude of strategies for managing your environment. A simple, first approach is to mimic your typical Windows NT 4.0 environment by having a few specific accounts with unlimited capability to administer your environment. Although this short changes the capabilities in Windows 2000, organizationally, it might make the transition to the new technology easier in the short run. In the long run, it can result in the difficult hurdle of taking away privileges when a more discriminating administrative model is put in place.

Beyond mimicking the Window NT 4.0 administrative model, a centralized administration strategy can take advantage of the features that Active Directory, Windows 2000, and the tools provide as part of the product offering.

Why a Centralized Administration Strategy?

As stated earlier, administration can be viewed to be composed of several components. In Table 13.1, you can see an example of how the factors affect an interest in a centralized administrative model.

Table 13.1 **Centralized Administration Analysis**

Administrative Requirement	Disposition
Control	High need for control over the environment because lack of technological understanding and changes in the organization.
Demographics of Organization	Users are not sophisticated in use of technology and the training expense is not available at this time.
Security	Restrict access to confidential information on desktops and network.
Support Expectations	Users have a variety of needs, but most are use to a mainframe support through phoning a Helpdesk.
Flexibility	Does not have a known requirement for immediate changes to environment.

Centralized Administration Strategy Example

Based on the requirements described in the previous section, a centralized strategy should be implemented. The implementation includes the following implementation components.

The SDOU structure includes GPOs at the domain level to provide control for a three desktop-type lockdowns. The GPOs define three types of users. They are the general computer user who has all the basic user functionality. This includes the operating system, connectivity and access requirements, and base-level application support. The base-level application support includes the standard desktop applications and enterprise-wide horizontal applications.

The second level of desktop type is for the sales and managers in the organization who need to access applications that have specific financial information.

The third type of desktop is for IT. This desktop has access to the base-level applications and to the IT-specific applications that run the environment.

These GPOs would flow to each workstation based on inclusion in groups. Access to applications that fall outside the three desktop types would be applied to users based on inclusion in application-specific groups.

Administration would be held by a centralized group, and the division of responsibilities would be distributed in two tiers. The technical leads would have access to separate accounts for specific enterprise-wide changes and significant changes to the infrastructure. This would include items, such as bringing on a new server or changing GPOs and applying them to Active Directory. The second tier would permit administration for maintenance items like backups and additions, deletions, and modifications for accounts and computers.

In addition, the requirements call for a deployment of tools that support the centralized environment. This can be a multi-media support approach that includes a Web page for support and IT project status. A Helpdesk that is staffed at such a level where users find a real person, rather than voice-mail (most of the time) and also an implementation that supports remote control of each workstation.

Decentralized Administration Strategy

Another strategy is to move administrative capabilities and tools out as far as possible. Under this strategy, as much of the administration as possible is distributed to the end user. In some ways, this is happening on the Internet today. If you try to access some Internet sites, you need to register yourself and give them valuable demographic information. This is essentially "adding" you to the user database for the system. If the underlying theme of your strategy is to move to end user (or self) administration, the culture of your organization needs to be evaluated against the capabilities of the technology and the real impact. One way to evaluate your organization is to identify the cost of administrative support and the cost of the end user's time. If the value of the person's time exceeds the value of the administrator's time, this strategy probably does not make sense. A highly paid medical professional should probably not be burdened with the responsibility of administrative accounts if a more cost effective staff person is able to perform the task.

Another roadblock to pushing the responsibility out to the end user is the requirement for training. You need to ask those in the organization if this additional responsibility is going to burden the community too much.

Pushing the administrative responsibilities out from the center is best justified, if the end user or regional IT person can be more responsive to the users' or the organization's needs. We have seen an example of this with the advent of word processors. A typing pool or an administrative support person originally performed word processing. Today most executives perform much of their word processing themselves. The task of writing a document out and passing it to someone and then reviewing it, takes more time that it takes to write and proof the document yourself.

When distributing administrative tasks, you want to make the tasks more responsive to the user's needs. Here is an example to illustrate this point. An end-user is able to update part of the directory information through a Web page that has access to the directory. Because the user authenticates to the directory, Active Directory knows who the person is and permits updates to the individual's Active Directory entry. In this scenario, the end user can change only their information in Active Directory. Some fields are protected from change by Active Directory.

Why a Decentralized Administration Strategy?

A decentralized administration strategy is typically motivated by the responsiveness and accuracy of the task. Simple things, like updating your address or changing your password, take time when someone on the other end of the phone is there. The capability to perform the action is immediate when you are able to perform the action directly. Rather than listing to you spell your street address and thus create a possible inaccurate entry, a user that updates their address information is going to have their address entered correctly.

Table 13.2 identifies an example of the findings leading to a decentralized administration strategy.

Table 13.2 **Decentralized Administration Analysis**

Administrative Requirement	**Disposition**
Control	The need for control is limited. Users and organizations use the network and network resources as they would other utility services. The network responsibility ends at the plug in the wall. Desktops are the responsibility of the business units.
Demographics of Organization	Users are sophisticated. Everyone has their own PC or laptop.
Security	Restrict access to confidential information on desktops and network. Users are responsible for desktop data. IT is responsible for Network data.
Support Expectations	Users and organizations continue to be autonomous. They work with IT on network issues, but seek desktop support as an exception.
Flexibility	There is a high requirement for desktop flexibility and access to the network from multiple locations. New applications are brought up at will to the business unit level.

Decentralized Administration Strategy Example

The requirements described in the Table 13.2 lead to a decentralized administration strategy. A decentralized administration requires less work in developing and testing GPOs in the organization. There is still a requirement for policies to be applied to all workstations that are attached to the network and use network resources. Centrally, computer accounts and user accounts need to be created to give users access to the network.

Based on the previously stated requirements, the organization needs to develop procedures for allowing organizations to join the network. This should be as automated as possible. After inclusion in the network has been established, it is up to the business unit or user to identify the workstation unique capabilities that need to be put in place.

In this example, there are sophisticated user communities, but there are not seasoned IT professionals existing in the business units. This prevents us from creating an OU structure, and it prevents business unit IT professionals from establishing GPOs as part of their OU.

The level of administration distribution in this example includes the self-administration of accounts, directory information, group participation, and password reset. In the business units, administrative support personnel are given basic training in printer administration, application support, and basic troubleshooting techniques. Finally, the limited central IT staff rarely provide immediate problem resolution. The central IT staff is focused on project work.

Hybrid Administration Strategy

The third strategy is a hybrid strategy. This strategy employs components of both the centralized administration strategy and the decentralized administration strategy. From a centralized administration view, this strategy addresses enterprise-wide considerations, such as communication between organizations and defining minimum functionality standards. From a decentralized administration view, this strategy addresses the need for autonomy and enables business units to make changes as their business dictates.

Why a Hybrid Administration Strategy?

A typical hybrid strategy uses centralized management for network-wide operations and decentralized operations to the regional offices where they fit. Updates or maintenance of the information is performed by those who know the information and are most interested in keeping up to date. A simple scenario for the hybrid approach is to have the centralized IT staff architect new capabilities and establish the services. The centralized staff's concerns would be functionality, disaster recovery procedures, and capacity planning, to name a few. These are typically administered and controlled by the central IT organization, regardless. The regional organization performs the tasks that are specific to them. This would include adding and deleting users and monitoring capacity within the framework of the centralized administration staff. Table 13.3

illustrates how unique requirements can be considered and planned for locally by monitoring the capacity planning in the region. This approach might include a variety of scenarios based on how the company is organized.

Table 13.3 **Hybrid Administration Analysis**

Administrative Requirement	Disposition
Control	The need for control exists. Regional offices need autonomy, but they also want backup support for the organization.
Demographics of Organization	Users are sophisticated. Everyone has their own PC or laptop. There is IT support in remote offices.
Security	Restrict access to confidential information on desktops and network. Users are responsible for desktop data. Some data is restricted to regional offices that want their own security.
Support Expectations	Users and organizations continue to be autonomous. They work with IT on network issues, but seek desktop support as an exception.
Flexibility	There is a high requirement for desktop flexibility and access to the network from multiple locations. New applications are brought up at will to the business unit level. There is IT support in regional offices.

Hybrid Administration

In the hybrid administration model, the centralized IT organization works with regional IT organizations to divide responsibility. In the extreme case, the Windows 2000 environment mimics the Windows NT 4.0 environment with specific trusts between Forests.

In this example, based on the description in the Table 13.3, the requirements are satisfied by creating a centralized model that has regional domains. Each regional domain is administered by the central office and the regional office, but each office has the capability to create OUs in their domain as needed. The centralized organization can also provide GPO examples for use and suggest standards by example rather than by enforcement.

Administrative Models for Windows 2000 Using Active Directory

Active Directory provides the mechanism for administering a large enterprise and establishes unique administrative requirements throughout the organization. This section does not consider the potential complexity that is created by multiple administrative models, but it does review the capability for multiple administrative models.

The capability to establish multiple contexts for administration is inherent in the design of Active Directory. By establishing a variety of OUs, an organization can create the group policies, security groups, and administrative tools to permit specific administrative capabilities.

OU-Specific Administration

One strategy is to establish specific administration within an OU. There are several ways to implement this. The flexibility provided in Active Directory makes almost anything possible. This section looks at two scenarios. The first scenario is based on an organization that has three levels of a possible large multinational administration. The major geographies are autonomous, and inside of the geographies are locations requiring administration. Table 13.4 describes the organizational requirements and the impact on administration. Figure 13.1 is a picture of a European domain expanded in the context of this implementation. There is a corporate domain, a European domain, and a North American domain.

Table 13.4 **OU Requirements and Administrative Impact**

Region (Domain)	OU Implementation	Administrative Strategy
Europe (European domain)	OU for each country	Domains: No standards defined for the organization. European-unique security and desktop standards.
		OU: Complete administrative control within OU.
North America (North American domain)	OU for each time zone	Domain: NA security, desktop standards, standard applications, and enterprise applications.
		OU: Eastern, Central, Mountain, and Western. Regional administrators for maintenance. Little design authority in OU.

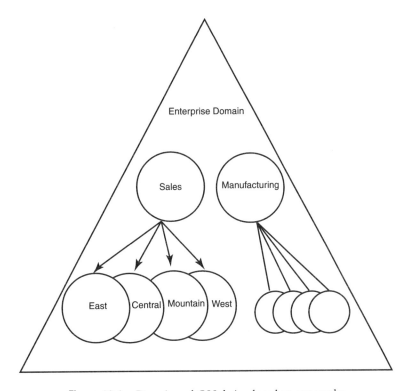

Figure 13.1 Domain and OU design based on geography.

The second scenario, in Table 13.5, is with an enterprise that is divided based on corporate function. This company has a single domain and has OUs for each of the corporate functions. Each corporate function has a its own resources defined by location. As an example, manufacturing has an OU for each manufacturing plant. At each plant, an administration team collectively manages the manufacturing OU and manages the contents of the OU based on their location. Under this same design, the marketing organization, which only exists at corporate headquarters, has an OU that is managed by the centralized IT staff. Figure 13.2 gives a subset of what the domain and the OUs look like. Each has their own number of OUs based on the organization. Associated with each location OU are users, computers, GPOs, and printers.

Table 13.5   **Domain and OU Based on Corporate Function**

Corporate Organization (OU)	OU Implementation	Administrative Strategy
		There is a single domain for the entire enterprise.
Finance	OU based on each physical office location	All the OUs are managed by corporate IS with input from a central administrator for Finance.
Sales	OU for each sales region	All the OUs are managed by corporate IS with input from a central administrator for Sales.
Engineering	OU for each manufacturing plant	Each OU is managed by the Engineering organization IT staff at each plant.
Manufacturing	OU for each manufacturing plant	Each OU is managed by the Engineering organization IT staff at each plant.
Corporate	Single OU for corporate headquarters	The Corporate OU is managed by central IT at headquarters.
Marketing	Single OU for corporate headquarters	The Marketing OU is managed by central IT at headquarters.

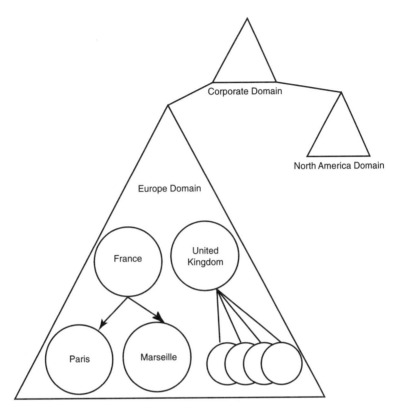

Figure 13.2 OU design based on organization.

In each of these examples, the administrative tasks are divided between the centralized staff and OU administrators.

The role of the OU administrator is dependent on the namespace design you have chosen. Each of the examples can be further customized. Within each OU, administration can span from full control to a dministration for specific tasks, such as changing passwords or adding users. If your OUs were based on specific application use, administrators would have OU administration only for the applications that they have administrative responsibility for. In any case, your OU structure design should complement the way you want to administer your environment.

Summary

Creating an administrative model is important for effectively managing your environment. Microsoft has clearly provided the tools to distribute your administration or to centralize your administration. With a careful analysis of your business requirements coupled with an understanding of the features available in Windows 2000 administrations, an administrative strategy for almost any scenario can be created.

Active Directory enables the delivery and security to support this powerful set of capabilities.

14

Windows 2000 Networking Services

WINDOWS 2000 IS UNIQUE COMPARED WITH MOST operating systems because it embraces a multitude of industry standard protocols and services for advanced networking. Some of these services are fundamental to your network, such as Transmission Control Protocol/Internet Protocol (TCP/IP), and some are complementary, such as Dynamic Host Configuration Protocol (DHCP), domain name system (DNS), Windows Internet Naming Service (WINS), and Quality of Service (QoS). In any case, the networking services you choose to implement and how you choose to implement them to achieve your business objectives is an important task as a Network Architect or IS Manager. As you plan your implementation of Active Directory, it is important to also focus on planning for the implementation of these network services.

Whether you need to implement a single local area network (LAN) for your business, connect multiple offices together forming a wide area network (WAN), or simply extend your network to provide support for remote users, suppliers, or business partners, Windows 2000 offers the advanced networking services required to meet your specific organization's needs. However, without an adequate understanding of how these network services should be designed and implemented, it is possible to deploy network services that can negatively affect the performance of Active Directory in your organization.

This chapter will explore some of the primary networking services contained within Windows 2000. This chapter introduces some of the core networking services of Windows 2000 and presents design scenarios common to many Network Architects and organizations, specifically TCP/IP and a subset of the TCP/IP protocol suite—DHCP. In addition, this chapter discusses how Windows 2000 advanced networking services can be implemented and configured to support the design requirements as well as what considerations to account for when implementing the services.

Windows 2000 Network Services

It is assumed that most readers have a solid understanding of Windows NT networking; therefore, most of this chapter focuses on the improvements Windows 2000 delivers. In other words, the focus is on the new features that Windows introduces, and how they can be used to meet your business objectives.

The Foundation: TCP/IP

TCP/IP is an industry standard protocol originally developed for the Department of Defense (DoD) in the 1960's. Since that time, businesses, manufactures, and standard bodies, such as the Internet Engineering Task Force (IETF), have embraced TCP/IP as the standard for implementing Internet technologies. Windows 2000 implements TCP/IP as the default protocol during the setup process and relies on TCP/IP for most of the functionality of components and services associated with the operating system. These components and services include Active Directory, DHCP, DNS, Internet Information Server (IIS), and WINS. Without TCP/IP, these Windows 2000 services will not operate.

With the widespread use of TCP/IP and the requirement to maintain a unique IP address for each network and each host on the network, IS organizations were presented with a significant management challenge. Network Managers had to maintain unique IP addresses for each device in their network and ensure that these addresses did not conflict with other addresses throughout their enterprise. In large organizations, this was a difficult task, and mistakes would often result in taking down a critical system or application, which affected business operations and productivity. To alleviate such problems, much time was spent maintaining IP standards and a database of IP addresses that associated computers and devices connected to the network with a unique IP address. To lessen the burden of maintaining this data, an industry standard was developed to provide automatic configuration of IP address information. This standard is called DHCP.

In addition to DHCP, Windows 2000 also includes automatic IP address configuration functionality called Automatic Private IP Addressing (APIPA). In the absence of a static IP address configuration or a DHCP server, APIPA will self-configure the Windows 2000 computer with an IP address from the range of allowable private IP addresses. APIPA will randomly select a unique IP address from the range, 169.254.0.1 through 169.254.255.254, and it will set the subnet mask to 255.255.0.0. This self-configuration greatly simplifies setting up a small home or business network. It is important to note, however, that the IP addresses in this range are not routable on the public Internet. Consequently, machines with IP addresses in this range cannot access the Internet without utilizing a proxy server or a firewall that does network address translation (NAT).

Windows 2000 DHCP Services

Microsoft adopted the DHCP standard and deployed it with Windows NT Server. This service has been expanded and improved with Windows 2000. The DHCP Server is an installable service that runs on top of Windows 2000 and is based on industry standards as defined by the IETF's "Request for Comment (RFC) 2131" and "Request for Comment (RFC) 2132." Since its introduction in Windows NT Advance Server 3.1, Microsoft has made many improvements and enhancements to the DHCP server.

Windows 2000 Server implements the DHCP server with several key enhancements. One of the more notable enhancements includes integrating DHCP with DNS so that DHCP servers and clients can register themselves with DNS by using the DHCP protocol. With this integration, the DHCP server can act as a proxy on behalf of the client to register both an address resource record (A record) and a pointer record (PTR record) for forward and reverse lookups through DNS. For more information on DNS, please refer to Chapter 8, "Designing the DNS Namespace."

Another important enhancement of the Windows 2000 DHCP server is the addition of advanced monitoring and reporting capabilities. Using the DHCP Manager (an MMC snap-in), Network Administrators can now graphically view statistical data of DHCP through the Simple Network Management Protocol (SNMP) and the Management Information Bases (MIBs). In this way, a Network Administrator can monitor the status of a DHCP server and determine how many addresses of the available DHCP address pool are available versus depleted or view performance information for the DHCP server in terms of number of leases processed, number of requests, and number of negative status acknowledgement messages (NACK) processed. When certain defined thresholds are reached, the DHCP server sends an administrative alert notifying Network Administrators of *yellow* or *red* conditions. For example, a yellow event is when the address pool has loaned 75 percent of addresses in the available range. A red event is when the address pool is completely depleted.

RFCs Related to BOOTP, DHCP, and NetBIOS Over TCP/IP

The following is a list of significant RFCs related to DHCP, DNS, and BOOTP:

RFC 1001— Protocol standard for a NetBIOS service on a TCP/UDP transport

RFC 1002— Protocol standard for a NetBIOS service on a TCP/UDP transport

RFC 1534— Interoperation between DHCP and BOOTP

RFC 1542— Clarifications and Extensions for the Bootstrap Protocol

RFC 2131— Dynamic Host Configuration Protocol

RFC 2132— DHCP Options and BOOTP Vendor Extensions

RFC2610— DHCP Options for Service Location Protocol

The Windows 2000 DHCP Server also incorporates support for vendor specific option classes and user option classes. For vendors, this means that they can leverage Windows 2000 DHCP servers to implement specific IP configuration options unique to that vendor, such as an option to dynamically flash a network card's BIOS. For users, DHCP scopes can be defined to detect certain types of network clients and then issue different IP configuration options for each client. For example, Windows 95 laptop users without an Active Directory client might need to be configured with shorter lease durations and the IP address of a WINS server. Windows 2000 Professional Desktop users, on the other hand, might require longer lease durations and might not need to use WINS for IP to NetBIOS address translation because Windows 2000 Professional clients can use Active Directory and DNS for this function. The DHCP service in Windows 2000 is able to detect the type of operating system on the requesting workstation and sends configuration information that is appropriate for the client. An important issue to note when designing a DHCP implementation: Some options will not be supported if there are multiple DHCP severs running on multiple operating systems in the environment. There are DHCP servers that run on UNIX and other operating systems that do not support all the option classes in the Windows 2000 DHCP server.

Other Windows 2000 DHCP enhancements include the capability to configure DHCP multicast scopes so that DHCP can be leveraged to configure a group of DHCP clients for videoconferencing, for example. Windows 2000 requires that all DHCP servers on the network be authorized as well. This prevents unauthorized DHCP servers from initializing and issuing incorrect addresses to requesting DHCP clients. With this feature, Network Administrators can eliminate situations where a developer accidentally installs a test DHCP server with a 10.0.0.0 scope that might conflict with other production DHCP servers in the enterprise. Finally, Windows 2000 Advance Server can implement Windows Clustering (based on the Microsoft Cluster Server), which will enable a Network Administrator to configure a virtual DHCP server for higher system availability. If a cluster node fails, users are transparently redirected to the other node in the cluster for IP address configuration—without adverse impact to operations or productivity.

In Figure 14.1, a Windows 98 laptop user, who travels from location to location, establishes a Virtual Private Network (VPN) connection over a shared IP network (ISP) and obtains IP configuration information (Default Gateway, DNS server, or WINS server) from a Windows 2000 DHCP server using a short (three day) lease. Similarly, a static Windows 2000 Active Directory desktop user establishes a LAN connection and receives IP configuration from a Windows 2000 DHCP server using a longer lease duration.

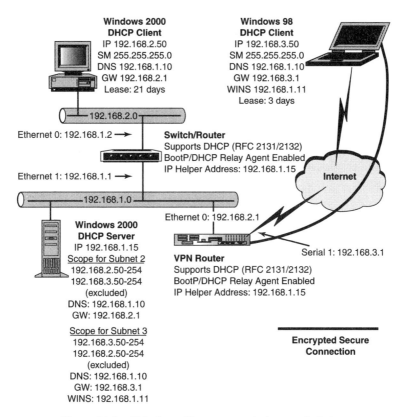

Windows 2000
DHCP Client
IP 192.168.2.50
SM 255.255.255.0
DNS 192.168.1.10
GW 192.168.2.1
Lease: 21 days

Windows 98
DHCP Client
IP 192.168.3.50
SM 255.255.255.0
DNS 192.168.1.10
GW 192.168.3.1
WINS 192.168.1.11
Lease: 3 days

192.168.2.0

Ethernet 0: 192.168.1.2 →

Switch/Router
Supports DHCP (RFC 2131/2132)
BootP/DHCP Relay Agent Enabled
IP Helper Address: 192.168.1.15

Ethernet 1: 192.168.1.1 →

Internet

192.168.1.0

Ethernet 0: 192.168.2.1

Windows 2000
DHCP Server
IP 192.168.1.15
Scope for Subnet 2
192.168.2.50-254
192.168.3.50-254
(excluded)
DNS: 192.168.1.10
GW: 192.168.2.1

Scope for Subnet 3
192.168.3.50-254
192.168.2.50-254
(excluded)
DNS: 192.168.1.10
GW: 192.168.3.1
WINS: 192.168.1.11

VPN Router
Supports DHCP (RFC 2131/2132)
BootP/DHCP Relay Agent Enabled
IP Helper Address: 192.168.1.15

Serial 1: 192.168.3.1

Encrypted Secure
Connection

Figure 14.1   This figure illustrates a typical network design,
comprising both desktop and laptop computers.

The desktop users are located on a separate subnet within a building, and they
need access to network resources and the Internet using TCP/IP. The laptop
users need access to corporate information and applications from a remote location.
To facilitate proper IP configuration for both user types, the diagram depicts how a
Network Architect could design their network to automatically configure and manage
their computers using Windows 2000 DHCP services.

There are a number of DHCP deployment considerations when designing your
network. These considerations will be explored in the next section. For example, if
remote users are located on a small LAN in a remote office that has a 56Kbps frame
relay connection to the corporate network, locating a DHCP server close to these
users is advised because of potential latency on the WAN network connection and the
inability of the workstations to connect to the network if they are unable to obtain an
IP address form a DHCP server.

Deploying Windows 2000 DHCP Services

Deploying DHCP in a Windows 2000 environment requires careful planning and consideration. You must account for the quantity and type of computers in your environment; the classification, work habits, and needs of the users who use these computers; and the relative location and access methods of users who access the information and network resources within your enterprise.

DHCP is so important to large IP networks that Network Architects spend as much time considering configuration alternatives as they do designing a backup and recovery strategy. DHCP and its adjacent service, DNS, constitute much of the foundation of a Windows 2000 network. Without a well-designed foundation, the stability and scalability of a network is compromised.

Consider the following situations:

- If a user cannot access the network to retrieve critical information or to run a business application required to place an order because of TCP/IP configuration problems, the entire business process is affected.

- If an administrator or Helpdesk support staff is bogged down with troubleshooting and supporting TCP/IP configuration problems and issues, they are wasting valuable time spent otherwise helping users work through issues running a new business application or preparing next year's budget for a new branch office network upgrade. A properly designed DHCP implementation helps to mitigate this type of situation.

- A server running DHCP in your network fails and client computers attempt to re-register themselves but can't, or they do so from a DHCP server across a slow wide-area link. Planning your network for fault-tolerance (including DHCP and other core Windows 2000 services), prevents your users from being negatively affected by these outages.

In any of these situations, spending effort, time, and money resolving TCP/IP configuration or management issues impacts a business' bottom line. If a Network Architect properly designs a Windows 2000 DHCP environment, deploying and supporting TCP/IP (with all its diverse configuration options and settings) becomes easy and manageable, saving valuable resources for more important business tasks.

Table 14.1 can be used to design your network for deploying Windows 2000 DHCP services. The table identifies key factors that impact a client workstation and then lists design considerations that need to be accounted for when deploying DHCP. When you account for these factors, you will be able to define the number and location of DHCP servers in your network and the configuration options each DHCP scope needs to contain.

Table 14.1 **Key Factors to Consider When Designing a DHCP Deploying Network**

Factor	Design Considerations
Network Size	Number of computers that need to be configured by DHCP (and those that can't or should not use DHCP).
Network Topology	Type and speed of network connections between users and DHCP servers.
Location	Within a building/floor, across a WAN link in a branch office, or across a dial-up or VPN link from home, a home office, or hotel.
Client Types	Windows 95/98, Windows NT, UNIX, Macintosh, and Novell.
Common DHCP Configuration Options (sample)	• Default Gateway (router) • WINS Servers (legacy clients) • DNS Servers, domain name
Monitoring, Reporting, and Security	Who will be able to add DHCP servers to the network? Who will administer DHCP? Thresholds, alters, and statistics.
DHCP Superscopes	Determine when to use these to avoid DHCP conflicts between a client and multiple DHCP servers.
Reservations	DNS servers, WINS servers, TCP/IP print servers, and UNIX clients that are configured using another method.
Lease Durations	Longer leases for stable networks that have a large address pool (for example, 10.0.0.0). Shorter leases for dynamic networks, or mobile laptop users who move frequently.
Routers	Which routers to configure? BOOTP/DHCP Relay agents and IP Helper addresses this.
Redundancy	Configure scopes to be split among servers (70/30 split).

Using Windows 2000 DHCP services, Network Managers can reduce the time and costs associated with configuring and managing IP hosts. With Windows 2000 and Active Directory, they are able to eliminate situations in which improper IP configurations can cause severe network outages and adversely impact business operations. Windows 2000 DHCP services are an integral part of Windows 2000; all organizations that use or plan to use Windows 2000 should design their networks with DHCP in mind.

WINS

WINS is an integral part of Windows. It enables mapping of NetBIOS computer names to IP addresses, just as DNS enables mapping of DNS host names to IP addresses. Before Windows 2000, WINS was a requirement for Windows-based IP networks. WINS provided IP address resolution so that users could easily browse for network resources within a Windows NT Domain, without having to know the fully qualified DNS name or the IP address.

Before Windows 2000, WINS could be difficult to configure and administer. Fortunately, Microsoft includes a new and improved version of WINS with Windows 2000. In Windows 2000, WINS is designed primary for legacy support of Windows 9x, Windows NT and Windows for workgroup's clients. When moving to Windows 2000, you will likely run in mixed-mode until all computers in your network are migrated to Windows 2000 or installed with an Active Directory client. In addition, it is important to note that there might be custom-built applications or third-party commercial applications that will require NetBIOS name resolution and, consequently, will require WINS. Administrators must complete an inventory of all the applications in the network environment before upgrading to Windows 2000 and determine if any of them require NetBIOS name resolution.

Because Active Directory uses DNS to identify computers, users, and other devices within your network, Windows 2000 no longer uses NetBIOS to identify computers, and so WINS is not required. However, because WINS is required for mixed mode, Microsoft incorporated some significant improvements to WINS in Windows 2000. Mixed-mode in Windows 2000 will be discussed later in this chapter. Table 14.2 describes some of the new features and enhancements to WINS in Windows 2000.

Table 14.2 **New WINS Features in Windows 2000**

Feature/Enhancement	Description
Persistent Connections	Enables WINS replication partners to maintain a persistent connection with each other for improved replication.
Manual Tombstoning	Eliminates propagation of undeleted records.

Feature/Enhancement	Description
Improved Management	WINS is now managed using an MMC snap-in, allowing for easy, customizable task pads to be created and distributed to network administrators.
Improved Filtering and Searching	WINS was always very difficult to manage and troubleshoot in large networks. These improvements make it easier to filter views and quickly search for records based on specific criteria.
Dynamic Record Deletion and Multi-Select	Both dynamic and static records can now be deleted, and support for selecting multiple records for deletion has been added.
Record Verification	Ability to quickly check the WINS database for consistency has been added. In prior versions, it was very difficult to verify the state of a WINS database.
Export Function	You can now export the WINS database to a CSV file for manipulation by Excel and other tools.
Fault-Tolerance	Added support for specifying more than two WINS servers on Windows 2000 and Windows 98 clients.
Dynamic Re-Registration	Clients can re-register without having to reboot the WINS server.

Similar to DNS and DHCP, WINS requires careful planning. Many of the same principles apply to WINS as they do to DNS and DHCP. For example, WINS lookups across a slow network link can cause delays when browsing for network resources. Consider locating a WINS server at each end of a slow WAN link. Consider fault-tolerance as well. Initially, it is recommended as an industry best practice to install two WINS servers, a primary and a backup, as *automatic partners*. This is a new feature of WINS in Windows 2000. A best practice is to configure a WINS server and backup WINS server for every 10,000 computers on a network.

WINS, Mixed-Mode, and Native Mode

Until all the existing Windows NT Server Domain Controllers (DCs) and Windows 9x/NT clients are upgraded to Windows 2000 with Active Directory, it will be necessary to maintain WINS for backward compatibility. This transitional period is referred to as *mixed-mode*. This is different from *Native Mode*, which relies exclusively on Active Directory and DNS for name resolution.

While in mixed-mode, Windows 2000 DCs present themselves as BDCs to down-level clients (clients running Windows 9x/NT). In this way, these DCs support both Windows NT/LAN Manager (NTLM) and Kerberos authentication protocols. After the upgrade to Windows 2000 is complete and the environment is migrated to Native Mode several changes take place:

- DCs no longer support the NTLM authentication protocol and process.
- The DC emulating the PDC no longer synchronizes with Windows NT BDCs.
- Windows NT BDCs can no longer be added to the Windows 2000 domain.
- Windows clients without Active Directory support, such as Windows 3.11 and Windows NT Workstation 4.0 clients, will not be able to utilize all the functionality of Active Directory.

WINS Interoperability

If using WINS with other services, such as DHCP and DNS, there are several considerations to be addressed for complete interoperability. For example, if you use DHCP, you should consider configuring your DHCP scopes to support WINS. This means using DHCP option 46 to identify WINS servers and using DHCP option 44 to define the client node type. In addition, you should consider setting your DHCP lease duration to coincide with the WINS renewal intervals. Doing so will eliminate lease traffic and prevent unnecessary WINS renewal processes.

For example, if you have a large number of NetBIOS clients who also use DNS for accessing the Internet, consider implementing WINS lookup on your DNS servers. Microsoft's DNS server supports this capability, as do many third-party DNS servers. This will allow WINS to be the final resolution point for client computers looking to resolve a host name that does not have a DNS entry.

WINS is a vital and important part of a Windows-based IP network. Although WINS has been known to cause great difficulties when it doesn't work correctly, more times than not, it is simply a matter of understanding how WINS works and configuring it correctly in the first place. Fortunately, Windows 2000 implements a new and improved WINS service, and because many enterprises will be running in a mixed-mode for some period of time, WINS interoperability and legacy support will continue to be an important part of your network design.

QoS

One of the most recent advances in networking is a result of work by vendors and independent software vendors (ISVs) for implementing techniques to improve the QoS on networks. These techniques are designed to improve the service quality of applications, especially when users are accessing the applications, which typically reside in a data center, across a WAN, or through a VPN connection across the Internet. QoS is implemented differently depending on the vendor and the device type you are configuring for QoS. For example, Cisco Systems implements QoS in release 12.0 of its IOS operating system for switches, routers, and remote access servers. Microsoft implements QoS in Windows 2000. Together, businesses can take advantage of QoS at almost every access point within a network.

Benefits of QoS

QoS is quickly becoming an important component of large, distributed networks. As voice and data networks converge, QoS becomes increasingly important because a Network Administrator will need to set higher priority for voice over IP (VoIP) traffic than traditional IP data traffic. For businesses to leverage their existing data network investments for voice and videoconferencing, the QoS must be near 100 percent, as is the case with today's traditional voice networks.

QoS enables businesses to maximize their network investments. QoS allows Network Administrators to set service levels for applications, users, groups and computers by establishing rules of priority on systems and network devices. QoS techniques control allocation of network bandwidth to applications so that higher-priority, or delay-sensitive applications, such as an Enterprise Resource Planning (ERP) or videoconferencing application, can achieve the service level that they require to run efficiently.

Realizing the full benefits of QoS requires an end-to-end approach. In other words, to fully implement QoS, a Network Administrator should implement QoS parameters from one end (the host computer) of the network to the other end of the network (the client machine residing in a branch office over a 128K frame relay link) and all points in between.

Consider the following example: A Windows 2000 Server runs SQL Server 7.0 and a packaged sales force automation application. It resides on a Compaq ProLiant server that is located in a corporate data center in Dallas, Texas. The company's distributed sales force must review, approve, and submit all orders by the 28th of each month. On the 28th of each month, the entire sales force dials-in to the corporate network using their laptops that run Windows 2000 Professional with an IPSec client for VPN connectivity through a local ISP. Because the sales force is distributed and uses the corporate VPN heavily during this time, a Network Administrator might want to implement QoS so that the orders are submitted on time, without having to contend with other corporate traffic, such as HTTP for Web browsing.

In this example, the goal was to guarantee a service level, implementing QoS for the application and for the network ensures that the orders are received before month-end closing. To implement QoS, the server running the application and the network devices connecting the server to the client need to detect the application traffic type and/or IP addresses of the server and clients and then direct the application traffic to a set of queues. These queues would then have an associated priority level that defines the rate at which the application data is submitted to the network and the rate at which the application traffic travels through the network. The Windows 2000 SQL Server would define a higher priority to the queue that stores the sales force automation application traffic, and the network devices connecting the server to the clients (for example, switch in the data center and the VPN router) would be configured with QoS priority so that the sales force automation application traffic is serviced with higher priority than other traffic types.

Windows 2000 QoS

QoS is implemented in Windows 2000 in several ways. For traffic prioritization, QoS is implemented using 802.1p, DIFFSERV, INTSERV, and others. This chapter focuses on 802.1p, DIFFSERV, and INTSERV. Because most LANs are based on IEEE 802 technologies, such as Ethernet, Token-ring, and FDDI, 802.1p is an important technique for implementing QoS. 802.1p is a technique that leverages part of the layer-2 (Media Access Control address) header of an 802 packet. This header field can be assigned eight levels of priority, which are then leveraged by switches, routers, and network adapters to assign service levels based on queuing priorities. DIFFSERV, on the other hand, is a layer-3 implementation of QoS that defines a priority level in the header of an IP packet called the DIFFSERV codepoint (DSCP). Routers can be configured for DIFFSERV QoS so that a consistent service level can be established from one point in the network to another. DIFFSERV is not as widely adopted as 802.1p, however, DIFFSERV is gaining momentum because it can sustain service levels for low-latency applications, such as videoconferencing. INTSERV is a QoS technique that defines a guarantee of service or a controlled load.

For example, configuring a series of routers in a WAN with INTSERV can produce a guaranteed level of performance in terms of latency. QoS can be set so that latency does not exceed 20ms, or a controlled load in terms of volume, which could mean all conversations between a client and server will comprise no less than 256Kbps throughput. Unlike 802.1p and DIFFSERV, INTSERV does not rely on an underlying queuing priority; it defines a service level control to an INTSERV class on each device. In other words, a router that supports INTSERV QoS service classes.

Implementing QoS on networks is typically accomplished using a set of protocols, policies, and management tools. QoS can be implemented using Resource Reservation Protocol (RSVP) and Subnet Bandwidth Manager (SBM) protocol. Each protocol provisions network resources are based on the QoS techniques (802.1p, DIFFSERV, and INTSERV) and the priorities defined by each technique. Windows 2000 implements QoS by leveraging Active Directory and group polices. In this way, a Network Administrator can use a customizable and familiar interface (such as MMC) and set QoS on any number of computers, users, and groups. In addition, Microsoft and Cisco have worked together to create Cisco Network Services for Active Directory (CNS/AD). CNS/AD will extend a Network Administrator's ability to assign policy to include Cisco network devices using Active Directory and group policies. CNS/AD eliminates the problem of having to have two different QoS technologies from two different vendors working together. Consequently, QoS is much easier to put in place.

One consideration when designing a QoS infrastructure for your environment is that not all computers, network interface cards, and routers will support the Network Driver Interface Specification (NDIS) version needed to implement QoS. NDIS version 5 is required to implement QoS on Windows 2000. This might require an upgrade to the network interface cards or other hardware in your network environment.

To implement QoS on Windows 2000, you must install the QoS admission control service through Windows 2000 setup. After it is installed, a MMC snap-in is created that allows a Network Administrator to assign QoS on an enterprise-wide basis or by subnetwork settings. Enterprise settings take the form of QoS settings to any authenticated user, or unauthenticated users. For example, you can apply a controlled load or a guaranteed service level to any authenticated user based on packets sent and received with certain flow limits on a single conversation or aggregated for all conversations. Settings include data rates in Kbits/sec, peak data rates in Kbits/sec, or duration in minutes. The default policy setting for data rate is 500Kbits/sec and full media speed (100Mbps) for peak data rates.

To implement QoS on a subnet, simply add the subnetwork's IP address and mask to the QoS admission control MMC snap-in, and then assign configuration to each subnet. Like with enterprise settings, it is possible assign traffic settings based on data rate, peak data rates, aggregate data rates and peak aggregate data rates. However, with subnetwork QoS settings, these settings are assigned to servers instead of users. It is possible to set logging for RSVP signaling and specify the log file location, number of log files, and log file size. In addition, you can initiate accounting and define additional advanced settings for election priorities on servers. QoS admission control for Windows 2000 can be installed for a domain tree or a number of domain trees in an Active Directory forest.

Figure 14.2 illustrates how you can implement QoS for 802.1p and INTSERV QoS techniques using RSVP signaling to control the amount of network resources allocated (and guaranteed) to the server and the sales users. Keep in mind that this example depicts using a third-party router and switch that also supports these QoS techniques so that end-to-end QoS can be realized. Also note that this example assumes QoS can be implemented at the ISP; an important point if you plan to implement QoS over a VPN, especially for videoconferencing and other low-latency applications.

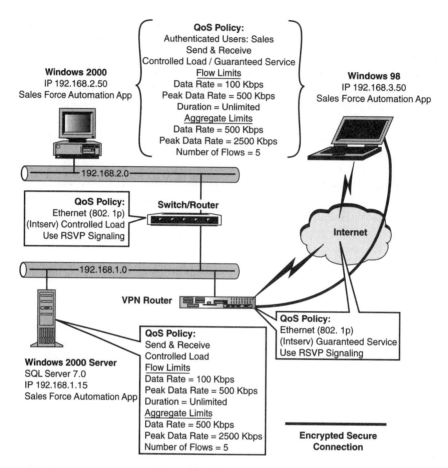

Figure 14.2   This diagram uses the previous example of the sales force automation application and applies it to a typical Windows 2000 network design, in which a group of sales users are located on a LAN and across a VPN tunnel through an ISP.

QoS is becoming increasingly important. Application service providers, for example, must be able to establish a guaranteed service level to their customers, which often comes at a high price because of the overhead involved in implementing QoS. Because QoS is a technique that assigns priority and policy to a network, a QoS-enabled network will require more planning and more overhead to achieve the service goals defined by the business and implemented by the Network Administrators. Generally speaking, the more a Network Administrator is willing to accept overhead in their network, the greater the ability to implement QoS. This translates to planning. If you require QoS on your network, expect that you will have to assess your network environment's capability and capacity to set and maintain the service level defined by your application and business environment.

With Windows 2000 support for QoS, enterprises and service providers can now implement QoS techniques on Windows 2000 platforms and establish service level guarantees for users and applications. Look for more QoS techniques to be implemented in Windows 2000. Because Active Directory can be easily leveraged to apply QoS policy throughout an enterprise, you can expect network vendors and ISVs to include Active Directory schema modifications and MMC snap-ins to support their network devices and *network-aware* applications.

One of the most important aspects of QoS in Windows 2000 is that the service is integrated into Active Directory. This integration means that Windows 2000 provides an application-aware network infrastructure. Through the QoS Application Programming Interface (API), vendors can update existing applications and develop future applications to communicate with network components to request the bandwidth needed for the applications to function properly. For example, telephony and video applications can utilize Active Directory-based policies to request more bandwidth for users in a specific OU when they access a videoconferencing application.

Summary

Windows 2000 and Active Directory provide advanced networking services. Windows 2000 is a powerful operating system and has been designed to use industry standards as the foundation for these services. Whether implemented in a pure-Windows 2000 environment in a LAN, or a mixed environment (which is typically the case with most large, distributed enterprises), Active Directory and Windows 2000 networking services offer improved management, networking, integration, scalability, and reliability.

Although this chapter focuses on Windows 2000 DHCP Services, WINS services, and QoS, it is important to point out that Windows 2000 offers a number of additional communication and networking services designed to address your specific network requirements. These include native support for Asynchronous Transfer Mode (ATM), IP Telephony and TAPI 3.0, VPNs, and much more. Chapter 16, "Developing a Remote Access Solution," focuses on remote access using Windows 2000 and Active Directory; VPNs are also covered in this chapter.

15

Developing a Network Security Strategy

THE SECURITY OF ACTIVE DIRECTORY IS CRITICAL TO the success of any organization in which Windows 2000 is deployed. Consequently, the management of security, with regards to access to the Windows 2000 environment as well as access to information in Active Directory, can define the success or failure of a Windows 2000 deployment.

Essentially, two security environments are relative to Active Directory. The first governs how users and resources gain access to the network, the Windows 2000 environment, and to the information in Active Directory. The second governs how security is managed for the data that travels across the network, between resources and users, or between clients and servers. The mechanisms by which these security environments are created and enforced often overlap.

Active Directory is the central repository for many of the security profiles for users and resources in Windows 2000. Group policies in Active Directory are used as the vehicle for security policy application and deployment. MMC is the tool by which security policies are developed.

Types of Security

Windows 2000 and Active Directory have three primary security mechanisms.

- Kerberos
- Public key infrastructure (PKI)
- IP Security (IPSec)

All three of these overlap in some ways and are distinctly different in other ways. They are used for different purposes in an Active Directory deployment. To design a security strategy that takes best advantage of the different security offerings in Windows 2000, it is important to understand the differences of the three primary security mechanisms.

Kerberos

Kerberos is the default authentication protocol utilized by Active Directory and Windows 2000. The version of Kerberos used by Windows 2000 is based on the Massachusetts Institute of Technology (MIT) Kerberos version 5 and has been extended to support public key authentication. Active Directory is the security account database for the Windows 2000 implementation of Kerberos.

Kerberos is a standards-based method of authentication. There are two primary versions of Kerberos: the version started and supported by MIT, and a variation now known as distributed computing environment (DCE) Kerberos. Microsoft opted to base the version of Kerberos in Windows 2000 on the MIT version because of its broad market acceptance. The Kerberos protocol provides several advantages over NTLM, the previous form of authentication in Windows NT.

- **Interoperability**—Kerberos provides a framework for interoperability with Kerberos implementations on other networks with different operating systems.

- **Client and Server Authentication**—Previously, with NTLM authentication, it was only possible for a client computer to authenticate to a server. However, it was not possible for a client computer to verify the identity of a server. Consequently, it was possible for someone to switch the server on the backend of a client connection and replace it with a different server than the one with which the client originally authenticated. Kerberos provides for mutual authentication, which enables clients to authenticate the servers to which they connect.

- **Efficient Authentication**—Kerberos provides for the authentication of clients by applications or file servers, rather than strictly by Domain Controllers (DCs), as was the case with NTLM authentication.

Kerberos authentication is provided via the exchange of secret keys between a client and server, or between a server and another server, on a network. The secret keys utilized in the authentication process never actually cross the network. Instead, they are used to encrypt information sent from one party to another. Another key is then used by the receiver to decrypt the information. The two keys used are known only by the two parties involved. One of the primary reasons the Kerberos protocol is so secure is that each participating party, whether client or server, in an authenticated session has its own encryption key. These keys are distributed by a key distribution center (KDC).

The KDC in Windows 2000 is integrated on a DC just like any other Windows 2000 service. The KDC utilizes Active Directory as the security repository of account information for all the security principals in the KDC realm. The concept of a realm in Kerberos is similar to the concept of a Windows NT domain. In Windows 2000, the Kerberos realm is referred to as a domain.

Every DC in the domain has a KDC running, as well as a copy of Active Directory. Consequently, it is possible for clients to access Kerberos authentication information from every DC. Although the Kerberos protocol specification does provide a definition for the replication of data between KDCs and security databases, Windows 2000 does not utilize Kerberos replication. Instead, it utilizes Active Directory replication.

For each security principal in the domain (user, client or server) the KDC stores a cryptographic key known only to the principal and the KDC. This key is used in Kerberos protocol exchanges between the KDC and the security principal. This *long-term key*, as it is known, is derived from the user's logon password.

If a client wants to access resources on a server, the client sends a request to the KDC for a *short-term session key*. This short-term session key is used by the server and the client during the pending session. The KDC encrypts a copy of the short-term session key for the client with the client's long-term key. The KDC also encrypts the short-term session key for the server with the server's long-term key. Both short-term session keys are then sent to the client in a single data packet. The KDC is the primary intermediary between security principals (clients and servers) in a Kerberos domain, as shown in Figure 15.1.

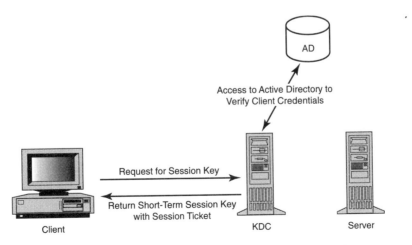

Figure 15.1 The KDC acts as an intermediary between security principals in a Kerberos realm, or domain, and session keys.

After the KDC has issued the encrypted session keys, the steps to establishing a session can be launched:

1. The server's short-term session key, which is sent to the client, is embedded in a data string called a *session ticket*. The session ticket and the short-term session key are the data that has been encrypted by the KDC with the long-term key shared with the server.

2. Now that the client has a short-term session key and a session ticket, it can make a request to the server to open an authenticated session. To do this, the client sends the server a message consisting of the session ticket and an authenticator, which has been encrypted with the short-term session key.

3. If the server receives a session request from the client, it decrypts the session ticket with the long-term key that it shares with the KDC and extracts the short-term session key. It then uses the short-term session key to decrypt the client authenticator. The server can then be certain that the client is trusted by the KDC, the security authority for the domain.

One of the advantages of Kerberos over NTLM authentication is that clients can ask for mutual authentication, as shown in Figure 15.2. If this has been requested by the client, the server uses its copy of the short-term session key to encrypt the timestamp from the client's authenticator information and sends the encrypted packet back to the client as the server's authenticator.

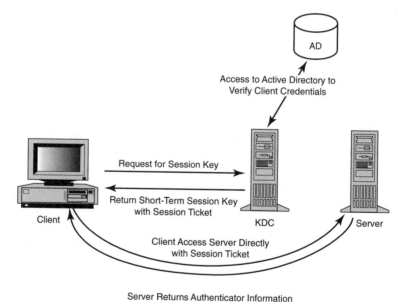

Figure 15.2   The client sends the encrypted packet, including the session ticket, to the server. The server decrypts the packet and, if requested by the client, can send back to the client an authenticator.

Ticket Granting

Another aspect of Kerberos authentication that is important to understand is the concept of a *ticket-granting ticket* (TGT). Each time that a user logs on to a workstation, the long-term key is calculated by the Kerberos client on the workstation. The password is converted to a cryptographic key and is then passed to the KDC for authentication. The KDC then retrieves another copy of the user's long-term key from the security database, Active Directory. This ticket is compared with the ticket received from the client. If the two tickets are the same, the KDC returns a session ticket for the KDC, known as a TGT, to the client. The use of a TGT enables the KDC to respond to requests for other session tickets from the client without having to retrieve the user's password from Active Directory each time a new session is required. This helps to limit the load on the DC hosting the KDC and to increase performance for the client.

Inter-Domain Authentication

In previous versions of Windows NT, it was necessary to establish explicit trust relationships between domains for clients and servers to establish authenticated sessions if the client was in one domain and the server in another domain. With Kerberos authentication, this is not the case. With Kerberos authentication in place, it is possible for a client to obtain a TGT from a KDC in one domain and use it to request a session ticket from a KDC in another domain, using an explicit trust between the two domains.

Authentication across domain boundaries is enabled by the sharing of an inter-domain key between domains. This occurs automatically between Windows 2000 domains in the same Forest. This can also be configured manually by establishing explicit trusts between domains. After the two domains have exchanged inter-domain keys, the ticket-granting service of each KDC is registered in as a domain security principal in the security database of the other KDC. After this has happened, the ticket-granting service in each domain can treat the ticket-granting service in the other domain as a regular service for which clients can request session tickets.

If a client requests access to a service that is in another domain, the KDC in the user's domain responds to the client's request with a TGT encrypted with the inter-domain key. This is called a *referral ticket*. The client then uses this referral ticket to request a session ticket from the KDC in the other domain.

PKI

In the previous section, Kerberos was examined as an encryption and authentication protocol. The basic assumption with Kerberos authentication is that the cryptographic key that is used to encrypt a packet of data is the same key that is used to decrypt it. This is known as *symmetric key cryptography*, or *secret key cryptography*. A cryptography system based on a PKI is fundamentally different from Kerberos. PKI relies on encryption and authentication based on keys that are not symmetrical. Every participant in the encryption/decryption process has a pair of keys—one public and one private. Users make their public key available to other users who want to send encrypted data. This data can then be decrypted by using your private key.

In addition to being able to encrypt data without a prior exchange of secret or symmetrical keys, public key cryptography also enables the use of digital signatures. Digital signatures can be used to verify that a document, or email message, was originated by a specific user. The users can "sign" the message with a digital signature that has been encrypted by the private key in a key pair. The public key can then be used to validate whether the signature originated from the private key and has not been altered.

Certificate Authority

In the case of Kerberos, symmetrical keys can be exchanged between the users of the cryptography system because each user trusts Active Directory and the KDC as a security authorities. Each user can trust that when the KDC delivers a session ticket for a specific service, it is the correct ticket. In the case of public key encryption, there is no mechanism for explicit trust, such as the KDC, between parties in the encryption process. Consequently, a trust broker must be established. This trust broker is commonly called a *Certificate Authority* (CA) because the most common way to verify the authenticity of public keys is via an accompanying certificate.

A CA issues certificates that are digitally signed by the issuer (the CA) and attests to the validity of the public key and the identity of the key's owner. The certificate typically contains additional information about the key's owner, such as what company they work for and what their contact information is.

An example of a public CA is VeriSign, which issues certificates for individuals wanting to encrypt and sign email and documents. As public key encryption becomes more widespread across the Internet, more and more companies are beginning to implement their own CAs, or they are beginning to utilize the services of other organization's CAs.

PKI in Windows 2000

In Windows 2000, PKI does not replace the need for Kerberos as the default authentication protocol. Instead, PKI is utilized as an extension of the security service provided by Kerberos. PKI can provide for scalability and extensibility beyond what Kerberos provides in a Windows 2000 domain environment.

The first basic element of the PKI in Windows 2000 is the Microsoft Certificate Services, which provides the mechanism to establish a CA for the organization. Certificate Services manages the issuing of certificates to validated users and verifies that all certificates issued are consistent with the public key security policy for the organization. The service also manages relationships with other external CAs that might be trusted by the PKI in the organization.

For example, in Wadeware, there might be a need to provide external vendor access to a server in the finance department to submit invoices on a monthly basis. The administrators for Wadeware can establish a trust with the vendor's external CA; this then enables all client certificates issued by the vendor's CA to be used for authentication to resources in the Wadeware domain environment.

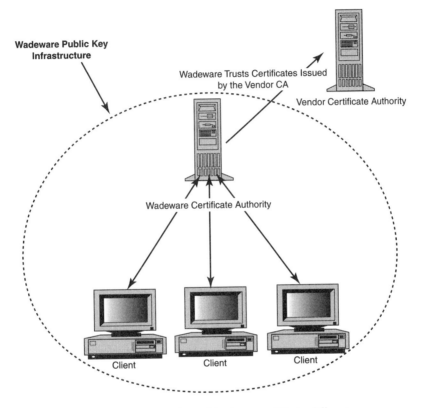

Figure 15.3   Trust relationships between CAs in different organizations can provide a mechanism for granting access to organization resources by users from a different organization.

The PKI within Windows 2000 is based on the concept of a CA hierarchy. A CA hierarchy is based on the parent-child relationships that are established between CAs. A parent-child relationship stipulates that a CA, which has issued a certificate, is trusted by a root CA. This way, any other CA has only to verify the validity of a certificate by contacting the root CA, not by having to navigate the CA hierarchy.

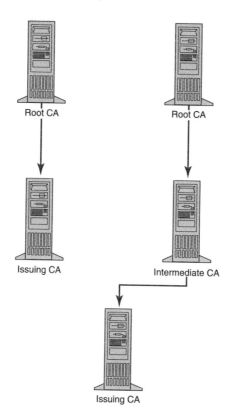

Figure 15.4 Windows 2000 PKI is based on the concept of a CA hierarchy. A hierarchy provides for the rapid validation of certificates by contacting a root CA and issuing CAs. Intermediate CAs pass along requests by issuing CAs to root CAs.

The concept of a CA hierarchy in Windows 2000 requires that there is a plan established for when and why to segment the CAs in an organization. There are essentially three reasons why CAs should be segmented into a hierarchy. These reasons tend to follow the same logic for dividing the domain structure into multiple OUs; however, there are also some key differences.

- **Geographic Distribution**—Organizations might divide CAs in to a hierarchy based upon geographic segmentation of network resources and users. If there were slow wide-area network connections between geographic locations, it would be necessary to place a CA at each geographic location so that clients could seek certificate validation without a dramatic impact to performance. In this type of configuration, there is usually a root CA based at the organization headquarters, which would trust all the regional CAs, as seen in Figure 15.5.

- **Business Segmentation**—As with the distribution of organization units discussed earlier in the book, it might be necessary to distribute the CA hierarchy according to the business segmentation of the company. In the case of Wadeware, it might be necessary to have a CA for the manufacturing department, a CA for the Sales department, and a CA for the mergers and acquisitions group. All these CAs are trusted by a root CA, which is managed by the Information Technology (IT) department, as seen in Figure 15.6.

- **Load and Usage**—It might also be necessary to segment a CA hierarchy based upon the measured or expected load that is placed on the CAs or by the type of function that the CA performs. One CA might be used for issuing and verifying certificates for email, whereas another is used for external vendor network authentication. The types of security policies and the client load on these CAs would differ greatly, and so, it would be wise to segment them in to a CA hierarchy, as seen in Figure 15.7.

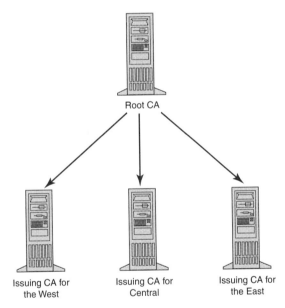

Root CA

Issuing CA for
the West

Issuing CA for
Central

Issuing CA for
the East

Figure 15.5 A CA hierarchy based upon geographic distribution of network users and resources. This example has a CA for each regional location and a root CA at headquarters managed by the IT department.

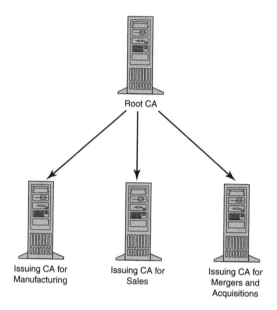

Figure 15.6   A CA hierarchy based upon business segmentation.
Because each business unit requires a different security policy and a different set
of criteria for issuing certificates, it is simpler to administer if there is a CA hierarchy.

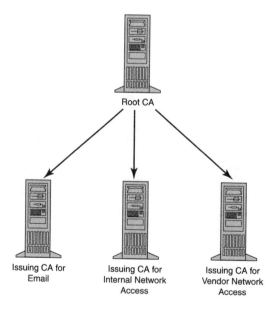

Figure 15.7   A CA hierarchy based upon the types of usage and load that
are placed on each CA. One CA is issuing and authenticating certificates
for email, whereas the other is authenticating users for network access.

Windows 2000 PKI and Microsoft Exchange

One of the first applications that organizations find for the PKI in Windows 2000 is integration with the key management services in Microsoft Exchange 2000 and later versions. By leveraging PKI and public key encryption, it is possible to provide Exchange and Outlook users with S/MIME (secure MIME), which includes encryption and digital signature capability. By deploying Windows 2000 and Active Directory, it is possible to provide the integration of secure and signed mail between disparate Exchange organizations.

IPSec

IPSec is a security mechanism that can be leveraged in a Windows 2000 environment with practically no impact to users and with minimal need for additional training. The reason for this is that IPSec is a security protocol that exists entirely below the transport level, and it is transparently inherited by all applications over the transport level. IPSec supports network-level authentication, encryption, and data integrity.

The IPSec protocol definition provides for the encryption of all data traffic that crosses a network from one host to another. To do this, IPSec uses an authentication header and an encapsulated security payload for each data packet. The authentication header enables the receiving host to identify that the sending host is indeed the desired host. The encapsulated security payload ensures that the data, which is received, has not been tampered with since it was sent.

IPSec relies upon a combination of both secret key cryptography and public key cryptography. In the case of an encapsulated security payload, only the sending and receiving hosts know the secret key for encryption and decryption. As with Kerberos, if the authentication data is valid, the receiving host knows that the data came from the sending host, and that it was not tampered with during transit.

To create the authentication header, two hosts on a network exchange public information. The public information of each host is then combined with its own secret information, and the result is the shared-secret value. This is known as the Diffie-Hellman technique. After the authentication header has been created, the sending host then uses data encryption standard-cipher block chaining (DES-CBC) to generate a random number that is used with the shared-secret value to encrypt the encapsulated security payload.

Because IPSec is completely transparent to users and to applications on the network, it is entirely up to the Network Administrator to decide when IPSec security policies should be applied. Security policies can be assigned to the default domain policy, the default local policy, or to a customized policy that the administrator creates. When hosts log in to a domain, they automatically assume the properties of the default domain and default local polices, which includes the IPSec policy assigned to the domain.

To establish security policies for a Windows 2000 and Active Directory implementation, administrators should follow three steps:

1. **Evaluate network traffic patterns**—All the network traffic in an organization follows specific patterns. Time sheets are sent from employees to the finance department on a regular basis—every two weeks. Sales forecasts are sent from field-based sales representatives to the VP of Sales every month. All the different communication patterns require different levels of security.

2. **Develop security profiles for each traffic pattern**—After the administrator has identified all the different types of data traffic on the network and the patterns that the traffic follows, it is now possible to develop security profiles for each of these patterns. For example, it might be decided that all the traffic sent between members of the organization's executive committee should be encrypted or that all the timesheet data being sent to the finance department should be encrypted.

3. **Build security policies**—After the security profiles for the traffic patterns have been established, it is time to use the Windows Security Manger MMC snap-in to build security policies for each profile.

Choosing the Right Security

Now that the basic differences in the three main security mechanisms in Windows 2000 have been discussed, the types of security you should plan to use as you are designing your implementation of Active Directory will be addressed. At the beginning of this chapter, we identified that there are essentially two different types of security relative to Active Directory and Windows 2000:

1. Security for access to the network environment and Active Directory resources

2. Security for the data that crosses the network between hosts on the network

Kerberos and PKI are security mechanisms for regulating access to the environment, whereas IPSec is a security method for regulating the data on the network.

Kerberos Compared with PKI

As the default protocol for Windows 2000, Kerberos is also the most widespread security protocol used in initial implementations of Active Directory. It requires relatively planning and preparation before implementing Active Directory, as long as there is no need for you to integrate the KDC in Windows 2000 with a KDC that already exists as part of a Kerberos realm outside of Windows 2000.

With the current release of Windows 2000, it is possible to intermix Windows-based and non-Windows-based Kerberos implementations. For example, it is possible for a Windows 2000 client to authenticate to a KDC that is Kerberos version 5 compliant running on UNIX. In addition, it is possible for a non-Windows client to authenticate to a Windows 2000 KDC, as long as the client supports Kerberos version 5.

More planning is needed if there is a requirement for two Kerberos domains to trust each other, and one domain is based on Windows 2000, but the other is not. It is possible to establish explicit Kerberos trusts between the two domains. However, security principals in the non-Windows domain do not have the necessary authorization data that the Windows 2000-based service requires. Consequently, it is necessary to use the users and computers management tool in Active Directory to map each external security principal to a specific internal Active Directory security principal (user).

Because mapping hundreds or even thousands of external user accounts to internal accounts might be a limiting factor in utilizing Kerberos security for external users, this is an excellent example of when to use public key authentication rather than Kerberos. If an organization has an external vendor with which it needs to exchange data on a regular basis, it is possible to implement public key authentication for the external vendor rather than establishing a Kerberos trust. A CA would be established, which trust certificates from the CA of the external vendor. These certificates can then be used to grant access to resources on servers in the Windows 2000 domain.

In addition, as pointed out earlier in this chapter, a PKI should be implemented if there are plans or requirements for users of the network email system to digitally sign or encrypt mail. Kerberos does not provide for a digital signature capability.

When to Use IPSec

Evaluating when to use IPSec is a different process than evaluating when to use Kerberos or PKI. IPSec is primarily used for network traffic that is internal to an organization. In addition, because it is transparent to users and applications, it is a protocol that is used when administrators feel there is a need for additional security for the data that is traveling across the network, rather than authenticating who is actually accessing the information or resources in the organization.

It is prudent to be cautious, however, when implementing IPSec in an organization. There are a few guidelines to follow to limit any impact on network and host performance.

- Implement host-to-host encryption only if absolutely necessary. It is better to implement a scenario whereby not all the hosts in a specific subnet need to encrypt traffic to each other. Rather, they only need to encrypt traffic if it is destined for a host outside of the subnet.

- Critically evaluate if IPSec is required at all. No matter how streamlined the protocol, IPSec introduces increased latency in the performance of the network and each host on the network. If what you are trying to accomplish with IPSec can be accomplished with firewall, it is preferable.

Summary

Active Directory provides a rich security framework to meet the security needs of most organizations. As discussed in this chapter, the most difficult aspect of designing a security strategy for Active Directory and Windows 2000 is not identifying what can be done, but rather which security tool to use to meet your security needs. Kerberos and PKI address the need to secure access to a computing infrastructure, whereas IPSec maintains the integrity and security of data that transits that infrastructure.

16

Developing a Remote Access Solution

I N TODAY'S INFORMATION AGE, ALMOST EVERY organization requires some form of remote access computing as a normal course of daily business operations. Whether you are in field sales on the road, a telecommuter working from home, a small branch-office manager, or an executive dialing-in from a hotel to gain access to important information, remote access is a critical business function. It is one that is common-place, and one that is relied upon by all users.

Remote access technologies have matured significantly over the past several years. Today, manufacturers and independent software vendors (ISVs) are developing new remote access technologies to take advantage of Web technology. Some examples include using a Web browser to remotely access systems and network equipment as a way to check status or to configure and manage these devices. No longer do you have to install a "fat" application/client (one from each device vendor) on your local machine only to find that they consume too much of the local computing resources or that they conflict with other applications on your system.

Remote access has become a standard Information Technology (IT) service require-ment for all enterprises—large and small. This fact presents many challenges for Information Systems (IS) organizations because they have so many factors and vari-ables to consider and so many product alternatives and implementation approaches to define. Remote access has become a core part of a business's IT environment; users expect it to be secure, reliable, high-performance, and available all the time.

Using Windows 2000 and Active Directory, organizations now have a number of distinct advantages to leverage with regards to remote access. Although Active Directory is a new component of the Windows 2000 product, adding more features and complexities to consider than prior versions had, much of the capabilities required to create a flexible and manageable RAS are built-in. IT decision makers should take comfort with Windows 2000's remote access capabilities because it enables IS managers and architects, who are struggling with the challenges of remote access, to design and implement a tailored solution that meets their specific business requirements.

This chapter presents a strategy that can be used to develop a RAS based on Windows 2000 Active Directory. It explores the specific technologies that Windows 2000 employs for remote access, and it discusses remote access alternatives and considerations for Active Directory.

Remote Access Strategy

Determining how you deliver remote access services to your users can be difficult and involves many complex decisions. By applying a structured approach to the design and deployment of a RAS, you can ease these difficulties and implement a solution that is targeted to your organization's specific needs. The following is a proven strategy for developing and deploying a viable RAS that meets your business objectives. This strategy has been successful, especially in larger projects that focused on complex issues, such as remote access.

This implementation strategy is very similar to that discussed in Chapter 17, "Developing an Implementation Plan." (See Figure 17.1 from that chapter.) The same terminology is used in both places, and both chapters use the same structure. The steps are the same; just the details are different.

- **Phase I Requirements Definition**—This phase defines specific business and technical requirements.

- **Phase II Discovery and Analysis**—This phase identifies available technologies, alternatives, options, risks, dependencies, and assumptions.

- **Phase III Design**—In this phase, conceptual design maps the requirements to the available technologies, detailed design defines the solution specifications.

- **Phase IV Lab**—This phase validates the design and demonstrates the solutions capabilities in a controlled environment. Detailed design is modified in iterations until all the requirements are met.

- **Phase V Pilot**—This phase demonstrates solution in a semi-production environment and tests the implementation approach for the subsequent production deployment.

- **Phase VI Deployment**—This phase, typically, deploys the solution by group or by location, depending on size, needs, and services being delivered.

This chapter focuses on the first two phases, because much of what is determined in these phases dictates the forthcoming solution and defines the activities for the last three phases. If you use this strategy to build and deploy your RAS, your chances of developing a comprehensive solution to meet all your business and technical requirements increase.

Requirements Definition

The first step in developing a RAS is to define your remote access requirements. Clearly defined and documented requirements make all the difference between a successful solution and a failed solution. Without defined requirements, you might build a solution that meets the needs of your mobile sales force, but that does not account for your remote administration needs or for your branch-office locations that are planned for occupancy next year.

Because Windows 2000 is built on standards, many of the remote access components that you need to build a standards-based solution are incorporated into the product. Examples of these components include: a public key infrastructure (PKI), based on X.509 certificates; Windows terminal services; and a Virtual Private Network (VPN) capability, based on Point to Point Tunneling Protocol (PPTP) or on Layer 2 Tunneling Protocol (L2TP) and IP Security (IPSec). Windows 2000 provides remote users with single sign-on access to network resources because it leverages Active Directory as the central security authority, which authenticates remote users and applies policy and permissions to computers, users, and groups within an organization.

If you are defining your requirements for remote access, you need to evaluate your specific business needs, such as

- How large is the remote access population?
- Where are the remote users concentrated?
- During what times and in what time zones will users be accessing the network?
- How restrictive does your network need to be for remote access?
- What are your business policies and security policies regarding remote access?

These questions, and more, need to be identified and defined before you determine what specific technologies you need, and how these technologies need to be employed to satisfy your business requirements. Typically, requirements, like the previously listed examples, are determined by first identifying the key customer stakeholders, such as the IT Director or CIO, and the business unit sponsors who require and use this service. After they are identified, you need to develop an interview questionnaire, and then schedule a series of facilitated meetings (individually or as a group) to define (list) these requirements. After they are listed, you would then need to group them into similar requirements, establish the priority for each, and then build a consensus that these requirements are the requirements from which your remote access strategy and solution should be developed.

If you understand the habits and needs of your remote users, you can begin to define remote access system requirements and define how Windows 2000 Active Directory needs to be configured and deployed to support your mobile work force. By understanding these requirements first, you avoid making costly mistakes and eliminate integration issues down the road.

Discovery and Analysis

Performing a thorough examination of various remote access products and technologies, using the defined requirements from Phase I as your base line for consideration, helps you to design and deploy a viable RAS.

Nothing is worse for a user than to have a corporate computing culture of "ease and flexibility," only to find that if they use remote access, they must dial a single long distance phone number that inevitably seems to be busy, and then they are presented with three separate sign-on requests using three unique user IDs and passwords. Worse, they then spend additional time completing expense reports to get reimbursed for remote access expenses when traveling to Europe for an important convention, when all they really needed was a file from the corporate network that took 3 minutes to download, and over 20 minutes and two support calls to obtain!

Doing a comprehensive discovery of technology options and alternatives and then mapping those against the requirements for remote access, a process we call a *gap analysis*, yields a technology direction. In this way, you ensure these typical user frustrations are avoided because you have developed a strategy for remote access that meets your remote users' requirements in the best possible manner.

Determining exactly what remote access technology you need to meet your remote access requirements is a critical and necessary first step to designing a functional solution for your users. Fortunately, Windows 2000 has many of these inherent remote access technologies built-in. The job of a solutions architect developing a solid remote access strategy is to fully understand the product features and capabilities, to know how they are deployed and managed, and then to determine what additional components are needed to round-out a complete solution.

To help you identify which remote access technologies are available and required for your specific business needs, the sections that follow discuss popular remote access technologies and present specific context for remote access product and technology selection. Unlike identifying which server to purchase and how much memory to install, defining a RAS with all its intricacies might require some external validation or support. Do not hesitate to consult outside expertise in this area; the money spent now is well worth it in the end.

Remote Access Technologies

During the discovery and analysis phase, you need to consider several components to construct a solid RAS. Applying the International Standards Organization's (ISO's) OSI model to a RAS enables us to easily associate these components and their relative relationships. Table 16.1 describes many of the common remote access components and protocols as they relate to the OSI model. If you understand each component and their specific relationships, it is easy to identify which components you need and which components you already have.

Table 16.1 **Common Remote Access Components as Related to OSI Model.**

OSI Model	Common Remote Access Components	Windows 2000 Remote Access Features
Layer 7	FTP, SMTP, HTTP, RLOGIN, DHCP, BOOTP	Active Directory, FTP Server, DHCP Server, Quality of Service
Layer 6	Lightweight Presentation Protocol	
Layer 5	LDAP, DNS, NetBIOS	DNS Server, Active Directory, WINS
Layer 4	TCP, NetBIOS, UDP	
Layer 3	IP	Routing and Remote Access Services
Layer 2	CHAP, PPP, PPTP	Routing and Remote Access Services
Layer 1	Analog, ISDN, ADSL, Frame Relay	

Access Methods and Standards

Manufacturers and ISVs continue to develop innovative RASs that incorporate additional functionality and features to improve security, management, and performance over slow links. Standard bodies, supported by leading manufacturers and telecommunication vendors have adopted several technologies for remote access, including faster analog dial-up access speeds (28.8–56 Kbps) using V.90 modems over the PSTN network. In addition, *basic rate ISDN* is a fast data service offered by Telcos—faster than typical analog modems, with top speeds of 128 Kbps—but deployment in the US is slow and expensive and throughput is typically not fast enough for today's multimedia Internet.

Recently, standard bodies, such as ITUT, have adopted an informal name for a technology called asymmetric digital subscriber line (ADSL), known as G.Lite or Universal DSL. The G.Lite standard (officially, G.992.2), or ADSL, is becoming a popular method for providing high-speed connectivity to residential communities or small office/home office (SOHO) over traditional "copper" networks.

ADSL is capable of speeds as slow as 64 Kbps and as fast as 8 Mbps. ADSL is becoming a viable transmission mechanism for businesses and enterprise customers requiring high-speed remote access to connect remote users, SOHOs, and branch offices. ADSL is a necessary technology for the increasing demands of fast, reliable remote access. With bandwidth capabilities at speeds greater than T1 (1.54 Mbps), ADSL can be deployed inexpensively compared to traditional technologies, such as frame relay, Point-to-Point T1, and Fractional T1.

Competing with ADSL are broadband and wireless technologies. Broadband technologies from cable TV providers use cable modems over the cable television network to provide Internet access through a "supported" ISP. Cable modems provide excellent transmission speeds to residential communities and the SOHO; they are widely deployed for remote access to home users.

Alternatively, wireless solutions that use digital cellular, 900 MHz, or radio wave technologies offer excellent solutions for mobile users who are constantly on the move. Unfortunately, many of the wireless technologies deployed today do not offer the performance and reliability of traditional or broadband carrier technologies. As these technologies improve, you are able to choose from a variety of viable transmission mediums, including wireless, broadband, and satellite.

Bringing this all together, Windows 2000 is an operating system built on standards. Windows 2000 supports routing and remote access services (RRAS) that leverage all the remote access components previously listed. Furthermore, Windows 2000 Active Directory provides centralized administration of your remote access environment through MMC, and Active Directory delivers strong security authentication and encryption protocols to protect your corporate information assets while remote users access the network over the Internet. If coupled with the variety of transmission alternatives available to the market, businesses can now deploy a RAS that delivers users the flexibility to work securely from anywhere, at anytime.

Secure RASs

Widespread use of the Internet has led to the creation of the ISP. ISPs deploy a variety of network and security technologies designed to provide Internet and business-to-business connectivity to organizations and consumers around the world.

Today, ISP customers can establish a secure connection into their corporate networks using the ISP's shared IP network. This capability is called a VPN. For example, VPNs enable a mobile user, who uses his or her laptop on the road, to dial a local ISP and access critical business information and applications over the public Internet using secure encryption and authentication techniques. VPNs are quickly becoming the standard approach to connect mobile users, branch offices, and SOHOs to corporate networks. The cost savings achieved by deploying VPNs are tremendous, and organizations no longer need to be in the business of managing large modem pools and complex security systems and support processes.

Figure 16.1 illustrates a typical VPN. Keep in mind that a VPN is not a type of transmission service, such as analog, ISDN, or ADSL. VPNs apply secure connection technologies, such as L2TP or PPTP, to connect two or more entities together using a shared IP network and the Internet.

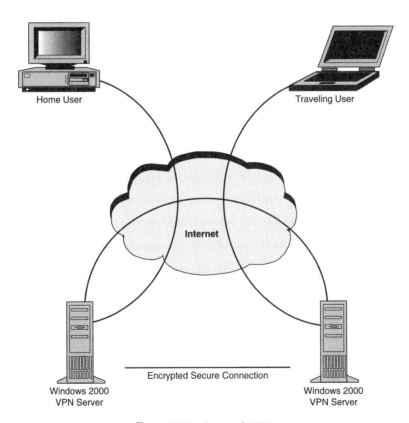

Figure 16.1 A typical VPN.

VPNs enhance data security over shared IP networks by authenticating remote users, and by encrypting authentication credentials and data. Both PPTP and L2TP support encrypted and plain text authentication. If a remote user is using L2TP and IPSec, authentication involves an exchange of certificates that prevents an unknown computer from falsifying themselves as an authorized network computer. Windows 2000 Active Directory provides native support for L2TP/IPSec and PPTP; these core components enable remote users to access corporate network resources over the Internet.

Another important aspect for VPN remote access is domain name system DNS. Active Directory uses DNS for a service location. If a remote VPN user requests access to information located on a corporate network over the Internet, they use the DNS name to authenticate with Active Directory, and they use encrypted certificates to establish a private "tunnel" to the desired information resource being requested.

Thin-Client Computing

Windows 2000 Terminal Services is an excellent feature for your RAS. All the Windows 2000 Server products (server, advance server, and data center) include Windows Terminal Services. Windows 2000 Terminal Services was co-developed by Microsoft and Citrix. Similar to the product WinFrame (from Citrix), Windows 2000 Terminal Services enables a Windows 2000 Server to operate as a multi-user application server, enabling remote users to run applications from the server using a single "thin" client application (or through a Web browser). It uses a presentation layer protocol called Remote Desktop Protocol (RDP) or a protocol from Citrix called Independent Computing Architecture (ICA). Because client workstations run the Windows Terminal Services client software, they do not need to have their business and productivity applications installed locally on their desktops or laptops.

Windows 2000 Terminal Services offers many benefits to an organization, such as lowering total cost of ownership and simplifying administration and management of a large, distributed computing environment. In addition, Windows Terminal Services can leverage legacy desktop and laptop equipment because it requires a small hardware/software profile to run your applications. In this way, applications run off the server, and the remote user is simply presented with redirected video, mouse, audio, and keyboard updates. Depending on your hardware, Windows Terminal Services can often provide greater performance than a traditional "fat" client, in which all applications and services run locally on the remote user's desktop or laptop.

Consider the following example. You have a large population of remote users with a variety of laptop configurations (make, model, CPU, memory, hard disk, OS versions, and applications). You know how difficult it can be to support these users and to maintain these computers. If they have a problem or they need to be upgraded to a newer version of an application, either they have to come to you (for example, fly in or send their computer to "corporate") or you have to deploy a technician to perform this service at their location—like at home or at the airport. Whatever the case, this situation takes time, extra personnel, and often frustrates the user, not to mention the technician.

If you were to deploy a RAS that leveraged analog dial-up (56Kbps), ISDN, and/or ASDL, coupled with VPN technologies, which provide secure, encrypted communications over a shared IP network and Windows Terminal Services, you could host most, if not all, of your Enterprise Resource Planning (ERP), productivity, and business applications on a "farm" (two or more) of Windows Terminal Servers located in a protected data-center. Moreover, as you need to make updates, make upgrades, or expand the environment, you only need to make those changes at your data-center.

Finally, another key advantage of Windows 2000 Terminal Services for remote access is the concept of "remote administration." Using Windows 2000 Terminal Services, as a means of providing secure and reliable remote access to servers located throughout a distributed enterprise, can be a tremendous service advantage and can reduce administration costs. Windows 2000 Server can not only operate as a multi-user application server using Terminal Services, it can also contain the Terminal Server client software, so that a remote administrator can manage the server using the same, proven technology that remote users use to run their business applications.

In this scenario, an administrator with a laptop running Windows 2000 Professional and the Terminal Server client software, could dial-up an ISP, establish a secure connection to the corporate network, and then remotely control a server or a network/system management console running the Terminal Service client. By doing this, the administrator can remotely manage almost every aspect of an IT enterprise.

The advantages of Windows 2000 remote access features are significant. Windows 2000, aside from all its other key benefits, can realistically be justified simply on the advantages it brings to your remote access computing needs.

Remote Access Considerations

Selecting which remote access components of Windows 2000 to implement, how to implemented them, and how to design your Active Directory tree to support and manage these components in the context of your enterprise can depend on many factors. For example, designing an Active Directory tree and namespace with remote users in mind has an impact on performance. To account for this, a well-designed Active Directory tree and namespace needs to consider the quantity and location of Global Catalog (GC) servers—the GC provides an indexed catalog that speeds searches for network resources, an important requirement for remote users. To understand some of these issues and dependencies, consider the following:

1. Who needs remote access in your organization?
2. Where do these users gain access from, one location or multiple?
3. What level of security does each user or group require, when accessing the network from each remote location?
4. Which applications/services does each user/group require?

    Applications and services to consider include off-line file storage and synchronization; email, contact management, calendar, group scheduling, enterprise resource applications; videoconferencing or IP telephony services; and local or remote printing.

5. Do any application services require, or benefit from, Terminal Services?

6. Do you use dial-up or VPN servers? For help making this decision, see the VPN server's sidebar.

7. If you are using a VPN, users can gain access to the Internet through the corporate network or from a split tunnel through the ISP (one PPTP or L2TP tunnel to the corporate network and another to the Internet)?

8. Do you need to connect remote locations, such as a small branch office LAN?

9. What Telco options are available at each location, and what are the bandwidth requirements for each site?

10. Do you use Windows 2000 RRAS and Internet Authentication Service (IAS), or do you use separate routing device, like a Cisco VPN Router?

11. How should you configure the Active Directory site topology to optimize access for remote offices over slow links?

12. Consider how you authenticate remote users, and what level of authentication and data encryption you require for

> The number and placement of Active Directory Domain Controllers (DCs) and GC servers is relative to the entry point for remote users and the network resources to which they require access.

> The authentication approach and the level of encryption affect performance and could alter your Windows 2000 Active Directory design.

> Microsoft PPP Encryption (MPPE) for PPP and PPTP connections, 40-bit or 128-bit.

> IPSec for L2TP connections, 40-bit data encryption standard (DES), 56-bit DES, or Triple DES.

VPN Servers

Consider implementing VPN remote access servers if using the Internet to access intranet-based resources is an acceptable risk, or if the connection to the Internet will support the maximum number of remote access clients.

VPNs should specify the number of PPTP or L2TP ports necessary to support the maximum number of simultaneous clients, the user accounts that are granted remote access, and the remote access policy restrictions.

VPN servers might be an acceptable solution if your remote-user community is highly distributed and diverse.

Dial-up servers might be an acceptable solution if your remote-user community is relatively small and located within a local calling area.

VPN servers are excellent if you need to provide controlled, secure access to business partners, such as a supplier. This is typically referred to as an extranet, or business-to-business communications.

Remote Access Policies

With earlier versions of Windows NT remote access, authorization was based on a check-box ("Grant dial-in permission to user") option in the User Manager, or in the remote access administration utility. You could specify callback options on a per-user basis as well. In Windows 2000, authorization is granted based on the dial-in properties of a user account *and* the remote access policies, which are both stored in Active Directory and replicated throughout the network.

Remote access policies are a set of conditions and connection settings that give administrators more flexibility in authorizing connection attempts. Windows 2000 RRAS and IAS both use remote access policies to determine whether to accept or deny connection attempts. With remote access policies, you can grant or deny authorization by the time of day and day of the week, by the Windows 2000 group to which the remote access user belongs, by the type of connection being requested, and by dial-up networking or a VPN connection requests. You can configure settings that limit the maximum session time, specify the authentication and encryption methods, set Bandwidth Allocation Protocol (BAP) policies, and detect a "slow network," thereby assigning policies for software installation, logon script processing, and group policy inheritance if a slow network is detected.

It is important to recognize that Windows 2000 Active Directory group policies and remote access policies offer much more flexibility to the administrator and the users than prior versions of Windows NT. However, implementing them requires a bit of time and effort to understand their implications and their affect on remote access users and groups.

For information, refer to Chapter 9, "Group Policies."

Summary

Remote access services are a vital part of an organization's computing environment. Almost every organization has some form of remote access requirement—dialing in from a hotel, convention, client site, business-to-consumer, and business-to-business communications. Windows 2000 with Active Directory offers significant performance and security improvements over prior versions of Windows NT, and it offers tremendous flexibility in how you design and configure your solution because Windows 2000 is built on industry standards. Whether you choose to implement a complete Windows 2000 RAS or to implement specific components of Windows 2000, one thing is certain; your remote users, home users, and branch office computing requirements continue to evolve and expand. Windows 2000 and Active Directory offer the core services—DNS, DHCP, IPSec/L2TP, PPTP, Radius, PKI, Active Directory Policies—which are required to deliver scalable, secure, and reliable remote access service to all enterprises—large and small.

As the work place "virtualizes" and the use of the Internet makes it easier for us to collaborate with others, developing a rock-solid RAS based on Windows 2000 improves intra-company communications and business productivity, enables collaboration across remote geographies and time-zones, and strengthens security if accessing information from remote locations over a shared IP network (Internet), which improves a company's bottom line.

17

Developing an Implementation Plan

AN ACTIVE DIRECTORY PROJECT HAS SEVERAL PHASES, each of which influences the outcome of the project. Active Directory design, in which Active Directory is defined so that it meets your organization's requirements, is a pivotal phase of the Active Directory project. If Active Directory design does not meet your organization's requirements, no matter what is done in the other phases of the project, Active Directory will come up short of fulfilling its promises. The implementation plan is another pivotal phase of your Active Directory project. Although you have a beautifully designed Active Directory, if it is not implemented properly, the design never allows Active Directory to meet you organization's requirements. Therefore, it is important to carefully plan the implementation of Active Directory. This includes proper project management from a Project Manager, realistic timelines, communication, organization, and well-defined user and management expectations.

Unfortunately, there is no simple cookbook implementation plan. Each implementation is different because each organization is different. This chapter touches on some of the components and approaches that can help you define a successful implementation plan.

Implementation Plan in the Overall Project

As mentioned several times in this book, there are multiple phases to any project. The implementation plan represents yet another phase of the overall Active Directory project.

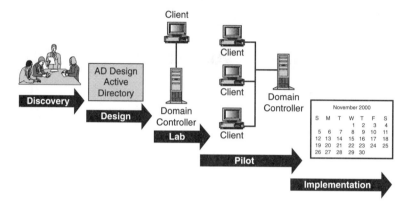

Figure 17.1 An overview of the implementation plan within the Active Directory project.

The implementation phase, which usually follows the lab and/or pilot phase, uses knowledge gained from these prior phases to build the implementation plan. The tasks necessary to implement the Active Directory design are discovered in the lab phase, and the nuances of rolling out Active Directory in your production environment are learned in the pilot phase of the project. All this knowledge goes into the development of your Active Directory implementation plan.

The pilot phase of a project is used to test the water. Active Directory design evolves out of the lab and into the production environment. A sample-set of users are identified, and the design is rolled out to those users. Thus, the pilot phase is in full swing.

The pilot phase has two purposes. One is to confirm that the Active Directory design functions in a pseudo-production environment as intended. The second is to gather information about how the design deploys to the pilot group. What is learned from the pilot deployment is then used to determine the best method for deploying the product across the enterprise.

Some other useful information gained during the pilot is the types of support and training necessary to make the pilot successful. Along with security and accessibility of resources, the amount of network bandwidth consumed by the pilot and the availability of piloted services are also types of information that can be gathered during the pilot and compared to what was recorded in the lab.

Implementing Active Directory Design

The implementation plan must implement Active Directory as defined in the Active Directory design. This means that the implementation plan itself should only specify how the components of Active Directory are going to be configured to create an Active Directory that mirrors Active Directory design. Actual Active Directory design decisions or components belong in the Active Directory design, not the implementation plan.

It is possible that the implementation plan itself might be more detailed and complex than the Active Directory design. Much of this depends on the current environment and how users and resources are going to be transitioned from any existing directory to Active Directory. If a directory exists within your organization, such as Windows NT or Novel (NDS), then upgrading from those technologies might be necessary to minimize user disturbance and to maintain the investment in directory data contained in the current directory service.

Implementation Team

The goal of the implementation plan is to take the Active Directory design and deploy it to the enterprise so that it meets the intended business and technical requirements of your organization. It can be tempting to change or interpret the Active Directory design in such a way that might inadvertently compromise the Active Directory design. This is one of the reasons that it's important to include members of the Active Directory design team on the implementation planning team. In most organizations, the Active Directory design team and the implementation team are going to be one and the same. However, in organizations where this is not necessarily the case, the Active Directory design team needs to be involved in the implementation to some degree. One option is to have the Active Directory design team review the implementation plan, commenting as to what degree it meets the Active Directory design. However, including Active Directory design team members on the implementation planning team helps ensure the implementation plan produces an Active Directory environment that meets the Active Directory design.

The Active Directory implementation planning team is implementation focused. As a team, it should include members who are responsible for implementing Windows 2000 across the enterprise. In addition to members of the Active Directory design team, the list of roles that are necessary to implement the Active Directory design includes project managers, system engineers, trainers, and testers.

Deliverables

The implementation plan can take many shapes, usually in the form of one or more deliverables. Some deliverables are detailed documents, which outline everything to be done and how they are to be accomplished. These types of implementation plans are usually for larger, more complex, environments. They can also be found in organizations that hire a consultancy to produce the implementation plan, which is then handed off to the organization for execution.

Other implementation plans are contained in a Microsoft Project plan. These implementation plans are schedule, resource, and task focused, but they do not give much detail on how the tasks are going to be accomplished. These simple implementation plans are usually found in smaller organizations and entail using the detail found in the Active Directory design to perform the tasks found in the project plan.

Make sure your implementation plan contains enough details about the design so that there is little room for interpretation, and those who developed the Active Directory design agree that the approach taken by the implementation plan meets the timeline and the other business requirements detailed in the Active Directory design.

Defining an Implementation Approach

Your implementation approach depends greatly on the systems that currently support your users. Chances are your organization already has one or more directories. Knowing if, and how, you are going to migrate from these directories helps define the implementation approach you need to take. For example, if you currently use Windows NT, then the likely path for implementation is through a migration of Windows NT accounts and resources to Active Directory. On the other hand, if your company uses Novell Netware 3.x, you implementation plan might not include a migration from Novell but a new Active Directory, employed with some form of coexistence established while the organization transitions to the new directory.

Strategy

One of the first steps in developing an implementation plan is to adopt an overall implementation strategy. This is something that has likely been thought through during the design phase, but should be solidified amongst the implementation team before developing the implementation plan.

There can be multiple ways to migrate from the current directory to Active Directory. Let's look again at the Windows NT example. There are at least three strategies that can be used to migrate from Windows NT to Active Directory.

1. **Upgrade in place**—The existing Windows NT domains are upgraded in place.

2. **Upgrade and Consolidate**—This is accomplished either by consolidating the Windows NT domains and then upgrading in place, or by upgrading in place and then consolidating Active Directory domains.

3. **Implementing then cloning the objects**—This results from installing a pristine new Active Directory domain topology and then using tools to move users, groups, and resources from Windows NT domains to Active Directory domains.

These approaches to migrating from Windows NT are described in more detail in Chapter 22, "Upgrading from Windows NT 4.0."

Each of these three strategies meets the needs of different organizations. Migrating from Windows NT to Windows 2000 is just that, a migration rather than an upgrade.

Based on your organization's current directory services and your need to maintain users' availability to resources and services, an implementation strategy should be chosen that takes you to your Active Directory design within the shortest amount of time and with minimal user disruption.

Pilot

The pilot phase of your Active Directory project is crucial to the success of implementation. Don't consider the pilot phase the first phase of implementation. Rather, consider the pilot phase a lab experiment that extends into the production environment.

This means that you need to choose a group of users who represent a sample of your user environment and who meet a certain criteria, such as users who are computer savvy, accept change, are patient, and are willing to provide feedback. These pilot users should have training in how Active Directory can be used and how it affects their working environment.

Identifying Pilot Users

Pilot users should not be Information Systems (IS) personnel exclusively. They should include, if possible, users from every part of the enterprise. MAC users, PC users, and administrators, to name a few. If your Active Directory design defines multiple organizational units (OUs) with corresponding group policies, then users in these OUs should be included in the pilot. If you have applications that rely on non-Windows-based systems, which survive the implementation to Active Directory, then users who use these systems should be included in the pilot.

If possible, the pilot users should be volunteers who are willing to participate in the pilot. Participation can include providing feedback and testing functionality. They should also understand that the availability of services might not be what they are accustomed to, but that there is support provided just for them. The pilot users should also understand that they are a part of a pilot implementation and not simply the first group selected for production rollout. Typically, there are things expected of pilot users that are not expected of other users within the organization. These expectations should be defined before the pilot phase begins.

Pilot User Support

How your pilot users are going to be supported should be well established before the pilot. This means the support, or Helpdesk, organization needs to have personnel ready to support the pilot users. If these support personnel are going to use Windows 2000 tools to support the pilot users, they become part of the pilot themselves. After the support infrastructure is in place, as defined by the Active Directory design, support calls should be documented along with their resolution. This information can then be used to train all the support, or Helpdesk, staff, before Active Directory is implemented to the enterprise.

Pilot User Training

The pilot phase also offers the opportunity to test the suite of training curriculum that the Active Directory design has identified. For both end users and administrators participating in the pilot, training curriculum should be established. The pilot gives you the opportunity to test this training to see if it is sufficient for your various types of users.

The Pilot Duration

The duration of the pilot depends on the complexity of the design and the scope of the project. The duration should be long enough to adequately test the current, as well as the additional, functionality provided by Active Directory and Windows 2000. The pilot can be extended if problems arise that would hinder implementation or put the design in question. Going back to the drawing board, or lab, should always be an option if the pilot does not go well. Although it can extend the timeline of the overall project, in the long run, going back to the drawing board might be necessary to ensure the success of the project.

What Should Be Learned from the Pilot

Again, the pilot is a test deployment testing the Active Directory design in production, the deployment process, user education and support, and the tasks necessary to configure the services that make up your Active Directory.

After the pilot has matured, take what you have learned and amend the Active Directory design to reflect your new understanding of how Active Directory works in your environment. You can make the changes required to meet your existing business or technical requirements, or you might make changes based on new business or technical requirements that you discovered during the pilot phase.

The other important learning experience to be gained from the pilot is that of deployment. The pilot is a small-scale implementation. Keep track of the tasks necessary to deploy your pilot services. These tasks are then expanded and become incorporated into the implementation plan.

Single Step Approach

One approach to implementation is the *single step* approach. This approach entails implementing Active Directory across the enterprise in a single step. Obviously, this approach only applies to small organizations with limited users and simple existing directory services.

After the Active Directory design has been tested in the lab, an implementation plan should be drafted that defines how the Active Directory design is to be implemented in your organization in a single step. Single step approaches are well-orchestrated efforts that include a well thought-out rollback plan. Before deciding on the single step approach, make sure it is practical for your organization.

Phased Approach

The more common approach to implementation is the *phased* approach. This approach assumes that it is not practical to implement Windows 2000 Active Directory across the enterprise in a single step. Therefore, Active Directory is rolled out in phases. Typically the phases include some preparatory phases, followed by phases based on geographic location, and finally, post-installation or clean-up phases.

Some of the phases included in the phased approach are

- Preparation of NT 4.0 domains
- Establishment of root domain and DNS services
- Phases based on geographic locations
- Demolition of NT domains
- Moving to Native Mode

What phases are required, and in what order, is difficult to determine without an Active Directory design. The method of determining the phases necessary for your organization should be based on the layout of your physical locations and the domain topology, as well as each location's requirements. In general, those locations or domains with limited users and resources are candidates for implementation in an early phase. Likewise, those locations that have applications that can immediately benefit from Active Directory should also be included in one of the early phases. On the other hand, those locations that have large numbers of users or that have application running on Domain Controllers (DCs) that can not be upgraded to Active Directory can be included in one of the final phases of implementation.

Defining a Set of Implementation Tasks

Defining a set of implementation tasks is the heart of the implementation plan. It is the tasks that make your Active Directory design come to life. The tasks are defined and then applied to specific geographic locations based on a rollout schedule. The categories of tasks include

- **Preparation Tasks**—prepare the enterprise for implementation.
- **Base Services**—are those tasks that establish the root domain and basic Active Directory services.
- **Coexistence Tasks**—prepare the existing directory services and resources for coexistence with Active Directory.
- **Geographic Location Tasks**—are the redundant tasks that are applied to each geographic location.

- **Post Rollout Tasks**—are the tasks that are applied to the enterprise after rollout is complete.

- **Coexistence Breakdown Tasks**—are tasks that breakdown coexistence and phase out the existing directory services. These tasks might take place several months after the rollout is complete.

The tasks that make up your task list depend on the type of rollout your implementation requires. For example, the set of tasks for a new installation of Active Directory is different than the set of tasks necessary for an upgrade or migration from an existing directory, such as Windows NT. This is because each approach is different in how you get from where you are to the prescribed design. Upgrading from Windows NT to Windows 2000 and Active Directory is a different process with different tasks than implementing a new Active Directory domain structure and cloning objects from Windows NT to the new Active Directory domain structure.

As always, after these tasks are defined, they should be tested in the lab to confirm that the end result is what is expected. This might take some additional time and resources, however, if lab testing ensures a smooth implementation, it is well worth it.

Preparation Tasks

The tasks to prepare for implementation include such things as readying the existing directory services to be migrated to Active Directory. Again, specific tasks depend on the type of implementation that you are planning to undertake and the end product described by your Active Directory design. In the case of a migration from Windows NT, such tasks might include

- Evaluating existing NT group structure and assuring that the existing Global Groups and Local Groups are necessary

- Inventorying NT group membership

- Accounting for existing NT accounts, their purpose, and their destination in the Active Directory domain structure

- Purchasing hardware required to support Active Directory design

- Upgrading any existing hardware that continues to be used to support Windows 2000 and Active Directory

- Collapsing NT domains if consolidation occurs before migration

- Installing and testing migration tools and preparing NT DCs as needed by migration tools

Base Services Tasks

Another set of tasks that must be defined are those that establish Active Directory in your environment. These tasks might include

- Installing the first DC in the forest
- Creating enterprise administrative accounts and delegating appropriate permissions
- Installing and configuring DNS, including integrating DNS into Active Directory if specified in your Active Directory design

Coexistence Tasks

Coexistence tasks define the steps necessary to establish coexistence between existing directory services and Active Directory. Where and when these tasks are performed depends on the type of rollout you are planning. If you have a multi-domain Active Directory and you are migrating from a multi-domain Windows NT directory, then these tasks fall just after each domain has been established. The list of tasks varies depending on the type of coexistence you require for migration.

For example, if you are installing a pristine Active Directory domain structure and then moving users between the existing Windows NT domains and Active Directory using tools, such as *ClonePrincipal*, then trusts need to be established. These trusts can be created manually, or in complex domain environments where there are many resource domains, you can use a tool, such as *NetDom*, to script the creation of trusts. On the other hand, if you are upgrading your NT domains in place, either to leave the domain topology as is or to move user objects after the domain has been upgraded, then the tasks necessary for preparing for coexistence are simplified.

Geographic Location Tasks

Geographic tasks are those tasks required to establish domain services in specific geographic locations. Each geographic location can be a domain in itself, or it can be part of a larger multi-location domain. In either scenario, there are two different sets of tasks depending on whether the domain is being established or whether the location is going to support additional DCs.

Establishing Domains

The first set of geographic-specific tasks is for establishing the domains in a multi-domain Active Directory. These tasks include

- Installing the first DC in the domain within the existing forest
- Creating sites as prescribed by the Active Directory design
- Creating the domain OU structure as prescribed by the Active Directory design
- Creating Group Policy Objects (GPOs) and applying them to sites, the domain, and OUs where appropriate

- Creating groups as prescribed by the Active Directory design
- Delegating permissions as prescribed by the Active Directory design
- Confirming directory configuration and schema partition replication with root domain
- Shipping hardware to remote location and configuring for localization.

Extending the Domains to all Locations

After the domains have been established, additional DCs are installed and configured and then located, as defined in the Active Directory design. The steps to ready these domain services might include the following:

- Install the DC and join the existing domain.
- Move the DC into the destination site.
- Configure site links with appropriate protocol, as prescribed by the Active Directory design.
- Confirm the domain, configuration, and schema replication.
- Install the DNS if defined in Active Directory design.
- Configure the DC as a Global Catalog (GC) server if defined in Active Directory design.
- Ship the DC if necessary, and then readdress to the local subnet. Confirm that the DNS has been updated.
- Deploy MMC snap-in(s) to the appropriate administrative workstation.

Again, this is not meant to be an exhaustive list of tasks for DC implementation. Modify this list to include the tasks that you had to go through when you implemented your Active Directory pilot.

Post-Rollout Tasks

Post-rollout tasks can be done at the end of the geographical implementation or during the implementation, whenever appropriate. These tasks center on deploying the services that are required by users or that are required to support your Active Directory. Such tasks include

- Implementing remote access to your Active Directory, as defined in the Active Directory design. This might include a Virtual Private Network (VPN) solution, a RAS solution, or both.
- Implementing network services, such as QoS.
- Installing scripts to be used to administer Active Directory. Administrators or Helpdesk personnel can use these scripts to maintain Active Directory.

- Implementing IntelliMirror as defined in the Active Directory design. This can include creating network installation points, and so on. More information on IntelliMirror can be found in Chapter 12, "Managing the Desktop."
- Installing and configuring the Active Directory Connector (ADC). If your organization uses Microsoft Exchange 5.5, you can populate your Active Directory with directory data from Exchange. The ADC is installed as described in the Active Directory design.
- Assigning Flexible Single Master of Operations (FSMO) roles as defined in Active Directory design.

Coexistence Breakdown Tasks

Some organizations might continue to coexist with existing directory services indefinitely. However, if you plan on decommissioning the existing directory services after the migration is complete, the final implementation task list includes those tasks required to de-configure Active Directory's coexistence with the old directory service.

In the case of Windows NT, this can include turning down the remaining Backup Domain Controllers (BDC) that are not going to be upgraded, and then configuring Active Directory to run in Native Mode never to support Windows NT DCs again.

Additional Implementation Plan Components

Along with the implementation of DCs, which make up the domains and sites in the Active Directory design, there are other components to an Active Directory implementation plan. Remember, the implementation plan must contain the processes necessary to implement the Active Directory design. Therefore, if there is an aspect to the Active Directory design that is not addressed in the implementation plan, the implementation plan is not complete.

Here are some additional sections that might be appropriate for your implementation plan.

Defining Rollback Plan

Don't consider a rollback plan pessimistic, rather consider it prudent. Although you go through the process of testing hardware, designs, and implementation tasks in the lab and then you go to the effort of running a pilot to confirm your procedures and prepare for implementation, there is always the chance your deployment will not go as planned. There could be any number of reasons you might want to rollback during a migration. What's important is that you have the ability to rollback if necessary. A rollback plan gives you that ability.

Take some time to consider what would happen during each phase of the implementation if you were to have to rollback. In some cases, all that would be lost is pride and man-hours. In other cases, it would be possible to lose data or cause an extended service outage.

Components of the rollback plan can be built into the implementation strategy. For example, if you are upgrading Windows NT 4.0 domains, it might be prudent to take a BDC from each domain off the network before the domain is upgraded. This way, if the upgrade goes south and the existing BDCs are affected, you will have the offline BDC to promote to a Primary Domain Controller (PDC) as part of a rollback plan.

Defining an Implementation Schedule

Scheduling the implementation project can be a difficult task. Some of the issues around scheduling your implementation project include the following:

- Determining task dependencies
- Placing tasks in order of predecessors to dependencies
- Calculating the number of business days from when the implementation begins to the project deadline, and subtracting at least one week
- Calculating the number of man-days required to accomplish the ordered tasks, and taking into account project milestones and possible simultaneous tasks
- Calculating the number of resources necessary to produce the necessary number of man-days in the number of business days until the deadline
- Building in slack time between phases for such things as travel time, unforeseen delays, vacations, sick time, holidays, hardware lead times, and so on

This is basic project management. Simplified, yes, but you should get the picture. In more complex implementations, utilizing the skills of a professional project manager can help the project run smoothly.

Defining Milestones

How you define milestones is dependent on your philosophy of project management. Some milestones are established between phases, to measure progress and to make adjustments as necessary. Other milestones are major dependencies during the implementation. Milestones might not be based on tasks but on geography. For example, if your enterprise spans multiple countries or continents, milestones might be established that break up the DC rollout phase by country.

Defining Dependencies

Dependencies are simply those tasks that must be performed before one another. In a project such as this, there are several dependencies based on the premise that a system is being built. As you learn more about Active Directory and test it in the lab, you begin to see the order in which things must be done to build your Active Directory.

Defining the Resources Required to Meet the Schedule

If you have limited resources, then the number of business days necessary to complete the project might have to expand. If you have unlimited resources, there are still dependencies and milestones that cause the project to extend over some period of time, which is in relation to the complexity of your environment.

Managing the Implementation Project

Project management is all about communication and organization. Although you might have a well-drafted implementation plan, if it is not executed well, the project will likely have problems. Tools as common as Microsoft Project can be used to manage tasks, resources, and schedules. Project methodologies, such as the *system life cycle*, can be used to conduct the Active Directory implementation. However your organization conducts its projects, planning, testing, communication, and organization will help ensure a successful implementation.

Summary

The implementation plan is but one step in the overall Active Directory project. The Active Directory design defines the environment. The lab confirms the design and allows for adjustments. The pilot tests the design in a pseudo-production environment and helps you build your implementation plan. The implementation plan makes your design come to life.

18

Windows 2000 and Exchange Server

ONE OF THE MOST COMMON AND SUCCESSFUL MICROSOFT BackOffice products is Microsoft Exchange. In many organizations, the Exchange messaging system brought Windows NT out of the workgroup and spread it across the enterprise. Exchange, as a messaging system, offered the benefits of a true client/server system with the convenience of centralized management. Able to support tens of users to tens of thousands of users, Exchange offers a scalable, standards-based messaging system that is packed full of functionality. If your organization uses Microsoft Exchange, the way that it coexists with Windows 2000 is an important part of your Windows 2000 and Active Directory planning process.

Exchange 5.5

The first version of Microsoft Exchange, version 4.0, was an X.400-focused messaging system. Exchange was based on the X.400 architecture with a message store, a message transfer agent, gateway services, clients, and a directory. The Exchange directory is an X.500-based directory that embraces many of the principals and functionality of X.500.

The Exchange directory is the focal point of communications between Exchange components, as shown in Figure 18.1. Before any Exchange component can communicate with another Exchange server in the organization, the component contacts the directory to obtain the component's address.

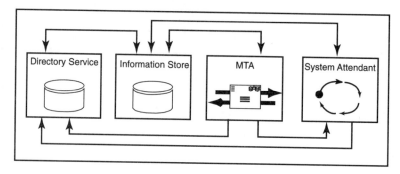

Figure 18.1   Exchange 5.5 core component communication.

The Exchange directory is a critical component of the Exchange messaging system. However, the Exchange directory is not a security sub-system. Rather, Exchange relies on Windows NT for its security services. Typically, a Windows NT user can only access Exchange objects for which the user has been granted the permissions. This creates an association between the Exchange directory and the Windows NT directory. The mailbox/NT-account association added complexity to the scalability of Exchange because two directories, each with their own requirements, are required to support the system across the enterprise.

As Windows NT evolved, it became apparent that the NT directory would have to be greatly enhanced to make Windows NT a contender in the data-center. Microsoft needed a directory service that could compete with the likes of Novell's Directory Service (NDS), another X.500-based directory service. The Exchange directory, already proven scalable, was chosen as the prototype for the Windows NT 5.0 directory. Hence, the Exchange directory evolved into Windows 2000 Active Directory. This means that Exchange administrators and implementers are going to see familiarities between the Exchange directory and Active Directory.

This also means that when you use Exchange 4.0 or 5.x with Active Directory, you are supporting two X.500-like directories in the same environment. Both directories employ a multi-master directory that replicates all the changes between Domain Controllers (DCs) or Exchange servers.

Fortunately, Microsoft provides an efficient tool to synchronize these two directories. This enables organizations to continue with the investment made in maintaining the rich data found in the Exchange directory. This also means that Active Directory can be populated with data from the Exchange directory.

Supporting Two Directories

Many organizations are going to migrate from Windows NT to Windows 2000 for the added value it brings to their organizations. Those organizations that also support Microsoft Exchange 4.0 or 5.x have the opportunity to upgrade to Exchange 2000, Active Directory-integrated version of Microsoft Exchange. However, after energy and budget has been spent on the migration to Windows 2000, it is likely that the upgrade to Exchange 2000 will take place sometime after the Windows 2000 migration project is complete.

This means that Windows 2000 Active Directory and Exchange 4.0 or 5.x will have to coexist. Two directories need to be maintained, supported, and synchronized. Users have access to two X.500-like directories and should be able to find the information they are looking for in either. This means that if a change is made to a user's phone number in the Exchange directory, the change should be synchronized as soon as possible to Active Directory. A user should not see two different phone numbers for the same user, depending on the directory the user queries.

Synchronization adds some complexity to supporting two directories. Before, when there was just Windows NT and Exchange, the information contained in each was mutually exclusive. For example, there was no phone number attribute in the Windows NT directory. Hence, synchronization between the directories was not an issue. However, with the Exchange and Active Directory directories, synchronization is necessary because your organization's directory data is duplicated across two directories and must be synchronized.

Active Directory Connector and Windows 2000

Microsoft provides the *Active Directory Connector* (ADC) with Windows 2000 as a means of synchronizing the Exchange 5.5 directory and Active Directory, see Figure 18.2. There are two versions of the ADCs. One that ships with Windows 2000, and one that ships with Exchange 2000. The Windows 2000 version synchronizes mail-enable objects between Exchange 5.5 and Active Directory. The Exchange 2000 version of the ADC not only synchronizes mail-enabled objects between the two directories, but it also synchronizes the configuration between the Exchange site and the Active Directory configuration partition. If Exchange 5.5 is to be supported by Windows 2000 and Active Directory and synchronization is required between Exchange 5.5 and Active Directory, the ADC that ships with Windows 2000 is one required. The version of ADC that ships with Exchange 2000 is discussed later in this chapter.

The ADC uses Lightweight Directory Access Protocol (LDAP) 3.0 to access and update each directory as changes are made. Currently, the ADC only synchronizes Active Directory with Exchange 5.5.

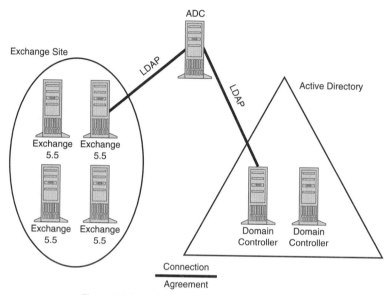

Figure 18.2 The Active Directory connector.

Connection Agreements

On the ADC, *connection agreements* are configured between each directory. These connection agreements define which objects are synchronized between each directory. Connection agreements also define which Exchange recipient containers synchronize with which Active Directory organizational units (OUs).

Connection agreements are configured with such parameters as

- Synchronization directory, which defines the direction synchronization in which occurs.

- Which containers in each directory are synchronized.

- A synchronization schedule, which defines the times at which synchronization occurs.

- What happens to deleted objects in each directory, and whether they are deleted in the synchronized directory or whether the deletion is logged.

- Whether the connection agreement is considered a *primary connection agreement*, which is the connection agreement that synchronizes new objects created in a directory. There is a primary connection agreement parameter for each synchronization direction. This parameter should only be specified on one connection agreement per Active Directory domain and on one connection agreement per Exchange site.

The configuration of connection agreements is simple and works well. However, there are instances in which the ADC design can be tricky. For example, an Exchange multi-site design might have been based on the top-level Windows NT domain topology of an organization, as seen in Figure 18.3.

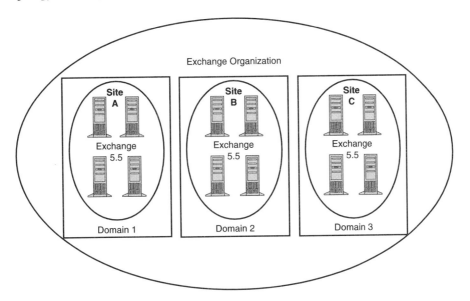

Figure 18.3 Typical multi-site Exchange organization.

If this organization upgrades from Windows NT to Windows 2000 and Active Directory, the three Windows NT domains are collapsed into two splitting the users of Domain 2 between Active Directory Domains X and Y, as in Figure 18.4.

Now that the Windows NT Domain 2 no longer exists, its users have been split between the two Active Directory domains, X and Y (assuming Domain 2 was not absorbed by a single domain). In this situation, you only want to synchronize the domain objects with the site that hosts those objects. In addition, you need to decide as to where new objects in each domain and site are synchronized.

- New objects created in Site A synchronize to Domain X. Also, new objects created in Domain X synchronize with Site A. Hence, the connection agreement between Site A and Domain X is configured as the primary connection agreement for the both the Exchange site and Active Directory domain.

- New objects created in Site B synchronize to Domain X. Therefore, the connection agreement between Site B and Domain X is configured as the primary connection agreement for the Exchange site.

- The connection agreement between Site B and Domain Y only synchronize objects that already exist in both Site B and Domain Y. This connection agreement is not configured as a primary connection agreement.

- New objects created in Site C synchronize to Domain Y. Also, new objects created in Domain Y synchronize with Site C. Hence, the connection agreement between Site C and Domain Y are configured as the primary connection agreement for both the Exchange site and the Active Directory domain.

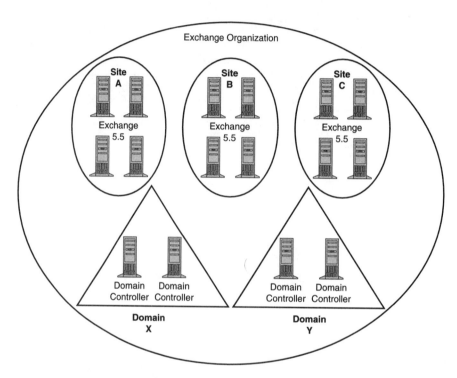

Figure 18.4 A typical multi-site Exchange organization after domain upgrade and consolidation.

With this configuration, connection agreements need to be defined between sites and domain that meet these requirements (see Figure 18.5). It is important to make sure all objects can synchronize with the corresponding directory container in which they belong. In addition, each site and directory must have a corresponding directory container in which new objects are created.

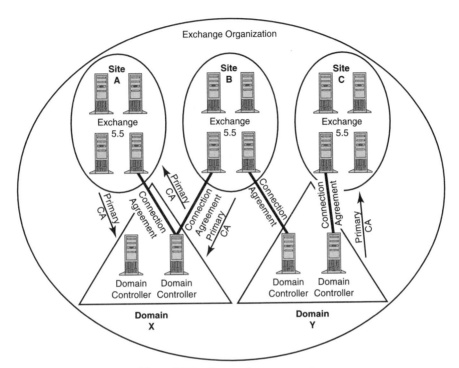

Figure 18.5 Connection agreements.

In this example, the primary connection agreements are configured so that new objects created in Site B synchronize with Domain X. The other connection agreements have been defined to meet the requirements previously defined.

ADC in the Lab

The ADC can also be used in your Active Directory lab. After you have designed one or more Active Directory domain topologies, you can use the ADC to import production data from your Exchange organization into the lab to test your Active Directory design(s).

This is done with one-way connection agreements from the production Exchange environment to the lab, as shown in Figure 18.6. After the directory data has been brought into the lab, you can test your Active Directory design. In addition, as changes are made to the Exchange directory, they are synchronized to the lab. After they are synchronized into the lab to the server defined in the Connection Agreement, they are replicated around the lab domain. This gives you the opportunity to see how Active Directory handles replication in your organization.

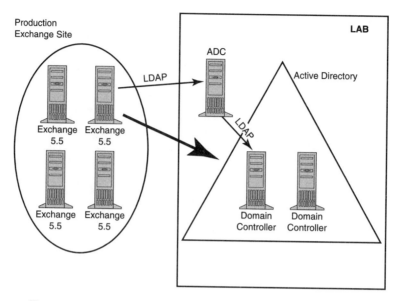

Figure 18.6 A lab using an ADC with one-way connection agreement.

Deploying the ADC

How the ADC is deployed also has to be planned and should be included in your implementation plan. This is important because the ADC changes the Exchange directory schema. If a connection agreement is created for a site for the first time, several attributes are changed and added to the Exchange schema. These schema changes to the Exchange directory are replicated to every Exchange server in the organization. Therefore, if you were to implement the ADC and its connection agreements to several sites at the same time, a considerable amount of Exchange replication traffic would occur across your organization. Hence, it is prudent to rollout the ADC in stages, allowing each site to replicate its schema changes before the next connection agreement is created. Create an ADC implementation schedule as part of your implementation plan, which addresses replication at a pace your infrastructure can withstand.

It is possible to install the ADC on an Active Directory DC. After this is done, the ADC does not need to communicate with the DC across the network for those connection agreements to the DCs domain. Rather, the ADC can open the LDAP session with the local DC. This reduces network bandwidth consumption by the ADC, but consumes DC resources. Whether this is prudent depends on the complexity of your environment, the number of changes made to your directories, and the size of your DCs.

Administration

Your Active Directory design should also define the way that your two directories are administered after synchronization is established using the ADC. If two-way connection agreements are created between the directories, changes can be made to either Active Directory or the Exchange directory. You might decide that all changes to mail-enabled objects, such as users with mailboxes, distribution lists, or custom recipients (Active Directory mail-enabled contacts), are done from the Windows 2000 Users and Computers management tool. The only thing that the Exchange administrator is used for is to change Exchange site configuration. Another option is for Exchange administration to take place as before, with all mail-enabled object changes made using the Exchange administrator. These changes would be reflected in Active Directory after it is synchronized.

The administration method you choose depends on the administration model that you currently have. If you plan to consolidate administrative tasks to groups of administrators who administer both users and mailboxes, then using users and computers to administer all mail-enabled objects is the best choice. If you plan to keep your current messaging system administration model, even at the mail-enabled-object level, separate from Active Directory administration, then segregating administration between users and computers, and the Exchange administrator is the best choice.

It is important to understand how the ADC works and how it is used in your environment. If your organization uses Microsoft Exchange, create a section in your Active Directory design for the ADC. This section should include how the ADC are deployed, what connection agreements exist, the frequency of synchronization, a way to monitor synchronization, and how the ADC is supported.

Competing Services

Windows 2000 and Microsoft Exchange can offer similar services. Another complication of supporting Exchange on Windows 2000 is deciding which services to offer on which system.

LDAP

If you host Microsoft Exchange on an Active Directory DC, two systems on the same computer are trying to use LDAP over Transmission Control Protocol (TCP) port 389. This causes TCP port contention and both services to fail. To avoid this, you should change the Exchange LDAP port to something other than TCP port 389.

After this change is made, everything should work fine; however, all LDAP clients that try to contact the Exchange server need to reference the new LDAP TCP port. For example, if you install Exchange on an Active Directory DC, change the Exchange LDAP TCP port to 390, configure an ADC connection agreement to the Exchange server, and then also specify the LDAP port on the connection agreement port 390.

SMTP

Windows 2000 comes with an SMTP host that can be used for several things, such as Active Directory replication between Active Directory DCs. Microsoft Exchange also has an SMTP host that can be used to connect Exchange sites or to communicate with foreign SMTP hosts, such as those on the Internet. If a Windows 2000 server supports an Exchange server, make sure that SMTP is only required by one of these systems. If the Exchange server running on Windows 2000 has the Internet Mail Service (IMS) configured, make sure the Windows 2000 SMTP host is not required.

Both a Windows 2000 Server and an Exchange server SMTP host can be supported on the same computer, as in Figure 18.7. This is made possible by changing the TCP port of one of the SMTP host from port 25 to another available TCP port. However, this means that the other SMTP hosts in this environment have to use that same SMTP port for communications.

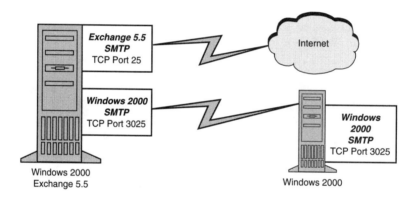

Figure 18.7 Two SMTP hosts on the same computer.

Although this is possible, it adds complexity to the configuration of your environment, and it should be avoided if possible.

Network News Transport Protocol (NNTP)

NNTP is another protocol that can exist on both Windows 2000 and Microsoft Exchange. To avoid port contention, as with SMTP, make sure that both Windows 2000 and Exchange are not both trying to use NNTP port 119.

It is also possible to change the TCP port associated with NNTP. The same rules and complexities apply that applied to SMTP.

Exchange 5.5 During the Upgrade

If upgrading from Windows NT to Windows 2000 Active Directory, special attention needs to be paid to user accounts and service accounts with regards to Exchange.

As you upgrade your NT domains, you want to make sure the association between the user's mailbox and NT account remains intact during the upgrade. This might influence the NT upgrade method you choose (see Chapter 22, "Upgrading from Windows NT 4.0," for more details).

If you upgrade your NT domain in place, the Exchange mailbox association should remain in place. If you intend to consolidate domains, which is likely, you need to consider whether it is possible to consolidate your NT 4.0 domains before the upgrade without breaking this mailbox/NT account association. If you are going to consolidate your domains after the upgrade, it is possible to upgrade your NT domains in place, to change your Active Directory to Native Mode, and then to use tools, such as *MoveTree*, to consolidate Active Directory domains. This should also keep your mailbox associations in place.

Whichever route you choose, lab testing plays an important roll in determining whether your Exchange mailboxes will maintain their associations with the proper Active Directory user accounts during the upgrade. This is yet another example of why lab testing is paramount to planning your Active Directory and to its implementation.

Exchange 2000

As different as Microsoft Windows 2000 is to Windows NT, Microsoft Exchange 2000 is to previous versions of Exchange. One of the most dramatic changes is that the Exchange directory has evolved (literally) into Active Directory. Exchange 2000 no longer supports its own directory. Rather, Exchange 2000 relies on Active Directory for *all* its directory services. This means that if your organization uses, or plans to use, Microsoft Exchange, you should consider the affect your Active Directory design decisions have on your Exchange organization. This section highlights some of Exchange 2000's design considerations for Active Directory.

Overview of Exchange 2000

In previous versions of Exchange, the Exchange directory was the focal point of the core components. Every Exchange component communicated with the directory for information required to fulfill their tasks.

In Exchange 2000, the directory is still a core component of Exchange. However, the objects and configuration that made up the Exchange 5.5 organization are now Active Directory objects. Mail-enabled recipients are Active Directory users, groups, and contacts. The equivalent Active Directory object and Exchange objects are defined Table 18.1.

Table 18.1 **Active Directory Object and the Equivalent Exchange Objects**

Exchange 4.0, 5.x Object	Active Directory Object
Mailbox	User
Distribution list	Distribution or security group
Custom recipient	Mail-enabled contact

Message transfer between Exchange 5.5 servers was done using RPCs within a site and using a connector between sites. Exchange 2000 no longer relies on RPCs for communications between servers within a site. SMTP is now the protocol used for intra-site communications. This means that every Exchange server is also an SMTP host.

The configuration of previous versions of Exchange was based on an X.500-like directory that consisted of an organization, which contained sites, which contained configuration information, servers, and mail recipients. This design was limited in that the site defined an administrative context as well as a routing context. If there is limited bandwidth between physical locations, sites need to be defined to support a connector, which could control messages between physical locations and compensate for the limited bandwidth. Because the site also defined the administrative context, those physical locations now have administrative boundaries between them, regardless of whether this was desired or not. Exchange 2000 resolves this by breaking apart the administrative and routing contexts. Exchange 2000 incorporates *administrative groups* and *routing groups* that, when in Exchange 2000 Native Mode, can be defined separately.

In Figure 18.8, administrative groups are defined based on the administrative model of the organization, whereas routing groups are defined based on the available network bandwidth between sites.

You notice in the preceding example that Exchange 2000 also uses the terms Native Mode and mixed-mode. Like Active Directory, which supports down-level DCs when in mixed-mode, Exchange 2000 when in mixed-mode also supports down-level Exchange servers. Only after Exchange 2000 has been switched to Native Mode can the full functionality of the product be realized.

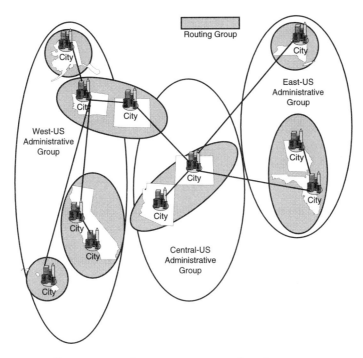

Figure 18.8 Administrative groups and routing groups.

Administrative Groups

Administrative groups are collections of configuration objects and servers. They can be created based on the administrative model of your messaging environment. In the previous example, in which there are multiple physical locations with limited bandwidths between them, there are three regional IS group locations in their regions. With Exchange 2000, it is possible to define an administrative group for each region, independent of the network and domain topology. By grouping servers and objects together in administrative groups, the administration of those objects can be granted to the appropriate administrators or groups, regardless of the organization's physical topology.

Routing Groups

Although administrative groups group servers and objects together based on an organization's administrative model, routing groups group servers together based on network topology. As with Exchange 5.5 sites and Active Directory sites, the server's within a routing group communicate directly with one another as needed, using SMTP. Servers within a routing group are assumed to have adequate bandwidth between them; therefore, no effort is made to conserve network bandwidth, either through scheduling or data compression.

To connect routing groups, *routing group connectors* are used. As with previous versions of Exchange, the routing group connectors include X.400 and SMTP connectors. Rather than a site connector, which used RPC, the routing group connector uses SMTP to move messages between routing groups. One or more messaging bridgehead servers, along with a delivery schedule, can be defined for the routing group connector.

Stores

Another advancement with Exchange 2000 is the capability to support multiple stores on a single Exchange 2000 server. This means that instead of having a single 50GB message store for 1000 users, the Exchange 2000 Server could support those same 1000 users on five 10GB message stores (assuming 50MB per user). The main advantage here is that each message store can be backed up and restored independently of the others. If one message store becomes corrupt, the other four stores continue to operate while the fifth message store is being restored. Furthermore, the restore time for that message store would be approximately one-fifth the time of the single 50GB store.

The stores defined on an Exchange 2000 server are divided up into storage groups. There can be up to 15 storage groups per system (plus one hidden used for restore). Each storage group can support up to six message stores, all sharing a single transaction log.

New Services

Exchange 2000 offers expanded functionality in many areas, such as Outlook Web Access and public folders. It also offers additional services, such as Instant Messaging, Video Conferencing, multi-media messaging, and the installable file system, which enables you to mount a network drive to a folder in the Exchange 2000 system, such as your mailbox or a public folder.

Exchange 2000 servers can also be configured to play a particular role in your messaging system. With Exchange 2000, you can configure servers to be *protocol servers* and *message store servers* with a front-end/back-end relationship, as in Figure 18.9. Protocol servers accept connectivity from any of the supported Internet protocols, such as POP3 and IMAP4, and forward the packets to the appropriate message store server. This way, you can have a group of protocol servers defined as front-end servers with multiple message store servers as back-end servers. Users need not know what Exchange 2000 server their mailbox resides on, they just need to connect to the front-end protocol server(s).

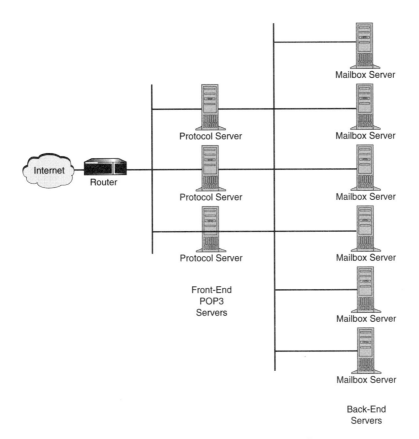

Figure 18.9   Front-end protocol and back-end mailbox servers.

Design Considerations

Exchange 2000 is the epitome of how an application, which is central to the enterprise, can rely on Active Directory for its functionality. Rather than an autonomous application that runs on top of the operating system, Exchange 2000 extends the functionality of Windows 2000 to provide messaging related services to users.

Fortunately, no major Active Directory design considerations are influenced by Exchange 2000. As it should be, the Active Directory design that fits your organization's business requirements also meets the requirements of Exchange 2000. However, some aspects of each design component should be noted.

Forest Design

Having just proclaimed that Exchange 2000 does not affect your Active Directory design, there is one exception. With previous versions of Exchange, it was possible to have an Exchange organization that spanned multiple sites, which in Windows NT domains were untrusted. As long as a single service account was used for each Exchange site and all the servers within the site were in a domain that trusted the service account's domain, there was no Exchange requirement for trusts between domains that did not span sites.

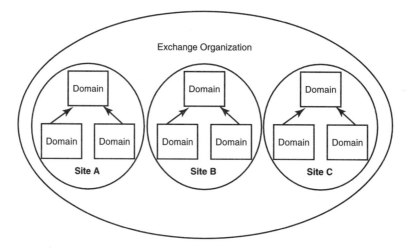

Figure 18.10   A single Exchange 5.5 organization with untrusted master domains.

This scenario is not possible with Exchange 2000. Active Directory is made up of a single Forest that hosts domains that all trust one another. That single Forest *is* the Exchange organization.

If upgrading this NT 4.0 domain model to Active Directory, you need to re-evaluate why you have multiple domains that are untrusted, and make one of two choices:

1. Decide having a single Forest with trusting domains does meets the administrative and security requirements of your organization and upgrade your Windows NT domain model to a single Active Directory Forest.

2. Decide that your organization must have separate security boundaries, schemas, configurations, and therefore, multiple Active Directory Forests.

Either of these choices will support Exchange 2000. However, if you choose to create multiple Forests, make sure that you and your organization understand the limitations multiple Forests place on Active Directory and Exchange 2000. You also need to develop a coexistence strategy between the two domains that supports message delivery and directory synchronization.

Domain Topology

The domain topology consists of one or more domains in one or more domain trees. The domain tree is defined by the domain name system (DNS) namespace assigned to the domains.

Exchange 2000 user–SMTP addresses are not affected by this namespace. A user in `northamerica.wadeware.net` can have the SMTP address of `user@wadeware.net` and `user@wadeco.com`, independent of the DNS domain address.

However, the *User Principal Name (UPN)*, which is a unique name in the Forest and can be used by the user to login from anywhere on the network, is by default `user@northamerica.wadeware.net`. This Forest-unique name assigned to each user object enables the user to login without knowing their domain. Some organizations might want to make the user's SMTP address the same as the user's UPN. This way, a user could log into the network using their suspected SMTP address.

Other organizations will want to avoid this. It would go against their security policy to have the user logon alias the same as the user SMTP alias. This would mean that when you know a person's SMTP address, you also know their logon alias. To add complexity to hacking a user account, the SMTP alias and logon alias are different.

Exchange 2000 does not affect the overall domain structure. It is possible to have Exchange 2000 routing groups span domains, with some Exchange 2000 servers in one domain and the rest in another domain, all within the same routing group.

OU Design

OU's are also Active Directory components that are not affected by Exchange 2000. User and computer locations within the domain are irrelevant to Exchange 2000. However, for organizational reasons, you might want to group all your domain's Exchange servers in an OU within your OU structure.

Outlook users, who use the Outlook Address Book, do not see OU's. Rather, Address Book lists are maintained by Exchange 2000 and are used by Outlook users to locate mail recipients. Address Book lists are built and managed by Exchange 2000, using LDAP filters. Several Address Book lists are pre-built and installed with Exchange 2000, and you can easily design your own custom Address Book lists.

Site Design

Active Directory sites are also, for the most part, unaffected by Exchange 2000. The design considerations that go into deciding what Active Directory sites to create also go into deciding what Exchange 2000 routing groups to create. The principals of Active Directory sites and Exchange 2000 routing groups are similar.

Exchange 2000 data conferencing services do assign a conference manager per Active Directory site. You can designate multiple conference managers within an Active Directory site. However, this is done only for redundancy purposes; only one conference manager can be active at a time.

Service Location

Remember that Active Directory clients require access to DNS, Active Directory DCs, and Global Catalog (GC) services to be authenticated by Active Directory. These same services are required for clients to access Exchange 2000 messaging services.

Exchange 2000 servers also need access to these services. As they communicate with one another, authentication, server location, and group expansion all require access to DNS, DCs, and GC services.

Make sure you place adequate services within close proximity to Exchange 2000 servers and clients.

Schema Modifications

Exchange 2000 makes approximately 650 changes to the Active Directory schema. These changes are made when the first Exchange 2000 server is installed in Active Directory. Additional attributes are also added to the Global Catalog (GC). This means that the Active Directory schema and configuration partitions need to have to replicate these changes throughout the Active Directory Forest. Hence, the first Exchange 2000 server should be installed at a time when the infrastructure can handle this amount of replications.

Another option is to run the Exchange 2000 setup with the /schemaonly switch. This switch does not install Exchange 2000, but only makes changes to the schema and configuration. Therefore, if your organization is going to implement Exchange 2000 after Active Directory has been deployed, it might be prudent to run the Exchange 2000 setup with the /schemaonly switch after the first few DCs have been implemented. This makes the Exchange 2000 modifications to the schema and configuration early so that as additional DCs and GC servers are implemented, these changes can be contained in the initial copy of these database partitions. Then, when you are ready to implement Exchange 2000, all DCs and GC servers have the changes necessary to support Exchange 2000.

Group Design

Exchange 2000 uses Active Directive groups for group messaging. Active Directory has both *security groups* and *distribution groups*. Both types of Active Directory groups contain users, contacts, and other groups. Both types of groups can be mail recipients, which means that you can send mail to both security and distribution groups. Security groups, however, can also be assigned permissions on network resources. This means that your group structure within Active Directory can be simplified. You don't have to create a distribution list for engineers and a Windows NT Group for engineers, and then maintain both. You can create a single security group, engineers, and assign it permissions on network resources and send messages to it. You want to make sure that you don't inadvertently grant a user permission to resources if you really intended them to be a member of the messaging group. Remember, if you put a user into a security group, not only will they receive messages mailed to that group, but they will also have access to the resources granted to that group.

There might also be groups of users for whom you want to group together only to receive messages and not to assign permissions. For these groups of users, you would use a distribution group.

The three types of groups, domain local, domain global, and universal groups can all contain different objects when in Active Directory mixed-mode or Active Directory Native Mode. Understanding the way that your organization uses groups is likely to be taken care of outside of Exchange 2000. When planning for Exchange 2000, you might need to add distribution groups, or even, security groups to supplement the group structure required to administer your Active Directory environment.

Universal groups are the most flexible of the groups. However, universal group membership is visible between domains. This means that the universal group's membership is published to the GC. Therefore, if you have a universal group with 1000 users that changes frequently, those changes are going to be replicated to all GC servers in the organizations. Global Groups, on the other hand, do not publish their membership to the GC. This means that users mailing to a global group from another domain are not able to see who is in that group. Hence, those groups whose membership is static and which needs to be visible across domains are a good fit for a universal group. Those groups whose membership is dynamic or which does not need to be visible across domains are a good fit for Global Groups.

Coexistence with Exchange 5.5

Exchange 2000 coexistence with Exchange 5.5 encompasses Active Directories coexistence with Exchange 5.5. This means that after you have established coexistence between Exchange 5.5 and Active Directory, using the ADC, extending that coexistence to include Exchange 2000 is not that complicated because the directories are already coexisting.

The Exchange 2000 Active Directory Connector

The user portions of the directories are coexisting, through the ADC, with a connection agreement. Exchange 2000 also requires coexistence between the configuration of Exchange 5.5 and Exchange 2000. This is accomplished with another type of connection agreement. The Exchange 2000 version of the ADC supports a *configuration connection agreement* that synchronizes the configuration of Exchange sites with the configuration of the Exchange 2000 administrative/routing groups.

This means that, before you install Exchange 2000 into an Exchange 5.5 site, you must have the Exchange 2000 version of the ADC installed. The Exchange 2000 setup program automatically configures a configuration connection agreement between the Active Directory domain and the Exchange 5.5 sites, as in Figure 18.11. This configuration connection agreement synchronizes the configuration of Exchange 2000 with *all* the sites in the Exchange 5.5 organization.

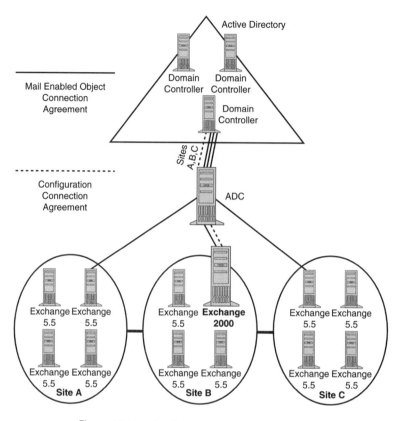

Figure 18.11   Configuration connection agreements.

The Site Replication Service (SRS)

The SRS is another piece of the coexistence puzzle. The SRS, for all practical purposes, is the Exchange 5.5 directory running on the Exchange 2000 server. This directory is *only* used to coexist with other pre-Exchange 2000 servers in the same organization.

When Exchange 2000 is installed into an Exchange site, the SRS accepts directory changes from other Exchange servers in the site. The ADC's configuration connection agreement then takes those changes and replicates them up to Active Directory.

The SRS can also accept changes from other Exchange sites. If the Exchange 2000 server is configured as the directory-replication bridgehead server for the site, it receives directory replication messages from other sites, and then replicates those changes, via RPC, to the other directory services in the site. Meanwhile, the ADC takes those changes from the SRS and synchronizes them up to Active Directory (see Figure 18.12).

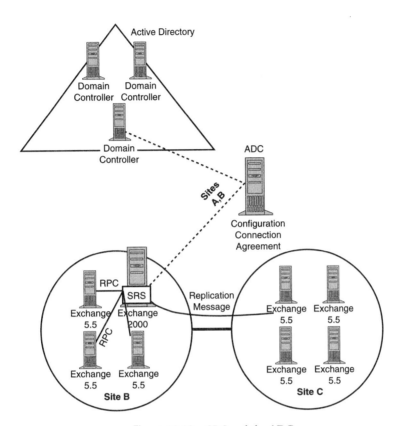

Figure 18.12   SRS and the ADC.

Thus, when installing an Exchange 2000 server into an Exchange site, making that server the directory replication bridgehead for the site makes directory replication to Active Directory more efficient.

Server Access

Exchange 2000 server uses GC services for many things. To reduce the burden on the GC servers in an organization, the Exchange 2000 server supports a directory access cache, *DSAccess*. If an Exchange 2000 server accesses the GC, the response is cached for a time (10 minutes). This helps reduce the burden placed on the GC servers by Exchange 2000.

Client Access

How Exchange 2000 clients access Active Directory depends on the client. The directory service proxy, *DSProxy*, process manages Exchange client access to Active Directory. If the Exchange 2000 system attendant starts, it uses DNS to locate a GC Server, which is then passed to DSProxy. DSProxy then acts on behalf of Exchange and Outlook97/98 clients that are accessing the Address Book by proxying the query to Active Directory. DSProxy refers Outlook 2000 and later MAPI clients to Active Directory for Address Book queries. After Outlook 2000 has been referred to an Active Directory server, the GC server is written to the client profile and all subsequent Address Book queries uses that Active Directory server.

Summary

Exchange 5.5 works seamlessly with Windows 2000 and Active Directory. With such tools as the ADC and SRS, Exchange 5.5 continues to be the reliable and scalable application it has always been. Exchange 2000 is one of the first truly Active Directory integrated applications in the BackOffice suite of products. By utilizing Active Directory, Exchange 2000 becomes an application that expands the functionality of Windows 2000 and Active Directory to include a rich set of messaging features.

19

Scripting with Active Directory

ACTIVE DIRECTORY IS, IN MANY FORMS, A DISTRIBUTED DATABASE. It has a schema. It has data values. It is replicated throughout your organization for use by administrators, end users, and applications.

With Active Directory, the Windows family of products is moving into a larger role within organizations. This new role provides Information Technology (IT) staffs with the ability to extend management and services to the entire enterprise through a single comprehensive view. Improved management of the enterprise is available through Active Directory, and scripts are efficient tools for managing the environment.

Benefits of Using Scripts

Using scripts provides several values to administrators. First, it provides clear documentation for what you are doing. If using a script for administration, you can always go back and reference exactly what you did.

Scripts provide a vehicle for logging exactly what you have done. By creating your scripts with logging, you are able to create an additional audit trail for what you are doing. This is a clear advantage over the point-and-click interface of a graphical user interface (GUI).

Scripts also provide a direct and quick interface to the directory. Rather than loading a GUI and traversing a tree with several clicks, you are able to get directly to the information with scripts.

Repetitive tasks do not require repetitive action if using a script. As an example, if you know that you are always going to use the same address when adding a user to the directory, you are able to create a script that always uses the same address. This also decreases user data entry errors. As you can see, the advantages of using scripts start to add up. A careful plan that includes well-documented scripts results in an easy and efficient customized administration toolset. The following list summarize the benefits of scripting:

- Clear documentation of administrative tasks
- Logging and documentation of tasks actually executed
- Quick and direct access to the directory
- Efficiency for repetitive tasks

Creating a Simple Script

Now that the benefits of creating a script for administration have been discussed, the next step is to create a script that modifies Active Directory.

Modifying the directory using scripts involves several parts. Without scripts, you can bring up the MMC and add the snap-in for modifying users and computers. After this is configured, you are able to select an object and modify the fields of the object online. If you perform this action, several items are taking place without your noting. First, the MMC snap-in is actually looking at the Active Directory schema. The schema includes the object names, the descriptive names, and the value or values for each object. As an example, if you open a user object and then look at the properties, there are many tabs of information. Looking at the General tab, there is the telephone number and email. Under the Address tab, you see the street, P.O. Box, state, and so on. With the descriptive name and the object name, you should be able to uniquely identify each field.

MMC Schema Snap-In

The Active Directory schema snap-in is available in the resource kit for Active Directory. This is found on the Server Install disc. You can install the resource kit by browsing the installation CD, going to the /support directory, and then the /tools directory, and then running 2000RSKT.MSI. 2000RSKT.MSI installs the Active Directory Schema snap-in that is used to look at the schema and to identify field names for modification.

A Simple Sample Script

Using the Active Directory schema snap-in and the Active Directory Users and Computers snap-in, you are able to look at the schema and view the fields for an object. A common practice is to change or modify the fields of an object. This example is designed to change fields for all the objects in an organizational unit (OU).

In this example, the business problem is that all the phone numbers and the addresses for all the users in a group have changed. There is a single switchboard number for the group and the office has changed locations for all the users in the GPLAB of Wadeware.

The Visual Basic script is designed to primitively modify the telephone number, street address, and zip code for all the users in the GPLAB OU. The state and city of the address have remained the same. To perform this task, the following script is created and named USERUPDATE.VBS.

```
REM userupdate.vbs
REM
REM
REM Subroutine Modify
REM   passes object that is a point in the tree
REM
Sub ModifyUsers(oObject)
Dim oUser
For Each oUser in oObject
Select Case oUser.Class
  Case "user"
    oUser.Put "streetAddress","1 Pennsylvania Avenue "
    ouser.Put "postalcode","98044"
    oUser.Put "telephoneNumber", "425-555-6666"
    oUser.SetInfo
  End select
Next
End Sub


REM Main program
REM
REM
Dim oDomain
Set oDomain=GetObject("LDAP://OU=GPLAB,DC=w2k,DC=Wadeware,DC=com")
ModifyUsers(oDomain)
MsgBox "Complete"
WScript.Quit
```

This script contains a body and a subroutine. The main program defines the domain object with the Dim statement. This is initialized with the GetObject routine that uses Lightweight Directory Access Protocol (LDAP) to locate the OU. ModifyUsers is called, using a pointer, to the location in the Active Directory tree that is defined by the LDAP path in the GetObject call.

The `ModifyUsers` subroutine takes the pointer to the tree location, and for each user at that point in the tree, it modifies the street address, zip code, and telephone number.

Testing the Script

This script can be easy to test. You need to create a working OU with a single user in it to begin. You can simplify this script even further by modifying only the telephone number. You are able point the script to the test tree by modifying the following line to point to the new point in the tree:

```
Set oDomain=GetObject("LDAP://OU=GPLAB,DC=w2k,DC=Wadeware,DC=net")
```

After you have made the changes to the script, the next step is to run some tests. You can do this by changing the phone number and by using the Active Directory Users and Computers MMC snap-in to validate the changes.

Using LDIFDE Utility

The LDAP Data Interchange Format utility is named LDIFDE. You are able to use this utility to manage the directory. You can export directory entries, import new entries, and change existing entries. This section describes how to export and change new entries.

Using LDIFDE, an administrator is able to create script files that can be used to perform maintenance functions. This section takes a detailed look at how to export, import, and modify existing entries.

LDIFDE has a long list of parameters. The first step is to understand some of the parameters and they can be used. For exporting, there are several parameters. They are as follows:

- `-I` is not used for export. Exporting is the default. `-I` is used for importing into the directory.

- `-f filename` is used to specify the filename to her the exported information is exported. The filename is also used on import to specify the information to be imported and from where.

- `-s servername` is the name of the server from which the directory information should be exported. The default for this field is the Domain Controller (DC) into which the system running the script is logged.

- `-c FromDN ToDN` is used to change the distinguished name (DN) of an object to another DN. The DN of an object is the unique name for the object in the entire active directory. As an example, the DN for a user, Bill Wade in the GPLAB OU in Wadeware's domain could look like - `CN=Bill Wade, CN=GPLAB, DC=Wadeware, DC=NET`. This is a handy way to export a file and to change where in the tree it is going. Another good use of this is if you are migrating from one domain to another domain.

- -v turns on the verbose mode. This is best used when testing a script. You are able to see exactly what is transpiring with the redirection log to a file.

- -j is used to specify the log file location. If you want to log the results of an export, you can also use this option.

- -t is used to specify the port number for access to the directory service. Port 389 is the default LDAP port.

- -d is used to specify the base DN of the search for the data export.

As an example, a simple command to export a single user to the directory is to run `ldifde -v -f output.lidf -d "cn=test user, cn=users,dc=Wadeware, DC=net"`. This command produces an output file called `OUTPUT.LIDF`. `OUTPUT.LIDF` contains the complete information for the user. This is depicted in the following listing:

```
dn: CN=test user,CN=Users,DC=Wadeware,DC=net
changetype: add
memberOf: CN=Testgroup,CN=Users,DC=Wadeware,DC=net
accountExpires: 9223372036854775807
streetAddress:
badPasswordTime: 0
badPwdCount: 0
codePage: 0
cn: test user
countryCode: 0
displayName: test user
givenName: test user
instanceType: 4
lastLogoff: 0
lastLogon: 0
logonCount: 0
distinguishedName: CN=test user,CN=Users,DC=Wadeware,DC=net
objectCategory: CN=Person,CN=Schema,CN=Configuration,DC=Wadeware,DC=net
objectClass: user
objectGUID:: 2UINsf7tD0WL9cl4wKnn4Q==
objectSid:: AQUAAAAAAUVAAAATWRJLufL3X0VJa9HgQQAAA==
primaryGroupID: 513
pwdLastSet: 125808936338153952
name: test user
sAMAccountName: testuser
sAMAccountType: 805306368
telephoneNumber: 425-555-6666
userAccountControl: 66048
userPrincipalName: testuser@w2k.Wadeware.net
uSNChanged: 130034
uSNCreated: 110608
whenChanged: 19990911215400.0Z
whenCreated: 19990904044032.0ZAs an example
```

Now that you have exported an entry, it is easier to see how directory entries can be changed and modified. There are three typical directory-entry actions that an administrator is interested in performing. The first is to add new users; followed closely by changing and deleting entries. The LDAP Data Interchange Format (LDIF) draft standard provides for each of these capabilities.

The LDIF draft standard is a proposed standard that describes a file format for modifying directory information. This file format is designed to be used for the import and export of directory information between LDAP directory services.

Adding Entries

To add an entry into the directory, you need to create a file that has the information that you want to add a user. This type of file can be easily created for a user using a script. The first step is to identify what you typically want in a file. For this example, the file to be used is intentionally simple. You can extrapolate from this to create a more sophisticated file to include the fields that you need filled out for each user.

A simple LDIF file includes the version number, the DN, the surname (SN), given name (GN), and the telephone number. The LDIF file also contains the control commands to identify the action that should be taken—add, modify, or delete. The following is an example of the file for adding a user.

```
version: 1
dn: CN=Doug Hauger,CN=Users,DC=Wadeware,DC=net
changetype: add
cn: Doug Hauger
givenName: Doug
sn: Hauger
distinguishedName: CN=Doug Hauger,CN=Users,DC=Wadeware,DC=net
objectClass: user
telephoneNumber: 425-555-9696
```

This file adds Doug Hauger to the directory under the Users container. The next step is to modify an entry in the directory. Modifying directory entries is a common task for administrators. Every time a user changes locations or phone numbers the directory needs to be changed.

Modifying a User

To modify a user, a file is created that identifies the object to be modified and that has the changetype value of modify. After the change timeline, the attribute or attributes that are going to be changed are followed with the new values for those attributes. The following listing shows how to change the telephone number, delete the postal address, and add a new street address for a user.

```
version: 1
dn: CN=Doug Hauger,CN=Users,DC=Wadeware,DC=net
changetype: modify
replace: telephonenumber
telephoneNumber: 413-555-9696
```

```
delete: postaladdress
add: streetaddress
streetaddress: 1 Pennsylvania Avenue $ Bellevue, WA $ 98004
```

Creating the Scripts

The LDIFDE utility provides a vehicle for modifying the directory. However, the challenge with this tool is the complexity that is required in creating the files. A simple mistake and the files do not work, or they perform the wrong action. This can happen if the wrong DN is specified or if the wrong field is specified. The potential for making errors is numerous. Therefore, it is important to test all scripts before use. The value of this type of tool is that it can be used to create a trial listing of the activities of the directory, and it can work to help distributed administration. Each of these is important in a large organization.

Creating LDIF Files

As was previously mentioned, creating the LDIF files can be complex and risky. The way to avoid this is to create an old batch file that helps you, and other administrators, create an LDIF file for the proposed task.

Changing the telephone number is a common task for users. To create a script that helps to create the LDIF file, you need to identify the key components of the file. If you are interested in changing the telephone number, you need to know the identity of the user whose phone number you are changing and how you want to change the phone number. You also want to understand any assumptions about your directory. As an example, does every user in the organization have a phone number associated with them, or are there some users who don't have phone numbers? With the batch file that is created for modifying phone numbers, the assumption is that every user in the directory needs a phone number. It might be the general number, but every user has a phone number associated with their directory entry. This is implied by the recursive nature of the script. This script does not contain any checks for exceptions.

After you have determined the minimal requirements and the assumptions, you are ready to start creating a batch file for creating the LDIF file. If you look at a typical example, the first five lines represent what is necessary for modifying a directory. This type of file can be created with the script in following listing.

```
Echo version: 1
Echo dn: CN=Doug Hauger,CN=Users,DC=Wadeware,DC=net
Echo changetype: modify
Echo replace: telephonenumber
Echo telephoneNumber: 413-555-9696
```

The problem with this script is that it changes Doug Hauger's phone number every time and to the same number. To change this, you create variables for the first name, last name, and phone number and you get the following script. This script named chtele, for change telephone number, creates a file based on the parameters passed to the script.

After the LDIF file is created, LDIFDE is called with the created file. To execute the script, type in **chtele Doug Hauger 425-555-9696 >> ad.log**. This also logs the file output in a log file for future reference.

```
REM
REM  chtele firstname lastname telephoneNumber  >> ad.log
REM
REM
IF "%1"=="" GOTO HELP
IF "%2"=="" GOTO HELP
IF "%3"=="" GOTO HELP
Del %1%2.tp
Echo version: 1  > %1%2.tp
Echo dn: CN=%1 %2,CN=Users,DC=Wadeware,DC=net >> %1%2.tp
Echo changetype: modify >> %1%2.tp
Echo replace: telephonenumber >> %1%2.tp
Echo telephoneNumber: %3 >>%1%2.tp
Ldifde -I -v -f %1%2.tp
IF 1==1 GOTO END
:HELP
Echo A parameter is missing
Echo ChTele Firstname Lastname TelephoneNumber
:END
```

Practical Use of LDIFDE

Using batch files and LDIFDE provides a set of tools that enable the logging of the directory administration and the controlled access to the directory. LDIFDE is practical as you move forward with a distributed administration model and as you build a family of batch files that facilitate in the administration. The manual creation of LDIF formatted files and the possibility for error make LDIFDE seem like an impractical administration tool, but careful thought and planning provide for a controlled access to the directory and the ability to log all transactions.

By eliminating the LDIFDE line, you prevent the actual attempt to import. Also, note that those without the proper rights to Active Directory are not able to modify the directory through imports.

With the new script file that you created, you are able to provide a mechanism for controlled administration. By distributing a script for various tasks, you give remote administrators the ability to send the appropriate files for use with LDIFDE. The scripts can be sent to a specific mailbox for remote administrators to review and execute once a day.

This provides you, the centralized administrator, with several advantages. You are able to control the changes to the directory and to audit the changes as they come into the mailbox.

With the capability to control the logging of each activity through the execution of LDIFDE in a batch file, you also have the ability to create an audit trail for each change to the directory. This avoids the questions later about who did what to the directory.

CSVDE Utility

CSVDE is another utility available for making changes to the directory. CSVDE is similar to LDIFDE for making changes to the directory except that it uses a Comma Separated File (CSV) file format as the input file for the changes. This is convenient if the directory information you have to work with is in Excel or in a database that has the ability to easily create a CSV file.

To add a user using the CSVDE utility, you would create a file that is similar to the following code:

```
Dn,cn,givenname,objectclass,samaccountname
"cn=billyboy,ou=user,dc=Wadeware,dc=net",billyboy,billyboy,user,billyboy
```

The first line is the header line, which identifies the parameter to each value in the subsequent line is set. Therefore, in this example, the DN is set to `cn=billyboy,ou=user,dc=Wadeware,dc=net` and `cn=billyboy`, the second value in line two.

This file, if used with the CSVDE execution line of `csvde -I -v -f filename`, adds `billyboy` to the directory in the user's OU.

Third-Party Tools

There are a variety of third-party tools that are available for directory administration through scripting. Directscript, from Entevo, provides ADSI compatible access to Active Directory for administration. Other vendors, such as Fastlane and Mission Critical software, provide software for Active Directory administration.

Summary

Scripting has long been the way to administer your environment in many computing environments. Active Directory takes Microsoft and Windows 2000 into and enterprise environment. In these large environments, the investment in scripting provides your staff with an efficient and effective way to administer your environment. This chapter provides a glimpse at the possibilities. By embracing scripting with your directory, you provide yourself with a powerful tool.

20

Designing Active Directory Hierarchies

T HE NAMESPACE HIERARCHY THAT DEFINES THE WAY IN WHICH Active Directory is implemented is critical to the success of an Active Directory design. The implementation of Active Directory is not successful if the namespace hierarchy is designed poorly or if it does not match the needs of the organization. In Chapter 11, "Active Directory and Scalability," Active Directory and scalability was discussed as it relates to the hierarchy of organizational units (OUs) and domains. This chapter reviews exactly what the components are that make up a hierarchy in Active Directory and how that hierarchy should be designed to match the needs of the organization in which it is being implemented.

Definition of a Hierarchy

An Active Directory hierarchy comprises of several elements. Depending on the design of the hierarchy, you can include all the elements or just a subset. The way that all these elements are combined determines the structure of the hierarchy. The elements of a hierarchy are

- Object
- OU
- Domain
- Tree
- Forest

Object

The most basic element of the namespace hierarchy is an object. Objects are the building blocks of the Active Directory structure. Objects can include, but are not limited to, the following:

- Computers
- Users
- Groups
- Printers
- Security policies
- OUs
- Applications
- Shared folders

In addition to these standard objects, it is possible to create custom objects. An example of a custom object is the user profile for an Enterprise Resource Planning (ERP) application that your human resources department uses. This profile might contain security definitions for the users as they apply to the ERP application. It might also contain definitions for the application modules, which the users have access to when they launch the application. If Active Directory is utilized as a repository of profile information for applications, it might be necessary to extend the Active Directory schema to accommodate new object classes.

Computers

Computer objects are the objects that define the properties of a computer machine account in the domain. The properties of the computer object might define the specific application settings on a machine or the individual users who have permission to access the machine.

Users

The user object defines, by the set of properties for user accounts, how resources are accessed within both Active Directory and the Forest. Specific properties include which groups the user is a member of, what time of day the user can access the network, and what the password expiration parameters are for the user. Many other parameters can be defined for each user object.

Groups

Groups define collections of specific user and group objects within the Forest. Groups can be used for security purposes, such as defining an administrative group that contains all the administrators who have rights to administer resources in the domain or Forest. Groups can also be used for administration purposes, such as defining a sales group that contains all the users in the domain or Forest who are in the sales organization, thus making it easier to assign access rights or applications policies to the sales force. In addition, Active Directory provides the ability to have groups that are mail-enabled. For example, a set of user objects for executive assistants and executive staff could all be collected in a single group, so that email could be delivered to them all by sending to a single mail alias.

In addition to using groups for security or administration purposes, groups in Windows 2000 can also be configured as distribution groups. This is significantly different from Windows NT 4.0. In Windows NT 4.0, it was not possible to configure a group as a distribution group for email. With Active Directory Windows 2000, it is possible to configure a security group as an email distribution group. This helps to eliminate the administrative overhead of having to maintain identical groups in the network operating system (NOS) directory and in the email system directory, as was the case with Windows NT 4.0 and Exchange Server 5.5.

Printers

Printer objects define the properties of printers in the Forest. Printer properties include the types of printer drivers, printer locations, and specific printer configuration requirements, such as whether a duplexer is installed on the printer.

Security Policies

Security policies are applied to objects in the directory. Security policies can control everything from the access rights that a user has for a specific resource to whether the traffic between two specific hosts on a network should be encrypted. Security policies in Active Directory are implemented as a subset of the Group Policy Object (GPO). In that they are applied to groups of directory objects, including users and computers. In addition, security policies can be applied directly to the local host machine using security templates.

OUs

OUs are both objects in the directory and the containers in the directory in which objects reside. OUs are discussed in more detail later in this chapter.

Applications

Applications can be registered in the directory as objects. By registering applications as objects, it is possible to assign security policies to the objects and to assign specific applications to specific groups of users. Applications either can be made available to users and groups, or they can be required. The distinction between the two is that in the first instance users, users can decide if they want to install an application or not. In the second instance, users, who are members of groups to which an application has been assigned, are required to accept the installation of the application.

Shared Folders

Shared folders are objects in the directory that identify the location and properties associated with file locations in the network environment.

OU

The next level of element in the Active Directory hierarchy is the OU. The OU is the container in which all the different types of objects can be grouped. If there is an object in Active Directory, it exists within the context of an OU, or a container. It is important to note that some of the containers that are set up in Active Directory by default are not OUs, and consequently, they cannot have group policies assigned to them. These include the containers for Users and Computers.

OUs are used for logical administrative groupings or for objects that are used to delegate administration within a domain. Although delegation of administration is one of the main reasons for developing OUs, it should not be the only reason. Several reasons for creating OUs are discussed later in this chapter. One of the most critical decision points in developing an Active Directory hierarchy is deciding whether to create new OUs.

Domain

A domain is defined by a common security context and policy, and it is unified by a single namespace within the directory hierarchy. This chapter discusses why and when to utilize a domain for segmenting objects in the directory rather than an OU.

Tree

A tree is a collection of Windows 2000 domains that fall under a contiguous and unified namespace, as illustrated in Figure 20.1. All the domains in a tree share a common security context and a Global Catalog (GC). This is also the case with domains in a Forest.

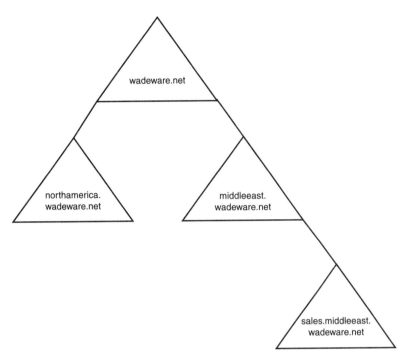

Figure 20.1 A domain tree comprising all the domains that participate in a contiguous namespace.

Forest

A Forest is typically composed of a single domain tree with domains unified under a contiguous namespace. If you create a single Windows 2000 domain, you also create a tree and a Forest. However, a Forest differs from a tree in that it can also contain multiple domain trees that do not participate in a contiguous namespace, as shown in Figure 20.2. In this example, the domain tree defined by `wadeware.net` does not share a namespace with `wadewarestuff.net`. However, they do share a common security context, a common directory schema, and a common configuration by participating in the same domain tree. The common security context is established by the default transitive trust, which is automatically established between the top-level domains of each tree.

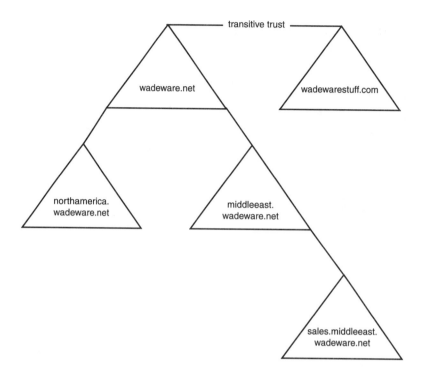

Figure 20.2 A Windows 2000 domain Forest is differentiated
from a single domain tree in that it can contain multiple
domain trees with discontiguous namespaces.

When to Use OUs

Deciding when to use OUs in your hierarchy design is the first step in determining
your Active Directory structure. Chapter 11 discussed that OUs should be used to
map the actual organizational structure rather than simply as a way to segment objects
for administration. This chapter examines when you should create a new OU and
when you should create a new domain instead in closer detail.

   The typical reason that the inexperienced Active Directory administrator creates an
OU is for delegation of administrative authority. This is because under Windows NT
version 4.0 and earlier, it was necessary to create a completely new domain truly delegate administrative authority. Now with the new concept of an OU, many administrators are tempted to pile OU on top of OU within a single domain to subdivide and
distribute the administration of objects. It is critical that this *not* be the starting point
for an administrator designing an Active Directory hierarchy.

Delegation of Administration

Delegation of administration should not be the primary motivating factor for segmenting the Active Directory hierarchy into multiple OUs. If that is the case, then what administration strategy should be used to delegate authority within an Active Directory hierarchy that has multiple administration requirements?

The starting point for defining an administration strategy for the delegation of authority should be the existing administration strategies for the organization. If your current company administration paradigm is one of distribution versus centralization, then that is where the design of the Active Directory hierarchy should start. However, that is only where it should start. The design process should continue with a critical examination of the existing administration configuration to ensure that it still meets the needs of the organization. Administration might currently be distributed to subsidiary organizations because that was the only model that could be supported under Windows NT 4.0. Now, with Windows 2000, it is possible to support a truly centralized model.

When examining your administrative model, it is important to consider the following:

- Identify all the administrative tasks that current system administrators carry out in all the different parts of the organization.
- Map the existing administrative tasks to the new functionality and, consequently, to the new administration tasks under Windows 2000.
- Identify which tasks will change with the implementation of Windows 2000 and Active Directory.
- Re-examine the administrative model to make sure that it still meets the needs of the organization.

For example, your organization might currently have a set of administrators who perform the task of creating new user accounts on the network and creating new mailboxes in Exchange. They are administrators for both the network and the Exchange environment. The administration model was set up this way because under Windows NT 4.0 and Exchange 5.5 it was easier to have mail administrators also be account administrators, so that they could create both the NOS account and the Exchange mailbox. Now, with Active Directory, it is possible to provide mail administrators with the ability to create user accounts in specific user OUs without providing them with complete administrative control of the domain.

In Active Directory, users, security groups, computers, and resources registered in the directory are referred to as security principles. (Please refer to Chapter 15, "Developing a Network Security Strategy," for a discussion of security principles and Kerberos.) Access control permissions can be granted and assigned to security principles. In this way, it is possible to restrict administrative control over specific objects in the directory without establishing multiple levels of OUs in which to store the security principles. However, this obviously is a tedious way to administer an environment if there are multiple security and administration policies to be applied to a wide number of security principles.

Consequently, OUs should be utilized for the segmentation of administration of security principles when there are a large number of individual user objects in the directory, and they require a diverse set of security policies for operation.

First-Level OUs

First-level OUs should be utilized for segmenting security principles and group policies in to units that are relatively static with regards to business requirements and administration requirements. As discussed in Chapter 11, first-level OUs can be based on the geographic segmentation of the organization in which Active Directory is being implemented. First-level OUs can also be based on organizational segmentation.

Design considerations for first-level OUs should center on how to apply administrative policy to the Active Directory hierarchy. If every user in the organization were to have the same access and administrative requirements, there would be little need for a segmented hierarchy with multiple first-level OUs. Because this is rarely the case, the reality is that there are multiple first-level OUs created for most organizations. First-level OUs should be utilized as home containers for most organization-wide group policies. It is possible to significantly reduce administrative overhead by establishing as many organization-wide group policies at the first-level of the hierarchy and enabling inheritance on second- and third-level OUs.

To establish your first-level OU structure, consider the following process:

1. Examine the current organizational segmentation of the organization. Determine if that segmentation will also be the future segmentation of the organization.

2. Map the geographic distribution of the organization. Determine if that geographic distribution is static or shifting significantly over time.

3. Identify which of the segmentations is least likely to change over time.

4. Build the first-level OU structure based on the segmentation identified in Step 3.

While planning your OU structure, it is important to note that OUs have no specific visible impact on users. OUs are exposed to users for browsing, but browsing should not be a design consideration when developing an Active Directory hierarchy. The OU structure is not exposed in the result set from query to Active Directory, by default. Furthermore, OUs are not exposed as part of the domain name system (DNS) service providing name resolution for Active Directory.

Application of Group Policies by OU

Group policies based on OUs are applied to objects in OUs from the domain root down. Consequently, if you have multi-level OUs nested within one another and multiple group policies associated with those OUs, client response time could be severely affected as the policies are applied at the time of logon.

Second-Level OUs

Second-level OUs should be used if it is necessary to segment resources, including both users and computers, into groups that are more granular than those implied by the delegation of security and administration discussed in the previous section. This might be required by the structure of the organization. For example, all the sales force might have the same security policies applied and they might conform to the same security model, but it might be necessary to isolate different sales groups based on geography.

When to Use Multiple Domains in a Single Tree

Identifying when to use multiple domains in a single tree, rather than multiple OUs in a single domain, is one of the hardest design decisions. Multiple domains in a tree share many of the same attributes that are shared between multiple OUs in a single domain. There is a shared Active Directory schema, security context, and namespace. So, why would you decide to implement multiple domains instead of implementing multiple OUs in a single domain? To make that decision, it is important to understand the characteristics of a multi-domain tree.

Schema

Multiple domains in a tree share a common schema. This means that the changes to the schema for the Active Directory database are written to the schema operations master and then replicated to other Domain Controllers (DCs) in the tree, as shown in Figure 20.3. By default, the schema operations master is the first DC in the Forest and the default schema is loaded on that DC when Windows 2000 is loaded for the first time. If changes are made to the schema on the schema operations master, they are replicated to every DC. Consequently, schema issues should not drive the decision process for selecting when to use multiple domains within an organization.

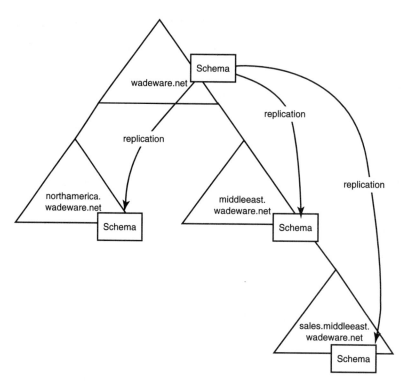

Figure 20.3   All domains in a tree share a common Active Directory schema.

Namespace

Just as they share a common schema, all domains in a tree share a common namespace. If the root domain for an organization is wadeware.net, then all child domains are a subset namespace of wadeware.net. Every child domain has exactly one parent domain. It is possible for a parent domain to have multiple child domains associated with it. Each level of the hierarchy is directly related in terms of namespace to the hierarchical level directly above and directly below. For example, below the root domain of wadeware.net there might be a child domain named northamerica. The namespace for this domain would be derived from the relationship with the domain above it. As such, the namespace for the domain associated with North America would be northamerica.wadeware.net.

This hierarchical relationship in the namespace is based upon the hierarchical relationship in the DNS protocol standard. This is the relationship that one DNS domain has with another, whether it is based on DNS supported in UNIX, on Windows NT, or on Windows 2000.

Business requirements for a hierarchical namespace in an organization might be a reason to implement a multi-domain tree. A large organization might require a multi-layered namespace that identifies attributes relative to the business model or business configuration of the company. Wadeware might need to have a namespace associated with business in North America and another namespace associated with business in the Middle East. This would require multiple domains in a tree and the namespaces would be `northamerica.wadeware.net` and `middleeast.wadeware.net`.

Security

All domains in a tree automatically share security trusts based on the Kerberos security protocol. In addition, they also share automatic transitive trusts with all other domains in the tree. This means that all users in a tree can access resources in all the other domains in the tree; as long as the proper access control lists (ACLs) have been set on the resources. The transitive trust is a two-way, secure relationship that exists between every child domain in the tree and their parent domain, as shown in Figure 20.4. This trust is established automatically when the domain is added to the tree. Transitive trust means that if Domain A trusts Domain B and Domain B trusts Domain C, then Domain A trust Domain C by way of the transitive trust of Domain B.

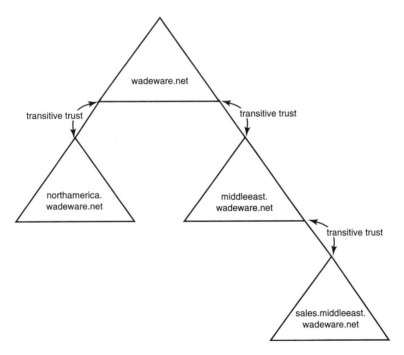

Figure 20.4   Transitive trusts between child domains and the parent domain.

Although every domain has an automatic transitive trust relationship when the domain is first created, it is also possible establish cross-link trusts between individual domains in the tree to improve the authentication performance. It is also possible to isolate a domain in the tree. Consequently, this is another significant reason why a multiple domain scenario might be appropriate versus a single domain scenario. It might be necessary to segment the administration of resources and users in a domain from users in other domains in the tree. This is something that is much easier to accomplish if the users and resources are segmented in to multiple domains rather than in multiple OUs within a single domain.

Replication Traffic

Replication traffic between DCs in a domain can also be a significant reason to consider a multi-domain tree. In a single domain, all changes made to Active Directory domain, including changes to all objects and properties, are replicated between DCs in that domain. This replication can be throttled and managed to a certain degree by implementing site architecture that overlays the domain structure. (See Chapter 10, "The Physical Topology: Sites and Replication," for a discussion on designing a site architecture.) However, all changes made to Active Directory data must still be replicated to all DCs.

In the case of multiple domains in a single tree, the only changes replicated between domains are changes to the GC server, configuration information, and modifications to the schema. If the Active Directory environment contains an infrastructure spread across multiple slow-speed WAN connections, a multiple domain tree should be considered.

When to Use Multiple Trees

Many of the issues previously described regarding multiple domains in a single tree also hold true for multiple domains and trees in a single Forest. All the trees in a Forest share a common schema and a common security context, through a two-way, transitive trust with the root domain for the Forest. The sharing of a common schema, common configuration information, and a common security environment is what distinguishes a Forest from a set of unrelated domain trees. However, some differences between a single tree and multiple trees in a Forest might drive organizations to consider the implementation of a Forest.

Discontiguous Namespace

Perhaps the greatest motivating factor in considering the implementation of a Forest with multiple trees, rather than a Forest with a single tree, is an organizational requirement for multiple namespaces. The need for multiple namespaces can arise for several reasons:

- The organization might be involved in a business that requires distinct and unrelated namespaces on the Internet, while still requiring centralized administration and organization-wide access to resources.

- The organization might be growing through acquisition and might not want to immediately dissolve namespaces inherited from businesses that have been acquired.

- The organization might be involved in partnerships in which the partner does not want to maintain an Active Directory structure and would like to leverage an existing Active Directory structure.

All these scenarios can be accommodated through the implementation of a single Forest with multiple domain trees, as shown in Figure 20.5. However, it is important to note that despite the fact that there is a discontiguous namespace in a Forest, there is still a single schema operations master to which all schema changes must be applied and there is a single GC for the entire Forest. It is possible to configure multiple DCs to be GC servers to host the GC.

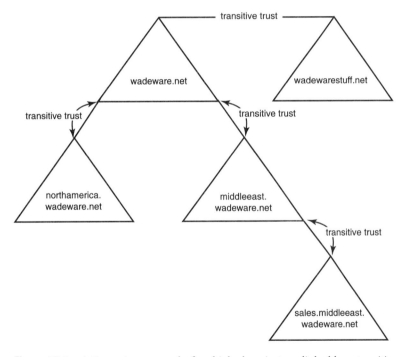

Figure 20.5 A Forest is composed of multiple domain trees linked by a transitive trust relationship from the root domain of each tree to the Forest root.

Access Control

Another reason to implement a Forest of multiple trees is to control access to resources by external users, such as partners or vendors. Organizations can set up partner or vendor user accounts in a separate tree in the Forest and make it easier for enterprise administrators to control access to sensitive corporate domain resources.

When to Use Multiple Forests

The decision to use multiple Forests in the design of an Active Directory hierarchy is one that should not be made lightly. Multiple Forest environments are possible to set up. However, they can be difficult and costly to administer. In most single organization environments, a multi-Forest Active Directory design provides no additional business value over a single Forest with multiple domain trees.

Why would an organization be required to implement a multiple Forest environment? The usual scenario is one in which one organization acquires another organization, and both organizations already have Active Directory implemented in a single tree configuration. There is no consensus or no business justification for recreating one of the trees in the context of the other.

The other scenario is one in which two business partners have Active Directory implemented, and they want to exchange information and access to corporate resources between the two companies. In this instance, the best solution would be to put in place a public key infrastructure (PKI), which would enable the sharing of public keys between the two organizations. Public keys can then be used to grant permission to resources in one domain for users in the other domain.

However, there might be the isolated case in which two Active Directory Forests must interoperate and share resources. When the needs cannot be met by PKI, it is possible to establish an explicit, one-way trust between Active Directory directories. By using explicit trusts, it is possible to grant users in one Forest access to resource in another Forest, as demonstrated in Figure 20.6. If an explicit trust is established between two Forests, it is important to actively administer the trust and to make sure that it is required for meeting the business requirements of the respective organizations. If these explicit trusts are established, it is necessary to create them between every domain in each tree that requires access to resources in another domain. Consequently, the process of establishing explicit trusts can become cumbersome.

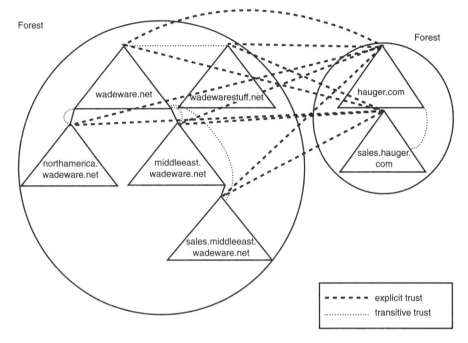

Figure 20.6 It is possible to establish an explicit trust between multiple domain Forests. However, as illustrated in the diagram, these trust relationships can be complex, can be hard to maintain properly, and should be constantly monitored to make sure they are still justified.

Summary

This chapter shows that there are many different ways to segment objects in an Active Directory hierarchy. On the one hand, you can configure a single domain with a simple OU structure. On the other hand, you can configure a multi-domain Forest with multiple namespaces and complicated multi-level OU structures. Windows 2000 and Active Directory are sophisticated enough to provide the flexibility to meet every organizational need. The deciding factors as to which configuration you implement are the business drivers for implementing Active Directory. If your business requires a complex security or access control model, or any one of the other factors that were discussed in this chapter, your Active Directory hierarchy will be complex as well.

The main point to keep in mind as you design your Active Directory hierarchy is that the more complicated the administration of the objects, including both users and computers, the more complicated the design will be. Although administration of the environment should not be a significant factor in designing the hierarchy as compared with the business drivers for your organization, it should be considered in the design process.

The next chapter discusses creating a lab environment in which you can test the Active Directory hierarchy you have designed.

21

Creating a Lab

IF YOU ARE READING THIS BOOK, YOU ARE MOST likely excited about the prospect of implementing Active Directory in your organization. You probably love technology and want to move to the latest and greatest as soon as it is available for prime time. The bulk of this book has addressed the process of designing Active Directory architecture and implementing that architecture in your organization. That implementation cannot occur, however, without the architectural design going through an extensive series of tests. Any organization, no matter how large or small, needs to test the Active Directory design before a full production rollout.

What should be tested? How should it be tested? How should the test results be measured? What qualitative and quantitative analysis should take place for the management of the organization to feel secure that Active Directory and Windows 2000 can be implemented in the production environment with minimal impact to the business? This chapter addresses the key issues involved in setting up a lab environment to test Active Directory.

Building a Lab Team

Before you begin to establish your lab environment, you must identify the groups and the individuals who will participate on the lab team. To guarantee success for the implementation of your Active Directory, it is important to include all the interested parties in the lab process. This is important because by including all the parties in the lab process, you enlist their support and buy-in for implementing and supporting Active Directory in production.

Who should be on the lab team? First, you need to identify a team manager. This should be an individual who understands lab testing and the stringent nature of following a lab schedule to meet implementation dates in production. The team leader is responsible for managing the schedule, the people on the lab team, the compilation of the lab results, and the presentation of those results to the executive management in the organization.

The second member of the team should be a technical individual who can understand and interpret the Active Directory architecture and develop a test plan for the lab. This individual should be experienced with lab work and should have the technical knowledge to identify the resolutions to issues that might arise.

Depending on the size of the environment, the next individuals on the team should be experts on the software and hardware in the environment. If the organization is large, hardware expertise and software expertise should be split among multiple individuals. For example, there might be an individual focused on testing Active Directory on the network, another individual might be focused on the server environment, and still another focused on testing the applications that are being used in the organization. If the organization is large, there might be an additional need for testers to run specific tests identified by the software and hardware experts.

The team should also include a representative from every major user group in the organization. These individuals should represent the major stakeholders in the organization who have a vested interest in the implementation and on-going functionality of Active Directory. The groups represented might include human resources (HR), finance, business units, executive management, and internal information technology. The individuals who represent these stakeholders need not participate in the actual testing of the product in the lab, but they should be included in regular team meetings so that they can report to their own groups on the progress of the lab tests. In addition, they should be directly involved in establishing the business requirements for the specific functionality of Active Directory.

One of the most important members of the lab team is the executive sponsor. Having an executive sponsor for the lab is critical. An executive sponsor can help to resolve issues that might arise during the lab testing process. Issues might include: obtaining a budget for implementing the lab, deciding when to drop functionality that proves problematic in lab testing, or when to seek further business justification for specific functionality. Again, as with the stakeholder representatives, the executive sponsor is not required to participate in testing, but he or she should be included in regular team meetings.

Developing a Lab Strategy and Methodology

Setting up a lab and testing Active Directory needs to be completed before production implementation. Developing a lab strategy and methodology needs to be undertaken, even before a lab can be configured. If your organization is relatively advanced in quality assurance programs, you might already have a lab strategy in place that you can utilize for Active Directory testing. If so, you are fortunate. Most organizations, no matter how advanced, do not have a comprehensive testing strategy that is employed on a regular basis.

Developing an Operational Acceptance Test Plan

One of the first goals of you should set as you begin establishing your lab is to put together a set of parameters concerning what you are testing in the lab. Typically, the results of the lab testing are presented to an operations group within your organization that accepts operational responsibility for the Windows 2000 network environment and Active Directory after it is implemented. Consequently, one of the best ways to establish a set of test parameters is to develop an Operations Acceptance Test (OAT) plan.

The OAT is fundamentally a negotiated contract between the team who is building and testing the Active Directory design and the operations group who administers the environment. The goal of the OAT is to establish a set of tests, which, if completed successfully, facilitate the implementation of the design in to production. Consequently, the plan should include testing for all the aspects of the plan with which the operations group is concerned.

To begin establishing your OAT, identify the following:

- Functionality to be tested
- Test parameters for each aspect of functionality
- Results expected from each test

When identifying the functionality to be tested, it is important to consider every aspect of the product. You are establishing a test plan for Active Directory, but Active Directory is directly impacted by the performance of the Windows 2000 network environment. Consequently, there might be aspects of Windows 2000 that also need to be tested. After you have identified the functionality to be tested, you need to build a test matrix.

Developing the Test Matrix

The test matrix should include an explanation of the functionality to be tested, how it will be tested, and what the expected result is. In addition, it should also include the business reason driving the need for the functionality. This is an extremely important aspect to consider during the OAT process. If there is no business reason to implement a specific aspect of the product, you will be hard pressed to justify the testing, design, and implementation of that aspect to business management. For example, you might decide that you want to test the integration of a public key infrastructure (PKI) with Active Directory. However, there might be no business reason for implementing PKI in your organization. There is no reason to conduct tests on functionality you won't be using. The converse is also true. You need to be sure to identify all business requirements for implementing a networking system and directory service and to map Windows 2000 and Active Directory functionality to the business. This makes it easier to justify the implementation of the product to the business management in your organization. After you have compiled the business justification for the functionality to be tested, it is time put together the test matrix. An example is shown in Table 21.1.

Table 21.1 **An Example of the Matrix**

Functionality	Business Driver	How to Be Tested	Expected Result	Result	Flag
Logon Authentication	Logon is required for access to environment.	Logon is performed from machines configured in the test environment.	Logon functions within acceptable parameters: Authentication takes no more than 5 seconds.	Logon took 4.5 seconds.	Green
Directory Search	Searching Active Directory for objects is required for integrating directory with the line of business (LOB) applications.	Populate the directory with 50,000 objects and perform a search for a single object.	Search for a single object should take no more than 5 seconds to find a single object in a 50,000 object directory.	Search for a single object in the directory took 8 seconds.	Yellow
Dynamic registration with DNS	Dynamic registration with domain name system (DNS) during the DHCP Dynamic Host Configuration Protocol (DHCP) configuration process reduces the overall total cost of administration.	Start up a workstation configured for DHCP and verify that dynamic DNS (DDNS) registration occurs.	During the startup process, the workstation automatically registers with the DNS server.	During the startup process, the workstation did not register with the DDNS server.	Red

In Table 21.1, three different flag types are listed. First, the logon test is performed, and the result is within the acceptable parameters for the test. No further action needs to be taken.

The second test, testing the search time for Active Directory, is completed, but it does not meet the acceptable results expected. However, the result is not severe enough to warrant a red flag. A yellow flag is set for the test. A yellow flag might or might not require further action. Depending on the acceptable variance in the test, action might be required.

The result of the third test in the example is more significant. The DDNS registration test results in a red flag. The client was unable to register with the DDNS server. If a red flag is registered during lab testing, it is critical that a path to resolution be established. In the preceding example, if the workstation is not able to register with the DDNS, it is not be able to properly function in the Windows 2000 environment. When establishing a path for resolution, remember to identify the following:

- Next steps for resolution
- Timeline for resolution
- Action to be taken if the issue cannot be resolved
- Lab team member responsible for the issue's resolution

Creating a Test Lab Environment

Creating an adequate test lab environment is important to establishing test results that accurately represent the performance you will find in your production environment. In that regard, the mantra for creating your lab environment should be "create a replica of the production environment." In an ideal world, the lab environment would be an exact replica of the production environment, down to the number of servers, the number of client workstations, the load on the network, wide-area network connections, external network links, and the number and variety of applications utilized by the LOB in the organization. In reality, it is impossible to create an environment that is an exact replica of the production environment. It is, however, possible to create an environment that accurately represents the same challenges that you might have in the production environment.

What do we mean by representing the same challenges that you might face in the production environment? Many aspects of the production environment can directly affect the performance of Active Directory after it is implemented. Chief among these factors is network performance and the available network bandwidth for directory access and replication. It is possible to replicate this in a lab environment by putting into place a WAN simulator and by producing load on the network with a device, such as a Network General Sniffer or some other network-testing device. Another aspect of the production environment that might affect performance is the number of user objects in the directory. Microsoft provides tools in the Windows 2000 resource kit to populate a test Active Directory environment with simulated user objects to simulate the load in a large production environment.

Conducting an Inventory

The first step to developing your lab environment is to conduct a complete inventory of your production environment. For a limited number of organizations, this is a simple task. Because of Y2K issues or other software implementation projects, some organization might already have a complete inventory available. For most organizations, this is not the case. Consider the extent of environment components that need to be inventoried:

- **Complete Network Environment**—Document your production network environment including all local area networks, all wide-area networks, and all external network connections, such as connections to the Internet and other network service providers.

- **IP Addressing Scheme**—Identify and document all the IP addressing information for the network. Locate and document all DHCP servers, DHCP scope configurations, and static addresses assigned to servers, workstations, and other active network components.

- **Router Configuration**—Document the configuration of the routers in the environment. Document any static route tables that have been set up. Identify the firmware and operating system levels implemented on each router. In some cases, it might be necessary to upgrade routers to become compliant with RFCs, such as RFC1542, for supporting BootP relay information.

- **Other Network Protocols**—Identify all other network protocols on the network, such as IPX/SPX, AppleTalk, and SNA.

- **Security Configuration**—Audit and document the security configuration of the production environment. This should include, but might not be limited to, access rights on files and network resources, firewall configurations, remote access restrictions, and internal network segmentation.

- **Workstation Configuration Policy**—Identify the different types of workstation configurations used in production and classify their use. If different workgroups have different configurations, document the business drivers behind the segmentation and the configuration details that map to the business drivers.

- **Applications**—Inventory all the applications in production and document any custom configuration information for each application. If certain applications are associated with specific groups, document what each group does with each application.

- **Administration Model**—Document the current administration model that overlies the existing production environment. Although it is likely that a different administration model is implemented with Active Directory, it is important to understand what is currently in place so that the delta between the two models can be documented, and a gap analysis can be conducted as part of the lab tests. What one administrator does today might be accomplished by multiple administrators following the implementation of Active Directory. The segmentation of administration must be tested in the lab.

Considering all the issues that need to be documented before testing, it is easy to understand why an inventory of the existing production environment is crucial and might be a time-consuming step in designing and implementing a test lab.

Designing and Implementing the Test Lab

After you have completed the inventory, it is time to begin designing and implementing the test lab. Where possible, utilize the same hardware and software that is in production. The biggest limitation to doing this is most likely budget restrictions for test equipment. Many organizations do not have an adequate budget for equipment and software for their production environment, let alone a test lab. If this is the case, consider creative ways of obtaining the necessary resources. If your organization is large enough, you might be able to secure loan equipment from hardware manufacturers. Consider the possibility of leasing equipment during the test phase. It might also be possible to secure budget from the LOBs in your organization for the test lab. Adequate testing is in the best interest of the LOBs, and they might be willing to budget accordingly.

As mentioned earlier, all network conditions should be replicated in the lab. For this, consider buying a network simulation device that can reproduce your network bandwidth and load, such as a 56K dial-up connection or a T-1 WAN link.

It is extremely important that the test lab is completely isolated from the production environment in the organization. You do not want actions taken in the test lab to adversely affect the performance or, worse yet, the actual configuration of servers in the production environment. Consequently, do not build two lab environments in two separate physical locations and then connect them by using the production local- or wide-area network.

Choosing a Lab Location

Finally, your lab environment should be located in a secure area. Do not place the lab in the middle of an open cubical where anyone can wander by and begin pounding on the keyboard of the root Domain Controller (DC) for the domain. If possible, put the lab equipment in the same sever room as the production servers. The production server environment is most likely in a secure environment with adequate cooling and power facilities.

Testing Hardware

After the lab environment is in place, it is time to begin testing hardware. The first step is to populate the OAT plan with the functionality to be tested, the method by which it will be tested, and the desired test results. To do this, identify each separate piece of equipment from the inventory documentation and document the functionality that will be affected by the implementation of Active Directory. With a router, for example, you should identify the following:

- Is the router RFC compliant? If so, test the DHCP relay functionality.

- Does the router support Quality of Service (QoS) networking? If so, test QoS functionality and service.

- Can the router be managed remotely? If so, test the management of the router by using the MMC and any associated MMC snap-ins provided by the vendor.

In addition to developing the test matrix for each individual network component, it is important to test functionality across components. This means verifying that the functionality that impacts multiple components on the network will not adversely affect any single component in the system. With the example of the routers, it is important to test that the router relays DHCP requests, and that it works properly with the DHCP server serving the DHCP requests from the DHCP scope.

Finally, as you populate the OAT, be sure to identify the expected results of each test. Identifying expected results for each functional aspect should be completed in the larger context of the entire system. For example, it is expected that all routers relay DHCP requests on to the DHCP server. It is also expected that they relay DHCP responses back to the client. In addition, it is expected that there is no undue load placed on the router or the network. All this should be documented in the Expected Results section of the OAT matrix. It is easy to see how the OAT can quickly become an extensive and critical document in the test process.

After you have completed populating the OAT for hardware, you can begin testing. Start by testing the underlying system functionality and progress to testing system-wide functionality.

Testing Software

As with the hardware test process, the software test process begins by populating the OAT with the functionality to be tested. Be sure to identify all the aspects of each software application that needs to be tested. For example, if you have an HR application that integrates with a back end database and exposes information in that database to users via the corporate intranet, your list might include:

- **User identification**—Does the application properly pull user identification from Active Directory?

- **Security context**—Does the application retrieve the proper access rights for the user from Active Directory? If appropriate, does the application integrate with Kerberos to utilize Kerberos authentication for resource access?

- **Network impact**—What impact does the application have on network traffic?
- **Windows 2000 compatibility**—Will the application function properly in a Windows 2000 operating system environment?

When identifying applications to test, be sure to consider all the applications in the environment, including all desktop productivity applications, all server applications, and all homegrown applications that might be in production in each of the LOB environments.

Documenting Test Results

A test lab is not worth implementing at all if the results are not adequately documented. For each set of functionality tested, be sure to meticulously document all the steps taken and all the results exactly as they occur in the test. Results that might appear minor or insignificant during the test might have a significant relationship to other sets of functionality tested later in the test process.

Make sure that each person involved in the test process has a lab notebook, and that they religiously document each result. This helps to identify issues that arise during the test process. In addition, this helps to mitigate any issues should any person in the test process be unable to continue testing. In the high-paced information technology environment, testers might be pulled off to other projects, might take another job within the organization, or might move on to another organization entirely.

One of the most important aspects of documenting the test results is to identify the level of severity in the delta between expected results and actual results. Functionality tests with a green result obviously can pass without comment. Yellow results need to be examined for severity, and a decision needs to be made as to whether or not they should be corrected and retested. Red results need to be scrutinized, and a plan of action for resolution must be created. Creating this plan should be a joint responsibility of the test lead and the team manager.

Presenting Lab Results

Finally, test results need to be presented to the organization. Presentation of test results is a way to demonstrate to the organization that the Active Directory design is ready for primetime and that implementation can begin. Presentation should start with the operations group that accepts responsibility for administering the environment after it is in production. A meeting should be called that includes all the major stakeholders from the operations group. Present both an electronic copy of the results as well as hard copy for the meeting participants to take away.

Following buyoff by the operations group, call a meeting of the executive staff to review the results. This meeting should be called by the executive sponsor for the test process. Be sure to also include a representative from the operations group, so that any questions regarding operational acceptance can be immediately addressed. In this meeting, it important to be concise and specific when presenting results. If there are any outstanding issues, be sure to identify them at the outset. If the testing has identi-fied aspects of the Active Directory design, which results in an impact to the business drivers of the organization, be sure to call them out. In addition, make sure that any action required by the executive staff is identified and specific action items are assigned. If LOB budgets must be increased to purchase additional equipment for the project, identify which investments are necessary and why. Clarity and action are critical.

Summary

In this chapter, I have provided an overview of how to implement a lab for testing your Active Directory design: build the team, develop a strategy, create the environ-ment, test, and then document your results. This entire process can play an important role in the implementation of Active Directory in your organization. It helps to estab-lish credibility for your project with the organization as a whole and with executive management. Most important, it is the place where you validate your design, and where you establish the need for more rework, or finally determine that you are ready to implement. Don't rush through the lab phase of your Active Directory project. It is critical to your success.

22

Upgrading from Windows NT 4.0

T HIS CHAPTER PROVIDES INSIGHT INTO MOVING to an Active Directory environment from Windows NT 4.0. Moving from Windows NT 4.0 to Windows 2000 and Active Directory is probably the most common migration. Microsoft has spent a bulk of their time preparing for this migration with tools and instructions to make it as simple as possible. Regardless of the environment or system from which you are migrating, the model used for this migration approach is similar to what you would use in any migration.

This chapter identifies the key goals you want to strive for in migrating to Windows 2000. This chapter includes information on how to prepare today for an upgrade later. You are also introduced to the upgrade process, upgrade approaches, upgrade scenarios, and phases of an upgrade project.

Reasons to Upgrade

Although there are many circumstances preventing individuals from upgrading to Windows 2000 and Active Directory immediately, several factors will drive individuals and companies to an early adoption of Windows 2000.

A single schema for the entire enterprise is one reason for moving to Windows 2000 and Active Directory. After you upgrade and you have all your down-level servers and clients upgraded into a Windows 2000 schema, you are able to publish printers, resources, and file shares. This is different from publishing in current Windows

NT 4.0 environments, because Active Directory provides the users with a direct way to find resources. As an example, if you try to find a local printer in Windows NT 4.0, you need to know that the domain and the server to find the printer to use. With a well-designed Active Directory, you are able to identify printers based on location or attributes.

Active Directory provides a single directory for many of the computing resources. As an example, the next release of Microsoft Exchange does not have a separate directory, but uses Active Directory for its directory.

With Windows 2000 clients available, you have the ability to browse for resources based on key attributes and/or key words.

Delegation of administration is another important reason to upgrade to Active Directory. This does not mean just delegation of administrators, it can also mean consolidation and segmentation in a centralized environment. With Active Directory, you have the ability to delegate responsibility in granular detail using group policies, MMC, and scripting. You might want to pull some administrative responsibilities into your Information Technology (IT) staff.

The Domain Controller (DC) locator service provides more efficient authentication. It is possible in a Windows NT 4.0 environment for users to authenticate to a Backup Domain Controller (BDC) across slow links simply because the BDC is returned by the Windows Internet Naming Service (WINS) server. With the DC locator service, a user is pointed to the closest DC based on response distance and network connectivity. The DC locator service returns the DC that is closest by domain name system (DNS) when querying for a DC. The capability provides the end user with the fastest response time possible. This has an impact on the user's experience with the environment.

Elimination of Windows NT 4.0's 40MB domain size limit provides organizations with the ability to have as many machine and user accounts as you need. Active Directory provides support for millions of objects.

Kerberos security provides for transitive trusts. With Kerberos security, your environment is more secure and standards-based. You are able to provide access and to integrate with third-party organizations. Extranet and vendor integration is possible with Kerberos security.

Kerberos is able to provide two-way authentication. This provides greater security than Window NT 4.0. With Windows NT 4.0, the user is authenticated to access server-based resources. This is still true in Windows 2000. In addition, with Active Directory and Windows 2000, the user is assured that the server you are connecting to is the server you intended. This is accomplished by sending you authentication that lets you, as the user, know that the network server or resource being accessed really is the resource you expect it to be.

Searching for resources across the enterprise is improved with the capability to search for resources based on specific attributes in Active Directory.

Fault tolerant multi-master DC model is part of Active Directory and Windows 2000. If one controller goes out, you still have a read/write copy of a DC available in the enterprise. Because each of the DCs can serve as a master, changes can be accepted and distributed throughout the enterprise. With a single Windows NT 4.0 Primary Domain Controller (PDC), a BDC must be promoted for changes to be accepted and distributed throughout the enterprise. This takes manual intervention.

Fewer, if any, explicit trusts are a feature of Active Directory and Window 2000. In a Windows NT 4.0 environment, you currently have user and resource domains to create and maintain. With the design of Windows 2000 and Active Directory, you don't need explicit trust relationships to have similar functionality in your environment. This decreases your maintenance costs.

Windows NT 4.0 has a flat model for groups. With Active Directory, hierarchical groups can be implemented. This provides for a more logical representation of the environment, possibly mapping real-world structures in the hierarchical group structures available in Active Directory.

Active Directory has snap-ins available for the MMC. This provides for the capability to create customized tool views and to integrate various snap-ins for a view of the environment that matches the way you want to manage your environment. Also available is ADSI for managing the directory through programs and scripts.

With the use of Lightweight Directory Access Protocol (LDAP) and DNS for name resolution in a Windows 2000 environment, your reliance on less reliable and efficient protocols like WINS can be minimized and eventually eliminated.

Project Phases

In moving to Active Directory and Windows 2000, there are distinct phases we recommend to minimize the impact to your organization. This generic approach can be used in any migration to Windows 2000. Later in this chapter, details on migration from Windows NT 4.0 to Windows 2000 are described.

The phases for migration are as follows:

- Discovery phase
- Design phase
- Lab phase
- Pilot phase

The first phase is the discovery phase. The discovery phase provides for understanding your current environment with the intention of migrating to Windows 2000. Although you are probably familiar with the architecture and operations of your environment, it is a good practice to kick your project off with a clean look at your current Windows NT 4.0 environment in the context of moving to Active Directory and Windows 2000.

In conjunction with your Windows 2000 and Active Directory discovery phase, you should create a requirements and discovery document. This document is a reference as you move through the other phases and can help in determining trade-offs should you need to eliminate capabilities during Phase 1 of the implementation.

The design phase is the phase in which you develop how you are going to implement to meet the requirements as defined in the requirements and discovery document. A product of the design phase is the Windows 2000 and Active Directory design document for use as a reference in the implementation. This document contains the configuration approach and standards defined for your organization. A simple example of a standard is the naming convention to be used for user objects or the location of DCs in your enterprise WAN. The design document defines the end-point for Phase 1 of your implementation.

The lab phase is the phase in which you validate your design. This is where you apply the design information to the expected use of the environment. As part of the lab phase, you should create a test plan and validation document that includes the results of the tests implemented.

Following the lab phase, which might include some changes to the design and redefinition of the features available in the Phase 1 implementation, is the pilot phase. The pilot phase typically includes two parts: a controlled pilot phase that is a small group of users using the new system in a production mode, and later a larger group that is representative of the user population.

Following the pilot phase is an upgrade phase. The critical step in the upgrade phase is creating a document that clearly outlines the procedures for implementing the upgrade.

Goals of the Migration

The goals of your migration from Windows NT 4.0 to Active Directory and Windows 2000 are maximum availability, minimal disturbance, minimized manual migration and support tasks, maintained security, and shortest timeline. Your objective in moving your users to the new environment is a clean implementation with the least impact to the user. This is important because the migration experience for the users has an impact on how they view the technology. Those first impressions are hard to overcome if they include a bad migration experience.

Preparing for the Migration and Active Directory

Training your administrative and design team is an important part of obtaining the technical details for implementing a new environment. For the early adopters, experienced Active Directory designers are hard to find. The best way to get up to speed is with training from Microsoft. This provides your staff with a strong foundation for moving forward with the methodology described in this book.

Revaluate Your Administrative Model

As part of preparing for Active Directory, re-evaluate your administrative model and determine how you are going to use group policies and the directory. With the flexibility of the tools and the granularity of administrative responsibilities that can be delegated, it is important to take some time to step back and determine how you want your environment administered.

Look at Current Windows NT 4.0 Groups

With your move to Active Directory, you want to take a close look at your current Windows NT 4.0 group structure and document it. Groups have changed with Active Directory and Windows 2000. There are four types of groups available in Windows 2000. The groups available in Windows 2000 is described later and depicted in Table 22.1.

It is important to understand the affect groups have when Windows is running in Native Mode or mixed-mode. You should also take the time to understand your use of local groups. After careful research, it is time take your findings into the lab, test the migration process, and validate that the proper access has been migrated or eliminated.

Upgrade Process for Windows NT 4.0

If migrating from Windows NT 4.0, several items need to be considered. They are the PDC upgrade, the resource domain upgrades, the actual upgrade steps, and the order of the domain upgrades.

When you upgrade the PDC, it becomes the first domain in the new Windows 2000 tree, and by default it is running in mixed-mode. Mixed-mode means that the system is emulating a PDC for the old domain for all the BDCs that still exist in the old domain (PDC emulation). Any changes made for a BDC on the old domain are made to the PDC just like in a Windows NT 4.0 environment.

"Mixed-mode" means that there are still Windows NT 4.0 DCs. "Native Mode" means that all DCs are Windows 2000. The PDC emulator continues to provide some services even in a Native Mode environment. For example

- Down-level client authentication
- Password changes are replicated preferentially to the PDC emulator
- Account lockouts are processed through the PDC emulator

The Windows NT 4.0 Security Account Manager (SAM) is uploaded into Active Directory. Windows NT 4.0 BDCs can be added while Active Directory is in mixed-mode. You also want to make sure that all the trusts that were in the previous environment are maintained. The mixed-mode PDC is still the account domain for the remaining Windows NT 4.0 systems.

Multiple PDCs

If you have multiple Windows NT 4.0 domains and thus multiple PDCs, the second PDC needs to be upgraded into the Windows 2000 tree. The way of accomplishing this is to upgrade the PDC into another domain in the tree. This provides for mixed-mode support while the BDCs are moved into the tree, and you eventually move to Native Mode.

Resource Domain Upgrades

If you look at the resource domains for upgrade, you need to consider why you originally created the resource domain. What was the requirement? A typical reason for the resource domain is need to avoid the possibility for a SAM size limitation violation. Another reason for the resource domain is delegation of administration. Both of these limitations have been overcome with Active Directory. Active Directory does not have the size limitations and organizational units (OUs) provide us with the ability to segment administration.

With the resource domains, you have a couple of upgrade choices. You can upgrade the resource domain in place. You can upgrade the resource domain into a new Forest and new DCs, move objects to the final Forest, and then decommission the old resource domain Forest. You can also restructure the resource domains into OUs.

Active Directory Upgrade Steps

The first step in upgrading to Active Directory is to establish the root domain. When you establish the root domain, you need to determine whether you are going to use an existing account's domain or establish a new domain. This is dependent on what your final Active Directory design is going to be. If you currently have two account domains, say one in Europe and one in North America, you might want to create a root domain and migrate the European and North American users into separate OUs in the root domain.

Accounts that are migrated to OUs have access to resources just as they had in separate domains.

After you have established the root domain, you want to upgrade the account domains first. By doing this you can quickly take advantage of some of the features of Active Directory. An example of one of the features that you can quickly put to use is the delegation of administrative control by breaking some of the Windows NT 4.0 domain limitations.

Following the account domain, you want to migrate the resource domains.

Order of Domain Upgrades

With regard to the order for upgrading the domains, you should consider the size of the domains and start out with the smaller ones first. This limits the potential impact to the end user.

If your larger domains are account domains, you should consider migrating these first. Migrating account domains first provides for easier administration.

After the size of the domains is identified, you should also consider whether a domain is going to be consolidated or just migrated and left largely intact. For those account domains that are being merged, you should wait until the end of the account domain migrations to perform those migrations.

Account domains can be merged by migrating users to a Windows 2000 Forest. The first step is to establish trusts to the Forest, so that you are able to maintain access to resource domains. Next, you need to create global groups in the new Forest for each global group that exists in the Windows NT 4.0 environment. After the trusts and global groups are set up, you migrate each user by using the ClonePrincipal to clone each user into the destination domain. You can move users from more than one domain into a single domain using this method.

With resource domains, you should migrate those domains in which the number of workstations is limited, followed by those domains that contain applications that use Active Directory. An example of this is the next generation of Microsoft Exchange. The next domains to be migrated are those resource domains that exists after the migration and finally those resource domains that are consolidated.

To migrate an Exchange resource domain to a Windows 2000 domain, you first create the trusts from the Exchange resource domain to the Windows 2000 domain. This permits users in the Windows 2000 domain to have access to the Exchange resource domain resources. You can use NetDom to identify the trusts that exist between the resource domain and the account domain. Next, you demote the application servers to member's servers and use NetDom to create computer accounts in the destination domain into which the member server is to be moved. Finally, you decommission the resource domain.

Tools for Moving Objects

There are several tools available for moving objects that are part of Active Directory. ClonePrincipal is a tool created to move users and groups between domains.

A SID history is an important part of any migration strategy. This utility is important because it enables you really move users. Remember, if you move a user between domains, you are really creating a user in the new domain and deleting the user in the old domain. This can create a problem, because when you do this you are creating a new SID, and the new SID is unable to access resources that are still in old resource domains.

To get around this, Microsoft has created a SID history for users so that the old SID can follow the user to the domain. This way, if the new user tries to access a resource in the old domain, it uses SID history to find the old SID, and it is granted access to the resource domain.

NetDom is a scripting utility used during the migration that enables you to build trusts and create computer accounts. For large organizations, this is handy when moving hundreds of resources. MoveTree is a utility to move objects between domains in a single Forest. This is used for upgrading a domain topology in place. These utilities are part of the resource kit. If the resource kit is installed, these utilities can be found in `c:\Program Files\Resource Kit`.

Approaches for Upgrading to Active Directory

Upgrading in place is taking your existing Windows NT 4.0 domain and installing Windows 2000 and Active Directory on the same machine. With this type of upgrade, you are ending up with the same type of topology that you started with. If this is true, you should be asking yourself some questions: "Am I really going to be taking advantage of the capabilities of Active Directory?" "Have you put enough time and effort into the Active Directory design to take full advantage of its capabilities?" "Are you able to do something with sites to mitigate network traffic to combine account domains?"

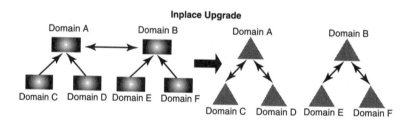

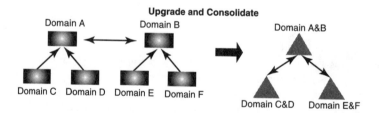

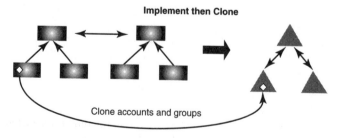

Figure 22.1   Upgrading approaches.

The next approach for upgrading to Active Directory is "upgrade and then consolidate." This approach includes upgrading the domains in place and then using tools to consolidate the domains to reflect your Active Directory domain design.

The most popular approach is to implement and then clone. This is great for organizations that want to leave their Windows NT 4.0 domain structure in place, bring in Active Directory in parallel, and then incrementally bring users into the new Active Directory domain structure. Microsoft has tools created to support this effort.

In-Place Upgrade Considerations

The in-place upgrade is the most straightforward approach for simple environments, but several items should be considered if taking on this approach. The first is the order of the account and resource domain upgrades. Typically, you want to upgrade the accounts first.

The DCs coexist so that you can make a gradual migration from Windows NT 4.0 to Active Directory and then convert from mixed-mode to Native Mode.

You should consider that all the Windows NT 4.0 objects become Active Directory objects through the migration process; therefore, it is a good idea to clean up your Windows NT 4.0 objects before the migration to prevent unnecessary clutter in the new directory.

Another consideration is the use of BDCs. You can create a BDC and keep it offline in case you need to retreat to the Windows NT 4.0 domains. With the BDC, you can promote it back to the PDC. Another approach before migrating the PDC is to create a BDC on a new box, take it offline to an isolated LAN, and promote it to a PDC. With the PDC, which is a reflection of your current Windows NT 4.0 environment, you can test the in-place migration with the real SAM.

A final note on the in-place upgrade is to review the trusts between Active Directory and Windows NT 4.0 domains to ensure that users maintain access to the resource that they need.

Consolidation

There are two ways to consolidate domains if moving to Active Directory. One way is to consolidate your domains first and then upgrade. The second way is to upgrade and then use tools to consolidate.

The problem with the first approach is that if you have multiple domains in the Windows NT 4.0 environment, there probably was a reason for it. If you had created multiple domains because of the size limit of the SAM, you probably won't be able to consolidate before migration.

If you are able to consolidate before upgrading, there are tools available from independent software vendors (ISVs) to support this. Microsoft provides the MoveTree tool for consolidating accounts into domains, based on your design.

A list of ISV tools is available at `http://www.microsoft.com/Windows/server/ deploy/directory/accessory.asp`. The list of companies providing tools includes NetIQ, Entevo Corporation, FastLane Technologies Inc., Master Design and Development, Mission Critical Software, NetPro, and Full Armor Corporation.

Consolidation Considerations

When you are consolidating, you need to consider the SIDs, because without the SIDs being migrated you will have difficulty accessing the resources that are in the old Windows NT 4.0 domain. Another consideration when consolidating is the affect on network traffic. If there are fewer DCs, traffic to the DCs could become a bottleneck. DNS changes might also be required during a consolidation if multiple domains, before consolidation, were represented in different namespaces that are also consolidated.

You should consider migrating users incrementally to minimize the impact of changes, at least in the early stages of the migration.

Before starting the migration, identify and test a rollback plan. This might be something as simple as creating a BDC and keeping it offline. You should be sure to test the capability to restore functionality with the BDC so that you are not trying to recover in a panic.

Implementing and then Cloning the Account Domain

If using the "implement then clone" approach for a migration, you should start by creating a new Forest. This clean environment is based on the Active Directory design that you have created.

The first step is to create trusts between the new Forest and the user domain in the Windows NT 4.0 environment. The trusts are from the Windows NT 4.0 domain to the Active Directory tree (see Figure 22.2).

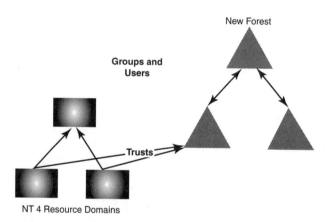

Figure 22.2 Resource domains trust both Windows NT 4.0 account domain and the new Windows 2000 domain.

After the trusts are in place, you need to clone the Groups and Users using the ClonePrincipal and SID history utilities.

Implementing then Cloning the Resourced Domain

When you start cloning resources, you need to consider that there are users in both domains. This requires that you establish a trust from the Active Directory domain to the Windows NT 4.0 domain so that users on the Windows NT 4.0 domain side can access resources in the new Active Directory tree (see Figure 22.3).

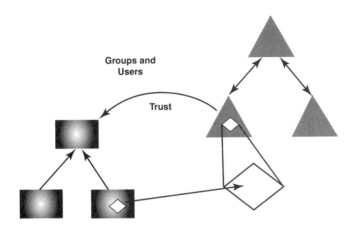

Figure 22.3   Move groups and users to a new domain.

After the trust is established, you want to clone the shared local groups using ClonePrincipal. Next, you want to move the servers into the resource domain. The tricky part is if you need to move a BDC. The way to do this is to take the BDC offline and promote it to a PDC. As a PDC, you upgrade it to Windows 2000 as part of the Forest; use DCpromo to remove the account information, and then make it a member server. Now, you can move the servers to the correct OU using NetDom. After all the servers are moved over, you can decommission the resource domain.

Active Directory Upgrade Scenarios

This section discusses the various migration scenarios. It looks at the single domain model, the master domain model, the multi-master model, and whether to go to Native Mode.

Single Domain

A single domain Windows NT 4.0 environment is the simplest environment to migrate from. You upgrade your PDC first, and then you upgrade your BDCs. After you have upgraded, reorganize objects into OUs as necessary and apply group policies to take advantage of Active Directory. Next, consider sites to control network traffic.

Master Domain Model

With a master domain model, you should upgrade the master domain first. If you are moving to multiple Active Directory domains, you can upgrade in-place. If you are going to have to a single Active Directory domain, your Windows NT 4.0 resource domain can be moved to the Active Directory domain, but you do need to create explicit trusts.

Multi-Master Model

With the multi-master model, you are able to upgrade into your ideal Active Directory domain model. In this scenario, Active Directory is addressing the issues that the multi-master model identified in large enterprises.

With this migration, you should build one tree with an empty root domain and build a domain tree for each master domain. The empty root domain provides the capability to have a contiguous namespace. The Forest, in which the master domains are located, has a common schema, configuration, and transitive trusts.

Account domains can be consolidated. A large single domain in Active Directory can be supported and does not affect end user authentication because of traffic, as long as there are an appropriate number of DCs, and they are distributed appropriately.

Account domains are consolidated by migrating account domains into separate domains in the same Forest. After an account domain is upgraded, the users and groups can be migrated to another domain in the Forest using ClonePrincipal for individual users, by user migration, or MoveTree for larger migrations.

Complete Trust Model

In this scenario, you need to understand why you have the complete trust model. Is it because your organization grew out of a departmental push for Windows NT? If so, you should create your ideal Active Directory design and upgrade to a single Forest with the empty root domain, similar to the multi-master model. If you have a complete trust model because of the business relationships that exist, you should consider the impact of a single Forest with trees or a multiple Forest implementation scenario.

When to Go to Native Mode

Several features point you to going to Native Mode. With Native Mode, you have more group types and group management with nested groups.

The availability and functions of groups are described in Table 22.1. The new group types are domain local groups and universal groups. Domain local groups are similar to local groups except that they are domain wide. Domain local groups enable access to resources in the domain. This is just like local groups enabling access to machine-specific resources. Universal groups have Forest-wide scope. Universal groups can give access to resources in the any domain in the Forest and to domains in other Forests, as long as the proper trust relationship exists.

Table 22.1 **Group Type Availability and Function**

Group Type	Mode Available	Function
Local Group	Mixed and Native	Access to machine-wide resources.
Domain Local Group	Native only	Access to domain-wide resources and can be used on any machine in the domain. They are limited to their local domain.
Global Group	Mixed and Native	Similar to Windows NT global groups. Domain-wide membership scope and can be given permissions in other domains.
Universal Groups	Native only	Membership and permissions Forest wide.

Native Mode removes the need for BDC replication traffic, and the PDC is eliminated. The SAM size limitation is lifted as well.

Staying in mixed-mode does not affect client access. There are a few reasons to stay in mixed-mode. They include not having adequate hardware to run Active Directory, wanting a fallback position, and not being able to upgrade BDCs because of applications that will not upgrade.

Summary

Moving to Active Directory is no simple task. However, this chapter provides reasonable scenarios for a successful upgrade. Moving to Active Directory in organizations provides potential logistical and technical challenges because of the rich feature set provided by Active Directory and Windows 2000.

Index

A

H

I

O

Windows 2000 Answers

This is the updated edition of New Riders' best-selling *Inside Windows NT 4 Server*. Taking the author-driven, no-nonsense approach that we pioneered with our Windows NT *Landmark* books, New Riders proudly offers something unique for Windows 2000 administrators—an interesting and discriminating book on Windows 2000 Server, written by someone in the trenches who can anticipate your situation and provide answers you can trust.

INSIDE
Windows 2000 Server

ISBN: 1-56205-929-7

Windows 2000
ESSENTIAL REFERENCE

Architected to be the most navigable, useful, and value-packed reference for Windows 2000, this book uses a creative "telescoping" design that you can adapt to your style of learning. Written by Steven Tate, key Windows 2000 partner and developer of Microsoft's W2K Training Program, it's a concise, focused, and quick reference for Windows 2000.

ISBN: 0-7357-0869-X

Windows 2000
User Management

Windows 2000 User Management is just one of several new Windows 2000 titles from New Riders' acclaimed *Landmark* series. Focused advice on, managing users and environments in your business.

ISBN: 1-56205-886-X

Advanced Information on Networking Technologies

New Riders Books Offer Advice and Experience

LANDMARK

Rethinking Computer Books

We know how important it is to have access to detailed, solutions-oriented information on core technologies. *Landmark* books contain the essential information you need to solve technical problems. Written by experts and subjected to rigorous peer and technical reviews, our *Landmark* books are hard-core resources for practitioners like you.

ESSENTIAL REFERENCE

Smart, Like You

The *Essential Reference* series from New Riders provides answers when you know what you want to do but need to know how to do it. Each title skips extraneous material and assumes a strong base of knowledge. These are indispensable books for the practitioner who wants to find specific features of a technology quickly and efficiently. Avoiding fluff and basic material, these books present solutions in an innovative, clean format—and at a great value.

MCSE CERTIFICATION

Engineered for Test Success

New Riders offers a complete line of test preparation materials to help you achieve your certification. With books like the *MCSE Training Guide*, *TestPrep*, and *Fast Track*, and software like the acclaimed *MCSE Complete* and the revolutionary *ExamGear*, New Riders offers comprehensive products built by experienced professionals who have passed the exams and instructed hundreds of candidates.

Windows NT TCP/IP

Windows NT TCP/IP
By Karanjit S. Siyan, Ph.D.
1st Edition
480 pages, $29.99
ISBN: 1-56205-887-8

If you're still looking for good documentation on Microsoft TCP/IP, look no further—this is your book. *Windows NT TCP/IP* cuts through the complexities and provides the most informative and complete reference book on Windows-based TCP/IP. Concepts essential to TCP/IP administration are explained thoroughly and then are related to the practical use of Microsoft TCP/IP in a real-world networking environment. The book begins by covering TCP/IP architecture and advanced installation and configuration issues and then moves on to routing with TCP/IP, DHCP Management, and WINS/DNS Name Resolution.

Windows NT DNS

Windows NT DNS
By Michael Masterson, Herman Knief, Scott Vinick, and Eric Roul
1st Edition
340 pages, $29.99
ISBN: 1-56205-943-2

Have you ever opened a Windows NT book looking for detailed information about DNS only to discover that it doesn't even begin to scratch the surface? DNS is probably one of the most complicated subjects for NT administrators, and there are few books on the market that address it in detail. This book answers your most

complex DNS questions, focuses on the implementation of the Domain Name Service within Windows NT, and treats it thoroughly from the viewpoint of an experienced Windows NT professional. Many detailed, real-world examples illustrate the understanding of the material throughout. The book covers the details of how DNS functions within NT and then explores specific interactions with critical network components. Finally, proven procedures to design and set up DNS are demonstrated. You'll also find coverage of related topics, such as maintenance, security, and troubleshooting.

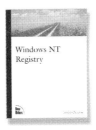
Windows NT Registry

Windows NT Registry: A Seetings Reference
By Sandra Osborne
1st Edition
550 pages, $29.99
ISBN: 1-56205-941-6

The NT Registry can be a very powerful tool for those capable of using it wisely. Unfortunately, there is little information regarding the NT Registry due to Microsoft's insistence that their source code be kept secret. If you're looking to optimize your use of the Registry, you're usually forced to search the Web for bits of information. This book is your resource. It covers critical issues and settings used for configuring network protocols, including NWLink, PTP, TCP/IP, and DHCP. This book approaches the material from a unique point of view. It discusses the problems related to a particular component and then discusses settings, which are the actual changes necessary for implementing robust solutions.

Windows NT Performance: Monitoring, Benchmarking and Tuning

By Mark T. Edmead
and Paul Hinsberg
1st Edition
288 pages, $29.99
ISBN: 1-56205-942-4

Performance monitoring is a little like preventive medicine for the administrator: No one enjoys a checkup, but it's a good thing to do on a regular basis. This book helps you focus on the critical aspects of improving the performance of your NT system by showing you how to monitor the system, implement benchmarking, and tune your network. The book is organized by resource components, which makes it easy to use as a reference tool.

Windows NT Terminal Server and Citrix MetaFrame

By Ted Harwood
1st Edition
416 pages, $29.99
ISBN: 1-56205-944-0

It's no surprise that most administration headaches revolve around integration with other networks and clients. This book addresses these types of real-world issues on a case-by-case basis, giving tools and advice on solving each problem. The author also offers the real nuts and bolts of thin client administration on multiple systems, covering relevant issues such as installation, configuration, network connection, management, and application distribution.

Windows NT Power Toolkit

By Stu Sjouwerman and
Ed Tittel
1st Edition
900 pages, $49.99
ISBN: 0-7357-0922-X

This book covers the analysis, tuning, optimization, automation, enhancement, maintenance, and troubleshooting of Windows NT Server 4.0 and Windows NT Workstation 4.0. In most cases, the two operating systems overlap completely and will be discussed together; in other cases, where the two systems diverge, each platform will be covered separately. This advanced title comprises a task-oriented treatment of the Windows NT 4 environment, including both Windows NT Server 4.0 and Windows NT Workstation 4.0. Thus, this book is aimed squarely at power users to guide them to painless, effective use of Windows NT both inside and outside the workplace. By concentrating on the use of operating system tools and utilities, Resource Kit elements, and selected third-party tuning, analysis, optimization, and productivity tools, this book will show its readers how to carry out everyday and advanced tasks.

Windows NT Network Management: Reducing Total Cost of Ownership

By Anil Desai
1st Edition
400 pages, $34.99
ISBN: 1-56205-946-7

Administering a Windows NT network is kind of like trying to herd cats—an impossible task characterized by constant motion, exhausting labor, and lots of hairballs. Author Anil Desai knows all about it; he's a consulting engineer for Sprint Paranet who specializes in

Windows NT implementation, integration, and management. So, we asked him to put together a concise manual of the best practices—a book of tools and ideas that other administrators can turn to again and again in managing their own NT networks.

Planning for Windows 2000

By Eric K. Cone, Jon Boggs, and Sergio Perez
1st Edition
400 pages, $29.99
ISBN: 0-73570-048-6

Windows 2000 is poised to be one of the largest and most important software releases of the next decade, and you are charged with planning, testing, and deploying it in your enterprise. Are you ready? With this book, you will be. *Planning for Windows 2000* lets you know what the upgrade hurdles will be, informs you how to clear them, guides you through effective Active Directory design, and presents you with detailed rollout procedures. Eric K. Cone, Jon Boggs, and Sergio Perez give you the benefit of their extensive experiences as Windows 2000 Rapid Deployment Program members by sharing problems and solutions they've encountered on the job.

MCSE Core NT Exams Essential Reference

By Matthew Shepker, MCSE, MCT
1st Edition
256 pages, $19.99
ISBN: 0-7357-0006-0

You're sitting in the first session of your Networking Essentials class, the instructor starts talking about RAS, and you have no idea what that means. You think about raising your hand to ask, but you reconsider—

you'd feel foolish asking a question in front of all these people. You turn to your handy *MCSE Core NT Exams Essential Reference* and find a quick summary on Remote Access Services. Question answered. It's a couple months later, and you're taking your Networking Essentials exam the next day. You're reviewing practice tests and keep forgetting the maximum lengths for the various commonly used cable types. Once again, you turn to the *MCSE Core NT Exams Essential Reference* and find a table on cables, including all the characteristics you need to memorize in order to pass the test.

BackOffice Titles

Implementing Exchange Server

By Doug Hauger, Marywynne Leon, and William C. Wade III
1st Edition
400 pages, $29.99
ISBN: 1-56205-931-9

If you're interested in connectivity and maintenance issues for Exchange Server, this book is for you. Exchange's power lies in its capability to be connected to multiple email subsystems to create a "universal email backbone." It's not unusual to have several different and complex systems all connected via email gateways, including Lotus Notes or cc:Mail, Microsoft Mail, legacy mainframe systems, and Internet mail. This book covers all of the problems and issues associated with getting an integrated system running smoothly, and it addresses troubleshooting and diagnosis of email problems with an eye toward prevention and best practices.

Exchange System Administration

By Janice Rice Howd
1st Edition
400 pages, $34.99
ISBN: 0-7357-0081-8

Okay, you've got your Exchange Server installed and connected; now what? Email administration is one of the most critical networking jobs, and Exchange can be particularly troublesome in large, heterogeneous environments. Janice Howd, a noted consultant and teacher with over a decade of email administration experience, has put together this advanced, concise handbook for daily, periodic, and emergency administration. With in-depth coverage of topics like managing disk resources, replication, and disaster recovery, this is the one reference book every Exchange administrator needs.

SQL Server System Administration

By Sean Baird, Chris Miller, et al.
1st Edition
352 pages, $29.99
ISBN: 1-56205-955-6

How often does your SQL Server go down during the day when everyone wants to access the data? Do you spend most of your time being a "report monkey" for your coworkers and bosses? *SQL Server System Administration* helps you keep data consistently available to your users. This book omits introductory information. The authors don't spend time explaining queries and how they work. Instead, they focus on the information you can't get anywhere else, like how to choose the correct replication topology and achieve high availability of information.

Internet Information Services Administration

By Kelli Adam, et al.
1st Edition,
300 pages, $29.99
ISBN: 0-7357-0022-2

Are the new Internet technologies in Internet Information Server giving you headaches? Does protecting security on the Web take up all of your time? Then this is the book for you. With hands-on configuration training, advanced study of the new protocols in IIS, and detailed instructions on authenticating users with the new Certificate Server and implementing and managing the new e-commerce features, *Internet Information Services Administration* gives you the real-life solutions you need. This definitive resource also prepares you for the release of Windows 2000 by giving you detailed advice on working with Microsoft Management Console, which was first used by IIS.

SMS 2 Administration

By Michael Lubanski and Darshan Doshi
1st Edition, Winter 2000
350 pages, $39.99
ISBN: 0-7357-0082-6

Microsoft's new version of its Systems Management Server (SMS) is starting to turn heads. Although complex, it allows administrators to lower their total cost of ownership and more efficiently manage clients, applications, and support operations. So if your organization is using or implementing SMS, you'll need some expert advice. Darshan Doshi and Michael Lubanski can help you get the most bang for your buck, with insight, expert tips, and real-world examples. Darshan and

Michael are consultants specializing in SMS and have worked with Microsoft on one of the most complex SMS rollouts in the world, involving 32 countries, 15 languages, and thousands of clients.

UNIX/Linux Titles

Solaris
Essential Reference
By John P. Mulligan
1st Edition,
350 pages, $24.95
ISBN: 0-7357-0023-0

Looking for the fastest, easiest way to find the Solaris command you need? Need a few pointers on shell scripting? How about advanced administration tips and sound, practical expertise on security issues? Are you looking for trustworthy information about available third-party software packages that will enhance your operating system? Author John Mulligan—creator of the popular Unofficial Guide to Solaris Web site (sun.icsnet.com)—delivers all that and more in one attractive, easy-to-use reference book. With clear and concise instructions on how to perform important administration and management tasks and key information on powerful commands and advanced topics, *Solaris Essential Reference* is the book you need when you know what you want to do and only need to know how.

Linux System
Administration
By M Carling, et al.
1st Edition
450 pages, $29.99
ISBN: 1-56205-934-3

As an administrator, you probably feel that most of your time and energy is spent in endless firefighting. If your network has become a fragile quilt of temporary patches and work-arounds, this book is for you. For example, have you had trouble sending or receiving email lately? Are you looking for a way to keep your network running smoothly with enhanced performance? Are your users always hankering for more storage, services, and speed? *Linux System Administration* advises you on the many intricacies of maintaining a secure, stable system. In this definitive work, the author addresses all the issues related to system administration from adding users and managing file permissions, to Internet services and Web hosting, to recovery planning and security. This book fulfills the need for expert advice that will ensure a trouble-free Linux environment.

GTK+/Gnome
Application
Development
By Havoc Pennington
1st Edition
492 pages, $39.99
ISBN: 0-7357-0078-8

This title is for the reader who is conversant with the C programming language and UNIX/Linux development. It provides detailed and solution-oriented information designed to meet the needs of programmers and application developers using the GTK+/Gnome libraries. Coverage complements existing GTK+/Gnome documentation, going into more depth on pivotal issues such as uncovering the GTK+ object system, working with the event loop, managing the Gdk substrate, writing custom widgets, and mastering GnomeCanvas.

Developing Linux Applications with GTK+ and GDK
By Eric Harlow
1st Edition
400 pages, $34.99
ISBN: 0-7357-0021-4

We all know that Linux is one of the most powerful and solid operating systems in existence. And as the success of Linux grows, there is an increasing interest in developing applications with graphical user interfaces that take advantage of the power of Linux. In this book, software developer Eric Harlow gives you an indispensable development handbook focusing on the GTK+ toolkit. More than an overview of the elements of application or GUI design, this is a hands-on book that delves deeply into the technology. With in-depth material on the various GUI programming tools and loads of examples, this book's unique focus will give you the information you need to design and launch professional-quality applications.

Linux Essential Reference
By Ed Petron
1st Edition
400 pages, $24.95
ISBN: 0-7357-0852-5

This book is all about getting things done as quickly and efficiently as possible by providing a structured organization to the plethora of available Linux information. We can sum it up in one word—value.

This book has it all: concise instructions on how to perform key administration tasks, advanced information on configuration, shell scripting, hardware management, systems management, data tasks, automation, and tons of other useful information. All of this coupled with an unique navigational structure and a great price. This book truly provides groundbreaking information for the growing community of advanced Linux professionals.

Lotus Notes and Domino Titles

Domino System Administration
By Rob Kirkland, CLP, CLI
1st Edition
850 pages, $49.99
ISBN: 1-56205-948-3

Your boss has just announced that you will be upgrading to the newest version of Notes and Domino when it ships. As a Premium Lotus Business Partner, Lotus has offered a substantial price break to keep your company away from Microsoft's Exchange Server. How are you supposed to get this new system installed, configured, and rolled out to all your end users? You understand how Lotus Notes works—you've been administering it for years. What you need is a concise, practical explanation of the new features and how to make some of the advanced stuff work smoothly. You need answers and solutions from someone like you, who has worked with the product for years and understands what you need to know. *Domino System Administration* is the answer—the first book on Domino that attacks the technology at the professional level with practical, hands-on assistance to get Domino running in your organization.

Lotus Notes and Domino Essential Reference

By Tim Bankes
and Dave Hatter
1st Edition
500 pages, $45.00
ISBN: 0-7357-0007-9

You're in a bind because you've been asked to design and program a new database in Notes for an important client that will keep track of and itemize a myriad of inventory and shipping data. The client wants a user-friendly interface without sacrificing speed or functionality. You are experienced (and could develop this application in your sleep) but feel that you need to take your talents to the next level. You need something to facilitate your creative and technical abilities, something to perfect your programming skills. The answer is waiting for you: *Lotus Notes and Domino Essential Reference*. It's compact and simply designed. It's loaded with information. All of the objects, classes, functions, and methods are listed. It shows you the object hierarchy and the relationship between each one. It's perfect for you. Problem solved.

Networking Titles

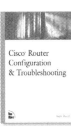

Cisco Router Configuration & Troubleshooting

By Mark Tripod
1st Edition
300 pages, $34.99
ISBN: 0-7357-0024-9

Want the real story on making your Cisco routers run like a dream? Why not pick up a copy of *Cisco Router Configuration & Troubleshooting* and see what Mark Tripod has to say? They're the folks responsible for making some of the largest sites on the Net scream, like Amazon.com, Hotmail, USAToday, Geocities, and Sony. In this book, they provide advanced configuration issues, sprinkled with advice and preferred practices. You won't see a general overview on TCP/IP. They talk about more meaty issues, like security, monitoring, traffic management, and more. In the troubleshooting section, the authors provide a unique methodology and lots of sample problems to illustrate. By providing real-world insight and examples instead of rehashing Cisco's documentation, Mark gives network administrators information they can start using today.

Network Intrusion Detection: An Analyst's Handbook

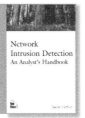

By Stephen Northcutt
1st Edition
267 pages, $39.99
ISBN: 0-7357-0868-1

Get answers and solutions from someone who has been in the trenches. Author Stephen Northcutt, original developer of the Shadow intrusion detection system and former Director of the United States Navy's Information System Security Office at the Naval Security Warfare Center, gives his expertise to intrusion detection specialists, security analysts, and consultants responsible for setting up and maintaining an effective defense against network security attacks.

Understanding Data Communications, Sixth Edition

By Gilbert Held
6th Edition
500 pages, $39.99
ISBN: 0-7357-0036-2

Updated from the highly successful
Fifth Edition, this book explains how
data communications systems and their
various hardware and software components work. More than an entry-level
book, it approaches the material in
textbook format, addressing the complex
issues involved in internetworking today.
A great reference book for the
experienced networking professional and
written by the noted networking authority
Gilbert Held.

Other Books By New Riders

We Want to Know What You Think

To better serve you, we would like your opinion on the content and quality of this book. Please complete this card, and mail it to us or fax it to 317-581-4663.

Name _____

Address _____

City_____State_____Zip _____

Phone _____

Email Address _____

Occupation _____

Operating system(s) that you use _____

What influenced your purchase of this book?
- ❑ Recommendation
- ❑ Cover Design
- ❑ Table of Contents
- ❑ Index
- ❑ Magazine Review
- ❑ Advertisement
- ❑ New Riders' Reputation
- ❑ Author Name

How would you rate the contents of this book?
- ❑ Excellent
- ❑ Very Good
- ❑ Good
- ❑ Fair
- ❑ Below Average
- ❑ Poor

How do you plan to use this book?
- ❑ Quick Reference
- ❑ Self-Training
- ❑ Classroom
- ❑ Other

What do you like most about this book?
Check all that apply.
- ❑ Content
- ❑ Writing Style
- ❑ Accuracy
- ❑ Examples
- ❑ Listings
- ❑ Design
- ❑ Index
- ❑ Page Count
- ❑ Price
- ❑ Illustrations

What do you like least about this book?
Check all that apply.
- ❑ Content
- ❑ Writing Style
- ❑ Accuracy
- ❑ Examples
- ❑ Listings
- ❑ Design
- ❑ Index
- ❑ Page Count
- ❑ Price
- ❑ Illustrations

What would be a useful follow-up book for you? _____

Where did you purchase this book? _____

Can you name a similar book that you like better than this one, or one that is as good? Why?

_____

How many New Riders books do you own? _____

What are your favorite computer books? _____

What other titles would you like to see us develop? _____

Any comments for us? _____

_____

_____

_____

Windows 2000 Active Directory 0-7357-0870-3

www.newriders.com • Fax 317-581-4663

Fold here and tape to mail

- -

Place
Stamp
Here

New Riders Publishing
201 W. 103rd St.
Indianapolis, IN 46290

 # How to Contact Us

Visit Our Web Site

www.newriders.com

On our Web site you'll find information about our other books, authors, tables of contents, indexes, and book errata.

Email Us

Contact us at this address:

nrfeedback@newriders.com

- If you have comments or questions about this book
- To report errors that you have found in this book
- If you have a book proposal to submit or are interested in writing for New Riders
- If you would like to have an author kit sent to you
- If you are an expert in a computer topic or technology and are interested in being a technical editor who reviews manuscripts for technical accuracy

nrfeedback@newriders.com

- To find a distributor in your area, please contact our international department at this address.

nrfeedback@newriders.com

- For instructors from educational institutions who want to preview New Riders books for classroom use. Email should include your name, title, school, department, address, phone number, office days/hours, text in use, and enrollment in the body of your text, along with your request for desk/examination copies and/or additional information.

Write to Us

New Riders Publishing

201 W. 103rd St.

Indianapolis, IN 46290-1097

Call Us

Toll-free (800) 571-5840 + 9 +4511

If outside U.S. (317) 581-3500. Ask for New Riders.

Fax Us

(317) 581-4663